TOURISM SECURITY

TOURISM SECURITY

Strategies for Effectively Managing Travel Risk and Safety

by

PETER E. TARLOW

ELSEVIER

AMSTERDAM • BOSTON • HEIDELBERG • LONDON
NEW YORK • OXFORD • PARIS • SAN DIEGO
SAN FRANCISCO • SINGAPORE • SYDNEY • TOKYO
Butterworth-Heinemann is an imprint of Elsevier

Acquiring Editor: Brian Romer
Editorial Project Manager: Keira Bunn
Project Manager: Priya Kumaraguruparan
Designer: Russell Purdy

Butterworth-Heinemann is an imprint of Elsevier
225 Wyman Street, Waltham, MA 02451, USA
The Boulevard, Langford Lane, Kidlington, Oxford OX5 1GB, UK

Notices

Knowledge and best practice in this field are constantly changing. As new research and experience
broaden our understanding, changes in research methods or professional practices, may become
necessary. Practitioners and researchers must always rely on their own experience and knowledge in
evaluating and using any information or methods described herein. In using such information or methods
they should be mindful of their own safety and the safety of others, including parties for whom they
have a professional responsibility.

To the fullest extent of the law, neither the Publisher nor the authors, contributors, or editors, assume
any liability for any injury and/or damage to persons or property as a matter of products liability,
negligence or otherwise, or from any use or operation of any methods, products, instructions, or ideas
contained in the material herein.

Library of Congress Cataloging-in-Publication Data
Tarlow, Peter E.
  Tourism security : strategies for effectively managing travel risk and safety / Peter Tarlow.
    pages cm
  1. Tourism–Security measures. 2. Tourism–Risk management. I. Title.
  G156.5.S43T37 2014
  910.68′4–dc23

                         2014012003

British Library Cataloging-in-Publication Data
A catalogue record for this book is available from the British Library

ISBN: 978-0-12-411570-5

For information on all Butterworth-Heinemann publications
visit our web site at store.elsevier.com

This book has been manufactured using Print On Demand technology. Each copy is produced to order
and is limited to black ink. The online version of this book will show color figures where appropriate.

Working together
to grow libraries in
developing countries

www.elsevier.com • www.bookaid.org

DEDICATION

May this book help in making my children's and grandchildren's world a safer and better place. May we all travel in safety and security, seeking to unite the world with caring and peace.

ACKNOWLEDGMENTS

No book comes about as the sole effort of a single author. This book is, of course, no exception. Numerous people from around the world encouraged me to write this book and without them I never would have given the time and effort necessary. I want to thank my colleagues in many parts of the world. My colleagues in tourism security, on both the academic and applied sides, not only encouraged me to write this book but also consistently reminded me of its importance. These people are too numerous to name, I can only hope that they know who they are and how much I appreciate their sage words of encouragement and caring.

I want to thank the editors of Elsevier who, each time I thought about dropping this project, knew how to prod me on and insisted that I write this book even when I could think of multiple excuses for not writing it.

During these many months of writing, there were several people who deserve special thanks. I want to thank the police officers that allowed me to interview them and publish their words. I want to thank my close friend and colleague, Charleston, South Carolina Police Chief Greg Mullen. Greg's words and wisdom have served me well and I am proud to call him my colleague and friend of many years. In a like manner, I want to thank the Director of the Dominican Republic's Tourism Police, now called CESTUR, General Justo Martín Amilcar Fernandez Tejada, along with Captain Dario Antonio and Coronel Ambiorix Cepeda Hernandez. These gentlemen are visionaries in the field of tourism security and it is a privilege and honor to work with them.

I also want to thank Dr. Camilo D'Ornellas of the Polícia Civil in Rio de Janeiro, Brazil. Camilo is one of the great minds in tourism security, he combines practical knowledge with academic wisdom. He has become a close friend and never fails to see reality for what it is.

I also want to thank my long time friend and colleague Ray Suppe of the Las Vegas Convention and Tourism Authority. Ray and I have worked together for many years on the Las Vegas International Tourism Security and Safety conference. Ray's strength of character and caring are tools that serve as a symbol for all who work in tourism security.

A special word of thanks goes to Nathan Smooha, my research assistant. Despite multiple academic tasks and personal challenges, Nathan has been a steady rock in aiding me in every aspect of this project. I pray that he has learned as much from me as I have from him and know that he will be a great success wherever life takes him.

Last but not least, I want to thank my family and especially my mother, grandchildren, children, and wife for all of their love and support. They are the true purpose for living and I want them to know how much I love and admire them.

CONTENTS

About the Author   xiii
Foreword   xvii
Foreword Two: Problems of Tourism Safety in Latin America   xxi
Introduction   xxv

1. **Introduction to Tourism Security**   **1**
   The tourism phenomenon   1
   Tourism terminology and history   2
   Modern tourism definitions   3
   Lack of a unified vocabulary   3
   Tourism as a social phenomenon   4
   Defining tourism security   5
   Classical and modern travel challenges   5
   Concepts of leisure and leisure travel   7
   Tourism security is more than criminal behavior   8
   Criminal acts and acts of terrorism   9
   Professional fears of addressing crime and terrorism   11
   Pre and post September 11, 2001   12
   Tourism safety, security, and surety in the post-9/11 world   14
   An overview of tourism surety: the pre-9/11 years   14
   The post-9/11 period   17
   TOPPs: the first defense against tourism crimes   19
   Summary   22
   References   22

2. **The Relationship between Tourism Security and the Economy**   **23**
   Part 1: How security, or the lack of security, impacts the tourism industry's
   economy   23
   Part 2: How tourism security must face the issues of shrinking budgets
   and how security personnel must do more with less   39
   References   47

3. **Hotel and Motel Security**   **49**
   Places of lodging in the tourism history   49
   Hotel security: The overview   50
   Common problems   51

Hotel challenges   52
Motel challenges   52
Bed 'n breakfast (B&B) challenges   53
Campgrounds and other lodging challenges   53
Lodging security in a consistently changing world   53
The role of the security officer   59
Dealing with the specifics of lodging security   62
Planning lodging security   64
Working with others   67
Around the hotel   69
Front desk and lobby area   69
Front desk personnel   70
Rooms and hallways   71
Food and beverages   72
The outside public areas   73
Pool and athletic safety   74
Other areas in the hotel   75
Outsourcing   75
Protecting the hotel's staff   76
Should an employee or guest become violent   77
References   78

4. **Risk and Crisis Management**   **79**
Introduction   79
Risk management   80
Why analyzing tourism risks is difficult   81
Crisis management   82
Performing risk management   85
A risk management model   86
Risk management guidelines   88
Alcohol and drugs and tourism risk   90
Drugs, tourism, and terrorism   93
The risk of food safety in tourism   94
Fire and tourism safety   96
Terrorism and tourism   98
Tourism, terrorism, and the media   100
From risk management to crisis management   103
Crisis recovery   106
References   108

5. Public Gathering Places

5. Public Gathering Places	109
Introduction	109
CCTV cameras at the casino and beyond	113
The casino security professional	115
Other places where people gather	121
History of meetings and conventions	121
Crimes at convention centers or trade shows	125
Some trade show/convention security procedures	127
Hazardous materials	128
Animals (pets) at trade and convention centers	128
Convention/trade-show center security and safety plans	129
Event security plan	130
References	135
6. Aquatic Tourism: Security at Beaches, Rivers, Lakes, and on the High Seas	137
Introduction	137
Beach/sea/river tourism	138
Criminal issues and issues of terrorism at aquatic locations	141
Cruise tourism	142
From the biblical text to the modern world	143
Other security issues specific to cruise ships	156
Other health issues	157
How passengers deal with cruise emergencies	163
References	165
7. Transportation: Travel by Air, Car, and Train	167
Introduction	167
The distinction between security and safety	168
Notable hijackings	168
Issues of commonality in hijackings	171
Counter-hijacking measures	172
Hardening the terminal	173
Greater examination of luggage	175
Making the plane itself more secure	177
Issues of fire at airports	178
Other suggestions in hardening air travel	179
Issues of health	179
Diseases carried from one nation or continent to another	181
Terrorism-based illnesses	185

Train travel as tourism   187
Bus tourism   190
Appendix: NTA's crisis management plan structure   193
References   197

8. Tourism Security Legal Issues   **199**
Tourism surety, standards of care, and the law   199
Issues of responsibility, legality, and standards of care   200
Making decisions   200
Standards of care   201
Legal vulnerability   202
Tourism law   203
Travelers' rights   207
Travel agents   207
Issues of travel law and travel agents   208
Additional issues for travel agencies   211
The airline passenger bill of rights   212
U.S. cruise passengers bill of rights   215
Train and bus travel   216
Fire codes   216
In Europe   218
Summary   219
References   221

9. Case Studies: Four Tourism Cities   **223**
Introduction   223
Tourism and freedom   223
Charleston, South Carolina   225
Las Vegas   235
The Dominican Republic   246
Tourist police   248
Rio de Janeiro   252
Summary   259
References   259

Afterword   *261*
Index   *265*

ABOUT THE AUTHOR

Dr. Peter E. Tarlow is a world-renowned speaker and expert specializing in the impact of crime and terrorism on the tourism industry, event and tourism risk management, and economic development. Since 1990, he has been teaching courses on tourism, crime, and terrorism to police forces and security and tourism professionals throughout the world. Dr. Tarlow earned his PhD in sociology from Texas A&M University. He also holds degrees in history, in Spanish and Hebrew literatures, and in psychotherapy.

In 1996, Dr. Tarlow joined the Bureau of Reclamation as the Hoover Dam's consultant for tourism development and security. He continued his involvement with the Bureau of Reclamation until December 2012. In 2000, due to interagency cooperation on the part of the Bureau of Reclamation, he helped to prepare security and Federal Bureau of Investigation agents for the Salt Lake City 2002 Winter Olympic Games. Dr. Tarlow also lectured for the 2010 Vancouver Olympic Games. He is currently working with police departments of the state of Rio de Janeiro for the 2014 World Cup Games and 2016 Olympic Games.

Dr. Tarlow has lectured for the Department of the Interior, the Department of Justice (Bureau of Prisons and Office of U.S. Attorneys-General), the Department of Homeland Security, and the American Bar Association's Latin America Office. He has worked with other U.S. and international government agencies such as the U.S. Park Service at the Statue of Liberty, the Smithsonian Institution's Office of Protection Services, Philadelphia's Independence Hall and Liberty Bell, and New York's Empire State Building. Dr. Tarlow has also worked with the Royal Canadian Mounted Police and the United Nation's World Tourism Organization, the Centers for Disease Control and Prevention, the Panama Canal Authority, and numerous police forces throughout the United States, the Caribbean, and Latin America.

In 2013, Dr. Tarlow was named the Special Envoy for the Chancellor of the Texas A&M University System. At almost the same time the U.S. State Department asked him to lecture around the world on issues of tourism security and safety. Also in 2013, he was asked by the President of the Dominican Republic to advise POLITUR (as of 2014 called CESTUR), the Dominican Republic's national tourism police.

Tarlow's fluency in many languages enables him to speak throughout the world (United States, the Caribbean, Latin America, Europe, Africa, the Eastern Pacific, and Asia). He lectures on a wide range of current and future trends in the tourism industry, rural tourism economic development, the gaming industry, issues of crime and terrorism, the role of police departments in urban economic development, and international trade. Dr. Tarlow trains numerous police departments throughout the world in TOPPS (tourism-oriented policing and protection services) and offers certification in this area. He provides keynote speeches around the world on topics as diverse as dealing with economies in crisis to how beautification can become a major tool for economic recovery.

Dr. Tarlow's research ranges from the impact of school calendars on the tourism industries to tourism ecology and business. These research interests allow him to work with communities throughout the United States. Dr. Tarlow researches how communities can use their tourism as an economic development tool during difficult economic times, and at the same time improve their local residents' quality of life. He also functions as an expert witness in courts throughout the United States on matters concerning tourism security and safety and issues of risk management.

Dr. Tarlow is a contributing author to multiple books on tourism security and has published numerous academic and applied research articles regarding issues of security including articles published in *The Futurist*, the *Journal of Travel Research*, and *Security Management*. In 1999, he coedited "War, Terrorism, and Tourism," a special edition of the *Journal of Travel Research*. In 2002, Dr. Tarlow published *Event Risk Management and Safety* (Wiley). He also writes and speaks for major organizations such as the Organization of U.S. State Dams, and the International Association of Event Managers. In 2011, he published *Twenty Years of Tourism Tidbits: The Book*. He has also recently published a book on cruise safety (written in Portuguese).

Dr. Tarlow has appeared on national televised programs such as *Dateline* (NBC) and on CNBC and is a regular guest on radio stations around the United States. He organizes conferences around the world dealing with visitor safety and security issues and with the economic importance of tourism and tourism marketing. He also works with numerous cities, states, and foreign governments to improve their tourism products and train their tourism security professionals.

Dr. Tarlow is a founder and president of Tourism & More Inc. (T&M). He is a past president of the Texas Chapter of the Travel and Tourism

Research Association. He is a member of the International Editorial Boards of "Turizam" published in Zagreb, Croatia; "Anatolia: International Journal of Tourism and Hospitality Research," published in Turkey; "Turismo: Visão e Ação," published in Brazil; "Estudios y Perspectivas en Turismo," published in Buenos Aires, Argentina; and the *American Journal of Tourism Research*.

FOREWORD

For over 20 years, Dr. Peter Tarlow has been one of the world's leading exponents and writers in the field of tourism and event security. I have enjoyed the privilege of being a fellow speaker with Peter at a number of conferences since 2004, in venues as diverse as Tel Aviv (Israel), Kingston (Jamaica), Kuala Lumpur (Malaysia), and Toronto (Canada). Peter is a brilliant and engaging speaker who simultaneously entertains and informs. His writings in English, Spanish, and Portuguese have been applauded by a wide audience of tourism academics and practitioners all over the world. Peter has successfully spanned the bridge between academia and the tourism industry in his presentations and writings.

Until the turn of the twenty-first century, security had been a dominant concern of specific sectors of the tourism industry. This is especially so for airlines and airports over many decades. Approaching tourism security from a holistic perspective is a relatively recent development. The 9/11 attacks on New York City and Washington in 2001 was the ultimate wake-up call that security was a core concern for all sectors of the tourism industry. Ritchie and Crouch, in their classic book *The Competitive Destination* (2003), identified tourism safety and security as a core attribute of a competitive tourism destination. Key global tourism associations including the UN World Tourism Organization (UNWTO) and the World Travel and Tourism Council (WTTC) now recognize the overriding importance of safety and security. The UNWTO, WTTC, and the Pacific Asia Travel Association have joined forces since 2012 to focus on educating and sensitizing the global tourism industry to enhance their attention to security issues.

The holistic approach to tourism security involves an interconnected chain with key links including airlines, airports, transit transport, trains, and railway stations, hotels and accommodation centers, events and event venues, tourist attractions and retail precincts, cruise ships and cruise ship ports, and tourist coaches and intercity bus stations. A cursory reading of the various links in tourism security suggests that each sector in the tourism, hospitality, and events industry has its own security challenges and threats. Destination planners and security specialists need to take a strategic approach to security, which factors all the links in the tourism security chain. In the accommodation sector there is the ongoing tension between guest security and the concept of a hotel as a center of hospitality and welcome to all.

This tension is both the attraction of hotels but also its vulnerability to terrorist attacks.

Many government destination-marketing bodies are reluctant to address the issue of destination security when promoting destinations to prospective travellers. In Southeast Asia, some tourism industry and political leaders see reference to security concerns in promotional media releases as a loss of face. It was an issue I was asked to refer to at a Tourism and Safety Security Conference in Thailand in November 2013. The approach the delegates adopted at that conference was that forewarning visitors of security risks and measures to minimize exposure would actually be seen as a positive reputation enhancement for the destination. To its credit, the Thai Tourism Authority has now endorsed the concept.

The state of tourism safety and security at destinations plays a major role in government travel advisories. Most major travel-generating countries provide detailed travel advisories for their citizens who travel abroad. As the primary role of any government is the protection of its citizens, governments employ and widely disseminate these advisories as an extraterritorial security measure. The Internet has enhanced the dissemination and by proxy the significance of travel advisories in the minds of international travellers.

In his books, articles, and conference presentations, Peter Tarlow has identified the many security risks that apply to each sector of the tourism industry. He has developed the TOPPS (tourism-oriented policing and protection services) in which local police at popular tourism destinations have been alerted to specific security issues that apply to tourists. Many of these problems stem from the vulnerability of tourists as naive, relatively wealthy and visible outsiders at most destinations. His work has been deservedly recognized throughout the world and due to his linguistic skills his expertise is currently in great demand in Latin America and especially Brazil, which is preparing to host the 2014 World Cup and the 2016 Olympic Games.

A holistic approach to tourism security starts with the individual tourist developing a sense of security awareness when they travel. It then extends to each sector of the tourism industry. Peter will navigate the complex avenues of tourism security, which encompasses events, hotels and accommodation providers, the transport sector, tourism attractions, tourism precincts, and tourism behavior. While headline-grabbing threats to tourism security tend to focus on terrorism and crime, the threat universe for tourism encompasses unsafe sex, drug use, spiking of drinks, lack of protection against disease, scams, vulnerability to risky behavior, and natural disasters.

Peter has lived and breathed tourism security for many years and has genuinely earned the coveted title of expert.

Dr. David Beirman
Senior Lecturer in Tourism, Management Discipline Group,
University of Technology, Sydney, Australia

FOREWORD TWO: PROBLEMS OF TOURISM SAFETY IN LATIN AMERICA

The tourism industry is one of the most important sources of wealth generation in the underdeveloped economies (Blake, Arbache, Sinclair, & Teles, 2008; Scheyvens, 2001). The literature reveals, however, that tourism does not come without a cost, and that within the tourism industry there are serious social pathologies (De Kadt, 1991). Because this problem is one that needs careful consideration, I want to thank Peter Tarlow for this valuable invitation to write a Foreword to his book on matters of safety and security. It is important to delineate the challenge and problems of Latin American policymakers in tourism if one wishes to ensure the stability of local economies, as well as the integrity of tourists. This poses an interesting question: To what extent can a nation that cannot provide security to its own people be capable of protecting its foreign guests?

Latin America's principal security issue regarding tourists has not been terrorism, but rather issues related to local crime. When we examine terrorism we note that it is based on the injection of fear into the body politic. Terrorists do not want to obliterate an entire civilization. Rather, they seek to sow panic so as to be able to negotiate with a stronger entity on a more equal footing (Howie, 2012; Korstanje, 2013). Terrorist cells seem to prefer extortion and panic as their weapon of choice. As ambassadors of their respective cultures, it is important for a nation to keep its visitors as far from danger as possible. Terrorists know this, and therefore do everything possible to create an unstable social atmosphere so that uncertainty will play a critical role. For example, one of the most terrible aspects of 9/11 was that the world became an unsafe place in which to be, for two main reasons. First, terrorists employed western technology against the visible symbols of the United States—the World Trade Center (economy), and also the Pentagon (military forces), a symbol of Washington's administrative power. Second, innocent people were killed to make others believe that the international diplomacy of the United States was wrong and weak. If the state was unable to protect its citizens, then the state should disappear. It is interesting to keep in mind that an event of this magnitude not only generated strong shock waves around the world but also in Latin America where the technological conditions to fight against terrorism are from the United States.

Although there has been a great deal of risk-related research over the last decade, since 9/11 there are relatively few academic studies dealing with the theme of (tourism) safety. Unlike risk, which can be subject to arithmetic algorithms, safety pivots in the organic image of tourist destination shows serious difficulties to be efficiently measured. In earlier research, both Korstanje and Tarlow have focused on the importance of understanding the dichotomy between real and perceived safety in tourism. Some tourism safety issues become overhyped (e.g., mad cow disease in Europe) and therefore may create states of paranoia for little or no reason, while other topics regarding serious risks are minimized. For example, many people fear an airplane accident, but statistically we are safer flying in a commercial plane than traveling by car. As Howie puts it, problems of safety correspond with its subjective nature. For laypeople, as opposed to experts, risks that threaten their ontological sense of control have further impacts than others that are likely more dangerous. Driving gives travelers a strong sense of control, whereas airplane travel provides uncertainty. Thus, we may state that, whenever mass media and journalists do not make a distinction between real and perceived safety, there tends to be a demand that the government intervene. We need further research to determine to what extent a government may attempt to fulfill all citizens' demands for security. History has witnessed how populist policies in these themes have led to terrible consequences when there has not been rational planning.

Tourism safety in Latin America has not evolved at the same level in all Latin American countries. For example, in Colombia, various administrations have historically struggled with organized crime; while in Argentina, there has not been a defined program to protect tourists either from acts of terrorism or from organized crime. Yet, although Argentines consider the problem of terrorism as being a United States or Middle East issue, they have experienced two major attacks killing almost 91 innocent citizens (Korstanje & Skoll, 2012). Although the Argentine government states that it recognizes the value of the tourism industry, it has no methods in place to keep its tourists safe. To better understand the development of risk perception on a country-by-country basis, it is necessary to understand the fears that each nation's citizens have. One way to understand national fears of risk is to analyze how much and what type of insurance the citizens of each nation choose to purchase.

Last but not least, the media and other responsible communication offices may protect or provoke a collapse of a tourist destination's image. Much of this perception is dependent on how news is transmitted.

Two main factors are of paramount importance to create an efficient plan of safety:

(a) the real probability of danger, which measures the real impacts of risk on a whole society

(b) the effects on social imagery, which measures the subjective perception of certain dangers.

Both of these two measurements are important for sustainable tourism programs. Policies based on the real probability of danger that ignore the power of communication are as useless as those articulated via perceived social threats.

There are three other factors that determine governments' urgency to mitigate risks in the tourist system: (1) the status of victims, (2) the probability of repetition, and (3) the threshold of control. Those events with a higher probability of repetition that affect children or vulnerable people terrify audiences in comparison with other negative events. These negative events have the most negative impact on tourist demands.

A visible threat may be taken into account to a lesser extent than those threats in which there is no known form of prevention, such as virus outbreaks or food pandemics. Furthermore, if the sanitary conditions are not adequate, then the impact may be such as to destroy almost overnight even a well-known international tourism "paradise."

Paradoxically, crime and terrorism generate each, in their own way, reactive adaptations. These adaptations occur when the probability of innocent victims rises. Along with a rise in state control, the public learns to adapt itself to the new situation consequently slowing down the process.

This may be one of the reasons why the public takes terrorism news less into account. This Foreword is meant to demonstrate the dichotomy between perceived and real safety and to shed light on the problems for policymakers to boost safe tourist destination images in these trying times. Tourism safety often depends on a locale's ability to project breaking news in such a way as to provide a more nuanced view of the event. Therefore, it is essential that both tourism professionals and academics work together with representatives of both public and private institutions to create tourism safety perceptions and realities.

Korstanje Maximiliano
Department of Economics,
University of Palermo, Argentina

REFERENCES

Blake, A., Arbache, J. S., Sinclair, M. T., & Teles, V. (2008). Tourism and poverty relief. *Annals of Tourism Research*, *35*(1), 107–126.
De Kadt, E. (1991). *Turismo:¿ pasaporte al desarrollo*. Madrid: Endymion.
Howie, L. (2012). *Witnesses to terror: Understanding the meanings and consequences of terrorism*. London, England: Palgrave Macmillan.

Korstanje, M. E. (2013). Preemption and terrorism. When the future governs. *Cultura, 10*(1), 167–184.

Korstanje, M. E., & Skoll, G. (2012). New York–Buenos Aires: Different solutions to the same problem: Terrorism and citizenry. *Rosa dos Ventos, 4*(1), 1–20.

Scheyvens, R. (2001). Poverty tourism. *Development Bulletin, 55*, 18–21.

INTRODUCTION

As I finish writing this book at the beginning of 2014, the world seems to be a very chaotic place indeed. In fact, there does not appear to be any one spot around the globe that does not have to face some form of danger or risk. From super-sized hurricanes (or typhoons) to earthquakes, from acts of terrorism to acts of crime, from social unrest to threats of war, tourism must exist and thrive in a world that often seems to have gone mad. Seeing the world through the eyes of the media, we cannot help but wonder how we make it to the next day and why anyone would travel. Yet, people continue to live their lives, travel, and find joy in learning about one another.

Perhaps what we perceive as modern madness has always been with us, and people in each generation saw themselves as living in a time of violence. Looking back on the twentieth century, the century in which modern tourism was born, we see a century filled with violence: acts of terrorism, genocide, war, and crime. Reading ancient texts helps us to put violence into a historical perspective. Certainly, the viewpoint that violence "covers the earth" goes as far back as Biblical times. Genesis notes that God destroyed the world through a flood, stating the reason as "the Earth was/would be corrupt and filled (would be filled) with violence before God. God saw the Earth and corruption was pervasive throughout the Earth" (Genesis 6:11–12, English Standard Version). Ironically, the violence causes not only the destruction of land life, but also the first cruise—a cruise to nowhere with Noah as its captain.

Just as acts of violence seem to have been born with the birth of humanity, so too have humans sought physical and mental ways to escape the horror of violence and add joy to their lives. Once again, the Biblical text clearly states that leisure is also a part of life: "And the heaven and the earth were finished, and on Saturday, God finished His work, which He had made, and He rested on Saturday (the seventh day) from all His work which He had made. And God blessed the seventh day and hallowed it" (Genesis 2:1–2, English Standard Version). Rest and leisure are not only necessary, but to ignore them is an offense against both God and the state. The sentiment that humans need more than merely the basics reaches its philosophical pinnacle in Deuteronomy where it states: "Human beings do not live by bread alone" (Deuteronomy 8:3, English Standard Version). In other words, what defines humanity is its ability to combine work with pleasure.

Perhaps it is this madness that provides the underpinning for leisure travel or tourism. Tourism is a road to personal escape. In a world in which many of us wonder about the direction that civilization is headed, tourism provides if not the answer at least the opportunity to clear one's head and to see the world through fresh eyes. Tourism, as distinguished from travel, is a leisure pursuit. A traveler, such as a business traveler, may have little choice as to where he or she goes. A soldier is also a traveler, but, more often than not, has no choice as to his or her destination. The tourist, on the other hand, has a choice. He or she makes a conscious decision as to where to go, where to stay within the destination of choice, and when to leave. Tourists, unlike visitors, literally vote with their feet.

Although mass or industrialized tourism is a relatively new field, for many countries other forms of tourism have been a valuable source of economic development. These lesser forms of tourism include the pilgrimage, the market, or fair-oriented tourism. Today, these specific forms of tourism have both a singular quality in the lone traveler and a massive quality as expressed by large trade shows and convention and pilgrimage cites such as the Hajj to Mecca. All these forms of tourism share the fact that they provide a nation with a venue with which it can showcase, to its own citizens and to the world, its culture, products, and even its political system.

Tourism is a unique industry in that it is one of the world's largest industries, and also perhaps the world's least-protected industry. For example, to quote the "World Travel & Tourism Council":

> *Travel & Tourism continues to be one of the world's largest industries. The total impact of the industry means that, in 2011, it contributed 9% of global GDP, or a value of over US$6 trillion, and accounted for 255 million jobs. Over the next ten years this industry is expected to grow by an average of 4% annually, taking it to 10% of global GDP, or some US$10 trillion. By 2022, it is anticipated that it will account for 328 million jobs, or 1 in every 10 jobs on the planet.*
>
> **(Travel and Tourism Economic Impact, 2012, Foreword)**

In reality, tourism is a composite industry composed of numerous smaller industries, and as such no one really knows the industry's true economic impact. Many of the numbers cited depend on which components are included in the industry and if we are to measure solely the direct impact of tourism or also its indirect impact.

In today's world, the cohort we call "tourists" and "travelers" may blend into new groups. A person may travel to a particular destination due to a business reason and then choose to stay longer, thus becoming a tourist. Likewise, a person may visit a specific location as a tourist and then return to invest in that locale and become a frequent traveler to, or investor in, that locale. Although the traveler and tourist may have different objectives, both suffer from some of the same sociological patterns. Both groups know what it is to be vulnerable, both may suffer from being in a state of anomie, and both are in a particular place but not of that place. Certain hypotheses used in this book are also valid for both groups. For example, it may also be hypothesized that the further a person travels from home, the more vulnerable he or she is to problems of cultural and linguistic differences that may impact on his or her sense of safety and security. The Spanish have a saying: *"para aprender hay que perder"* or "To learn one must be willing to lose." This means that we often do things, take chances, or accept risks that we might not take at home. Because we unfortunately live in a violent world, our "there" may be the local criminal's "here." The challenge is not only teaching visitors to be careful, but also the understanding that tourism security is as much about perceptions as it is about facts.

For example, the media may exaggerate the level of violence in a particular area, giving the impression that a locale has an excess of violence, or the media may create a false sense of security in which visitors are convinced that no matter what they do, nothing will occur. To complicate the situation, few places measure "nonevents," nor do they measure "nonreported events," leaving all tourism crime statistics as being open to debate.

What we do know is that reported violence can greatly impact a locale's tourism image, and in marketing a product such as tourism image is everything. Violence is to a society what cancer is to the body. Like cancer, it slowly gnaws away at a society's very fabric. When a society suffers from violence, fear enters, streets empty, and isolation overtakes the *joie de vivre* that is so essential to the world of tourism. Because tourism is a choice and not an obligation, fewer people will travel to places where they feel threatened. Often violence is accompanied, just as in the case of a physical ailment, with a sense of denial. Instead of confronting the problem, authorities simply deny it. Thus, a major threat to tourism is when its leaders believe that no matter what they do, people will come, that the level of violence simply does not matter. For too long a time, the tourism industry practiced some form or another of ostracism. That is, it took the position that if it saw no evil and spoke of no evil, that evil would not exist. Unfortunately, evil does exist and our visitors and tourists need protection from evil that comes in many forms and from many corners. In most other industries, security is considered to be a vital industry component. In tourism, on the other hand, many of its officials in the past labored from a schizophrenic position in which they feared violence against their clientele (visitors) and at the same time feared that overt protection of visitors would produce its own challenges and fears.

This schizophrenic industry position can be noted in many of the early studies about crime and tourism. In these studies, the authors assumed that tourists brought crime onto themselves, by the way that they dressed, spoke, and chose their jewelry. The assumption was that tourists were rich and that the locals were not and therefore tourism provoked jealousy due to conspicuous consumption. Put simply, the assumption was that the crime was the victim's fault. In the case of tourism, however, the media are attracted to incidents that involve visitors. The result being that the very thing that the industry has hoped to avoid, negative media publicity, becomes its reality.

Unfortunately, facts have a way of catching up with rhetoric. In tourism the public always has a choice not to come, and when tourism dries up, so do the businesses and public services that are dependent on tourism. Despite an often-heard popular myth, tourists do pay taxes in multiple forms, from room and entertainment taxes to transportation and sales taxes. The loss of tourism not only means the loss of revenue, but it also produces the perception that the community or locale that suffers from a lack of good tourism is not a good place to relocate a business. When the public refrains from visiting a locale due to fear of travel, social ills such as isolation may begin, cross-cultural fertilization ceases, and political and social accusations dominate the media and then creep into a locale's social climate.

The fight for civility then is the basis of tourism security and one of the reasons for having written this book. I wrote this book with the idea of not only providing additional tools for the tourism professional, but also with the hope that the lowering of violence will act to reinforce the principle that yes we are our brother's (and sister's) keepers; that it is our responsibility to make the world not only a safer place but also a better place. It is my hope that the book will inspire students of tourism science and professionals to do everything possible to promote a safe and worry-free travel experience so as to avoid suffering from the social cancer of crime and being damaged sociologically, morally, and spiritually.

Today tourism lives in a world that has come to know the continual horrors of terrorism and violence against tourists and visitors, against transportation and places of lodging. Every time a passenger passes through a metal detector, the visitor is reminded that we now live in a very dangerous world. For this reason, among others, tourism leaders have begun to address the issue of crime against visitors. This new awareness means that all forms of tourism security must cooperate and work together. The new world of tourism requires an understanding of the many aspects of tourism security and safety, from food safety issues to those dealing with potential pandemics, from issues of street crime to gang violence, from the illegal sale and consumption of drugs to acts of terrorism.

The first two chapters in this book deal with what tourism security is and how it impacts the economy. The book then moves onto types of security, from places of lodging to places of assembly. Other areas touched on are the threats of terrorism, legal threats, and issues of transportation. Finally, the book presents four case studies of two U.S. and two Latin American cities, comparing and contrasting each locale's tourism realities in its own words.

REFERENCES

Travel and tourism economic impact. (2012). *World Travel & Tourism Council*. Retrived from http://www.wttc.org/site_media/uploads/downloads/world2012.pdf.

CHAPTER 1

Introduction to Tourism Security

THE TOURISM PHENOMENON

Modern tourism is the world's largest peacetime industry, yet it often remains an enigma, not only to tourism scholars and professionals but also to those who are tasked with protecting visitors and the tourism industry. Tourism is something that everyone recognizes, but almost no one can define. There are almost as many explanations as to what tourism is as there are tourists.

While there may be scholarly debates over tourism's precise definition, there are still many areas of agreement. For example, most scholars will attest to the fact that tourism is about unique perceived experiences.

- Emotions are not necessarily connected to educational levels.
- Often, the higher the level of scientific reasoning within a society, then the more prone that society's members are to periods of irrational thought.
- In tourism, fantasy and reality may merge into a world of simulata. Simulata is the reproduction of reality in such a way that it mimics reality without being reality. A good example of simulata is the movie *Argo*, which is a movie about a movie.
- Security and safety have as much to do with our perceptions of them as they have to do with concrete data.

If we look at the United States, then we can note both facts and interpretations of facts. According to the World Tourism Organization (WTO), the United States ranked second in tourism arrivals with 62.3 million; France ranked first with 79.5 million arrivals (International Tourism & Number of Arrivals, 2013). However, if a person from, to use the Russian term, "the near abroad" chooses to use a French airport, is that person a tourist? Should a person who arrives at one Paris airport, and a few hours later leaves from another Paris airport, be considered a tourist? Do we define that person as a transient or a visitor?

Despite these statistical challenges, tourism is big business. In every U.S. state, tourism is either the largest or the second- or third-largest industry. If we assume that an export item is defined as "bringing money from place X to

Table 1.1 International Tourist Arrivals

1	France	Europe	79.5 million	77.1 million	+3.0%
2	United States	North America	62.3 million	59.8 million	+4.2%
3	China	Asia	57.6 million	55.7 million	+3.4%
4	Spain	Europe	56.7 million	52.7 million	+7.6%
5	Italy	Europe	46.1 million	43.6 million	+5.7%
6	Turkey	Europe	29.3 million	27.0 million	+8.7%
7	United Kingdom	Europe	29.2 million	28.3 million	+3.2%
8	Germany	Europe	28.4 million	26.9 million	+5.5%
9	Malaysia	Asia	24.7 million	24.6 million	+0.6%
10	Mexico	North America	23.4 million	23.3 million	+0.5%

Data taken from the World Tourism Organization for 2011.
www.indexmundi.com/facts/indicators/ST.INT.ARVL/Ranking (November 2, 2013).
Note: Different nations and organizations use different statistical methods and definitions of a tourist or tourist year, thus there will be slight variations in the numbers.
Source: 2013 tourism highlights (2013).

place Y," then tourism is also a major export item. Internationally, the tourism industry brings in millions of dollars, and it is one of the major job providers in many nations (Table 1.1).

TOURISM TERMINOLOGY AND HISTORY

The most common term employed among the industry's professionals is "travel and tourism." They use this term as if it were one word. Travel and tourism, however, are different from one another. Travel is one of the world's oldest phenomena. In a sense we can trace it back to the beginnings of recorded history. Humans, just as other species, have consistently wandered from place to place. Ancient men and women traveled to find food or escape danger, and they traveled due to harsh weather conditions or natural phenomena. Yet, few people saw travel as a pleasurable experience; in fact, travel was hard work. The entymology of the word *travel* reflects this difficulty. We derive the modern word *travel* from the French word *travail*, meaning "work," while the French derive *travail* from the Latin word *trepalium*, meaning an "instrument of torture."

For most of human history, travel was hard work and often torturous. Until the modern era (and even into the modern era), travelers never knew when weather conditions might turn "roads" into seas of mud. Robbers and kidnappers often ruled the nights, and pirates, stealing both goods and persons, were common fare. To add to travelers' woes, places of lodging were often cold and uncomfortable, they rarely provided privacy, and their food was irregular in both quantity and quality.

MODERN TOURISM DEFINITIONS

"Modern tourism" is one of those terms that most people understand, yet few people define well. There seems to be no definitive definition for "tourism." Tourism is defined as: "the practice of traveling for recreation; the guidance or management of tourists; the promotion and encouragement of touring; the accommodation of tourists" (*Merriam-Webster's Collegiate Dictionary*, 1993, p. 1248). Other scholars and tourism scientists present alternative definitions. For example, in the preface to *The Tourism System* (1985), David Pattison, then head of the Scottish Tourism Board, writes: "From an image viewpoint, tourism is presently thought of in ambiguous terms. No definitions of tourism are universally accepted. There is a link between tourism, travel, recreation, and leisure, yet the link is fuzzy..." (p. xvi).

However, Goeldner and McIntosh (1990) define tourism as: "the science, art, and business of attracting and transporting visitors, accommodating them, and graciously catering to their needs and wants" (p. vii). Later on, however, they state: "Any attempt to define tourism and to describe fully its scope must consider the various groups that participate in and are affected by this industry" (p. 3). The authors then describe four different scopes of tourism: (1) persons traveling for pleasure, (2) persons traveling for meetings or to represent another, (3) persons traveling for business, and (4) cruise passengers on shore (p. 6). In fact, we can reduce McIntosh and Goeldner's four categories into two, those traveling for pleasure or due to their own volition, and those traveling for commercial or business reasons.

On the other hand, Choy, Gee, and Makens (1989) in the work *The Travel Industry* define tourism by stating: "the travel industry will be defined as "the composite of organizations, both public and private, that are involved in the development, production, and marketing of products and services to serve the needs of travelers" (pp. 4–5) (Figure 1.1).

LACK OF A UNIFIED VOCABULARY

A review of the literature demonstrates that there is no one definition for the term "tourism," or any one single word to describe the industry. In the United States, travel or "travel and tourism" is the preferred colloquial,

The basic tourist model

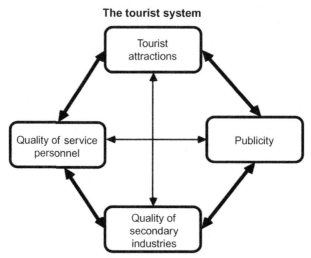

The tourist system

Figure 1.1 The tourism industry.

while in many other countries, the term "tourism" tends to dominate. Moreover, there is no set definition for the term "tourist" or how this phrase differs from others, such as visitor, or even day-tripper. For example, is a person who leaves his or her town to shop in a town nearby a tourist or a visitor? What if the same person stays in a taxable place of lodging? Are day-trippers tourists, visitors, or neither? What about cruise passengers who spend just a few hours in a port of call? What are they to be called?

For purposes of this book, a tourist is defined as someone who travels more than 100 miles (160 km) and stays at least one night in a taxable place of lodging or with family and friends. A visitor is defined as a person who earns his or her money in place X but spends it in place Y. A traveler can be a tourist, a visitor, or simply a person passing through a locale on his or her way to another locale.

TOURISM AS A SOCIAL PHENOMENON

Tourism is both a business and also a social phenomenon. In 2011, the economic volume of tourism equaled or, in some cases, surpassed that of oil exports, food products, or automobiles. So, tourism is a major player in international commerce. Not only is it a way to earn a relatively ecologically friendly income, but it also serves as a way for people from different parts of the world to gain a greater understanding of each other. The following figures, taken from the WTO, illustrate the importance of tourism.

Current Developments and Forecasts

- International tourist arrivals grew by nearly 4% in 2011 to 983 million;
- International tourism generated in 2011 was U.S. $1032 billion (€ 741 billion) in export earnings;
- UNWTO forecasts a growth in international tourist arrivals of between 3% and 4% in 2012.

(World Tourism Organization, 2012, Facts and Figures)

DEFINING TOURISM SECURITY

Considering how imprecise the terms "tourism" and "travel and tourism" are, it should not be surprising that in a composite industry such as tourism, the expression "tourism security" also suffers from the absence of a precise definition. This lack of precision with the terminology does not imply that tourism security practitioners are unaware of their major responsibility, which is to ensure both safety and security. What it does mean is that there are often questions as to who does what, as well as determining the boundaries of different roles. Just as in the case of law enforcement, police officers know that their job is fluid; they must always be prepared for the unexpected. Many police officers will state that their main responsibilities are to serve and protect anyone in their zone of duty, no matter where the person is originally from or how long he or she will stay in the area.

CLASSICAL AND MODERN TRAVEL CHALLENGES

While the nature of travel has changed over the course of time, the challenges facing modern travel are not new. At first, travel was just aimless wandering. By the Biblical period, two new aspects of travel had been added to the equation. Travel became necessary for international commerce, and pilgrimages began to emerge, providing not only a sense of the spiritual, but also a needed break from the drudgery of everyday life.

Ancient Middle Eastern texts, such as the Bible, tell of caravan traffic along the Futile Crescent (Babylonia to Egypt). Fairs were now common. At these fairs, people traveled to exchange goods, while the atmosphere of the fair added a sense of pleasure to the "travel" experience. From the first ancient fairs, the medieval fair was born. These early European fairs were not only places of commerce, but they also provided forms of entertainment, information exchanges, and relaxation. From the medieval period to the mid-twentieth century, travel underwent a transformation. Today, people travel for practical necessities, as well as to seek potential enjoyment. It is from this merging of necessity and enjoyment that modern tourism was born. Although tourism has numerous definitions, for the purposes of this book, we may see tourism as travel plus purpose, be that leisure or business.

Just as in the present day, many thieves in the past assumed that travelers would not be able to return to the sight of a robbery to pursue legal or punitive options, and that most travelers suffered from the disadvantage of unfamiliarity of place. Although, we can subdivide today's travelers into two categories—those who travel for pleasure (the leisure traveler) and those who travel for business—many of yesteryear's problems still exist today. Below is a partial listing of some of the reasons that travelers may become victims.

- Travelers often assume where they are going is safe.
- Travelers often lack proper details about their destination and the places through which they will pass on their way to their final destination.
- Travelers often have multiple destinations. This means that they may not even notice that they have lost something of value and when noticed may not have any idea as to where the object was lost.
- Travelers often forget objects of value or lose them along the way. Thus, the traveler may have no idea as to whether the object was lost or stolen.
- To travel is to take risks; travelers often take risks that they would not take at home.
- Travelers are often tired and/or hungry. Therefore, they may be thinking of immediate biological satisfaction rather than safety and security needs.
- Travelers do not know the place to which they are traveling (or through which they are passing), as well as the local population. Travelers may not know the local customs, tipping schedules, language, geography, and points of danger. Consequently, it is the traveler who is always at a disadvantage in a confrontation.
- Travelers often let down their guard or lower their level of inhibition.
- Travelers are on a schedule, so they often lower their standards of security and safety for the sake of staying within a specific time frame.
- Rarely are travelers willing to invest the time needed to file a police report, and they are often unwilling to spend the time and money needed to return to the site in order to testify against their assailant.
- Travelers are prone to become upset easily, leading to acts of rage.

- Few travelers are professional travelers, but most con artists and thieves are highly adept at what they do. In the competition between the traveler and the victimizer, the victimizer all too often has the advantage.

CONCEPTS OF LEISURE AND LEISURE TRAVEL

The idea of leisure travel is also far older than most people imagine. Under a sociological view, leisure was more than merely free time. As far back as Biblical times it was considered an activity that served to define human beings. The Biblical texts speak not just of free time but also of leisure. In the first chapters of Genesis, we read: "And the heaven and the earth were finished, and on the seventh day (Saturday), God finished His work, which He had made, and He rested on the seventh day from all His work which He had made. And God blessed the seventh day and hallowed it" (Genesis 2:1–2, English Standard Version). The Biblical writers saw leisure as more than simply work stoppage; instead, they viewed the concept of leisure as a positive precept that was ensconced in the Ten Commandments. Much of the social legislation of Western society was inspired by the idea that human beings were more than mere machines to be used and then discarded. Without the principle of time being a precious resource to be used and enjoyed, then tourism could not exist. The sentiment that humans need more than merely the basics reaches its philosophical pinnacle in Deuteronomy, where the text states: "Human beings do not live by bread alone" (Deuteronomy 8:3, English Standard Version). In other words, what defines humanity is its ability to balance our working world with pleasure. Hebrew social law even divides the concept of rest into destructive rest (*sikhuk*), restorative rest (*shvitah*), and productive rest (*nofesh*).

However, the Biblical idea of rest and relaxation did not exist without challenges. The rise of modern capitalism produced the notion that time is money, so to waste time was a "sin." The Industrial Revolution brought about the invention of machines that could work without rest. Therefore, rest and leisure stood in the way of economic progress. With the advent of the Industrial Revolution, the Protestant Ethic and Marxian thought were new ideas that began to define leisure. Both of these theories, in their own way, tended to see leisure as a poor use of time, as well as counterproductive to a healthy society. Thus, the Protestant Ethic, under the backdrop of the Industrial Revolution, tended to glorify work, and it saw southern European and Catholic traditions, such as the *siesta*, as examples of decadence. In some ways, these new social thinkers were correct. For example, the Spanish concept of the "hidalgo" meant that work was a social phenomenon about which one should be ashamed. The basic concept of the hidalgo was to exhibit great pride in having servants and in "doing nothing."

This same sense of leisure nothingness, which in classical Hebrew is called "*sikhuk*," also dominated much of classical Russian literature, such as *Anna Karenina*. Ironically, as history progressed, both Nazi and Marxist social thinkers came to despise the notion of leisure. The sign over Auschwitz, "Arbeit macht frei (Work makes you free)," is the most cynical transformation of leisure into a negative quality in history. Marxists, who hated the Nazis' view of the world, oddly arrived at the same conclusions. Marxists and neo-Marxists viewed leisure as periods of nonproduction in which the upper-class bourgeoisie took advantage of the working-class proletariat.

Marxists then stood in direct opposition to the Hebrew biblical *weltanschauung* (worldview). The classical neo-Marxist theorists assumed that leisure and leisure activities represented a manifestation of economic disparity between the wealthier tourist and the poorer members of the economy. From their perspective, leisure activities were nothing more than another means of bourgeoisie domination over the proletariat. This notion of leisure belonging only to the upper classes would later manifest itself in the neo-Marxist notion that the tourist was in many ways responsible for his or her own victimization.

TOURISM SECURITY IS MORE THAN CRIMINAL BEHAVIOR

To complicate matters further, tourism security deals with much more than just criminal behavior. Tourism professionals must continually fight against criminals who would seek to develop either a parasitic relationship with tourism or seek to take advantage of tourists and visitors. Visitors are often victims of acts that may not be illegal but are immoral and destroy a locale's reputation. For example, shop owners may bother (harass) visitors, without technically breaking the law, to the point where the visitors no longer feel comfortable. Furthermore, local mores and customs mean that what is acceptable behavior in one culture may not be acceptable in another. Often, these cultural clashes are likely to occur in places where multiple cultures, and diverse economic statuses, are placed within the same geographic locale or forced to intermix with each other.

To add to the difficulties, there is a general confusion between issues of security, safety, and, in this book, what we call "tourism surety." In a number of European languages, such as French, Portuguese, and Spanish, the same word is used for both security and safety. Security and safety experts do not always agree where one concept ends and another begins. For example, we speak of food safety, but if a person intentionally alters food so as to sicken someone else, then this act is no longer a food-safety issue but becomes a food-security issue. In the same manner, tourism specialists must worry about a traveler who deliberately carries a communicative disease from one locale to another for the purpose of harming others. Is such an act one of biological terrorism, a security matter, or an issue of safety?

CRIMINAL ACTS AND ACTS OF TERRORISM

As Brazil prepares for the 2014 FIFA World Cup Games and the 2016 Rio de Janeiro Olympic games, the country has been rife with criminal acts against foreign tourists. For example, *BBC News* ran the following headline "Brazil: Foreign tourist raped on Rio de Janeiro minibus." The article went on to state that "the (foreign) couple's identities and nationalities have not been disclosed," and that "Curbing violence is a major priority for the authorities in Rio, which is hosting the football World Cup next year and the 2016 Olympics" (2013, para. 3). Rio de Janeiro takes the problem of crime very seriously with what it calls a "shantytown pacification program" (*comunidades pacificadas*), yet the city has still not been able to solve the rape issue, with over 488 rapes having occurred in December 2012.

Table 1.2 shows some of the difficulties in determining criminal acts and how they differ from terrorism in the world of tourism. Table 1.2 also emphasizes how terrorism is not the same as crime. Crime is an antisocial form of capitalism, and as such, its end goal is economic gain. Terrorism, on the other hand, is political in nature. Terrorists may use economic methods to fund their actions, but their ultimate goal is political in nature.

Tourism has become a front-line battleground, not only for criminals, but for terrorism as well. Tourism sites, known as "soft targets," have often been successful objectives for terrorists. These acts of terrorism have taken place in both urban and rural settings, in countries considered "at peace" and in nations considered "at war." As a result, terrorism has impacted the world of tourism in multiple settings and on a worldwide scale.

The following is a partial list of places where terrorism has been launched against the tourism industry.

- Egypt
- Germany
- Indonesia

Table 1.2 Key Differences Between Acts of Tourism Crime and Terrorism

	Crime	Terrorism
Goal	Usually economic or social gain	To gain publicity and sometimes sympathy for a cause
Usual type of victim	Person may be known to the perpetrator or selected because he or she may yield economic gain	Killing is a random act and appears to be more in line with a stochastic model Numbers may or may not be important
Defenses in use	Often reactive, reports taken	Some proactive devices such as radar detectors
Political ideology	Usually none	Robin Hood model
Publicity	Usually local and rarely makes the international news	Almost always is broadcast around the world
Most common forms in tourism industry are:	Crimes of distraction Robbery Sexual assault	Domestic terrorism International terrorism Bombings Potential for biochemical warfare
Statistical accuracy	Often very low, in many cases the travel and tourism industry does everything possible to hide the information	Almost impossible to hide Numbers are reported with great accuracy and repeated often
Length of negative effects on the local tourism industry	In most cases, it is short term	In most cases, it is long term unless replaced by new positive image

Source: Tarlow (2001), pp. 134–135).

- Israel
- Jordan
- Kenya
- Mexico
- Morocco
- Peru
- The Philippines
- Spain
- United Kingdom
- United States

The one unifying factor between these nations is that they all have a success-ful tourism industry. Tourism professionals, along with students of tourism, have wondered what attracts terrorist organizations to tourism. Below are some of the reasons for this attraction.

- Tourism is interconnected with transportation centers, so an attack on tourism impacts world transportation.
- Tourism is a big business and terrorism seeks to destroy economies.
- Tourism is interrelated with multiple industries; thus, an attack on the tourism industry may also wipe out a number of secondary industries.
- Tourism is highly media oriented and terrorists seek publicity.
- Tourism must deal with people who have no history. Consequently, there is often no database and it is easy for terrorists simply to blend into the crowd.
- Tourism must deal with a constant flow of new people, so terrorists are rarely suspected.
- Tourism is a nation's "parlor" (i.e., it is the keeper of a nation's self-image, icons, and history). Tourism centers are the living museum of a nation's cultural riches.
- Terrorists tend to seek targets that offer at least three of the four possi-bilities listed below, and these same possibilities often exist in the world of tourism.
  1. Potential for mass casualties.
  2. Potential for mass publicity and "good media images."
  3. Potential to do great economic damage.
  4. Potential to destroy an icon.

PROFESSIONAL FEARS OF ADDRESSING CRIME AND TERRORISM

Traditionally, many tourism professionals have avoided addressing issues of tourism security and tourism safety altogether. There was a common (mis-placed) feeling among them that even speaking about these subjects would frighten customers. Visitors would wonder if too much security indicated that they should be afraid. Especially in the years prior to 2001, the industry often took the position that the less said about tourism security and safety, the better. From the industry's perspective, security professionals were nei-ther to be heard nor seen. For this reason, many tourism locales, prior to 2001, employed what was called "soft uniforms." The idea was to blend the security agent's dress with that of the locale's décor or theme.

For instance, hotels in Hawaii had their security agents use aloha-type shirts that matched the island's typical tourism dress code. Tourism professionals hoped that this blending of uniforms would permit low-profile security that would protect guests without their guests noticing that they were being protected.

In reality, nothing could have been further from the truth. For the most part, travelers and tourists, especially after September 11, 2001, tended to seek out places offering a sense of security and safety. Although a small minority of travelers seeks out dangerous endeavors, most visitors want to know what the industry is doing to protect them. They also wish to know how well prepared a local industry is if a security or safety issue should occur.

As noted above, although many academic disciplines make a clear distinction between security and safety, tourism scientists and professionals tend not to do so. Security is often seen as protection against a person or thing that seeks to do another harm. Safety is often defined as protecting people against unintended consequences of an involuntary nature. For example, a case of arson is a security issue, while a spontaneous fire is a safety issue. In the case of the travel and tourism industry, both a safety mishap and a security mishap can destroy not only a vacation, but the industry as well. It is for this reason that the two are combined into the term "tourism surety." As shown in Figure 1.2, tourism surety is the point where safety, security, reputation, and economic viability meet.

PRE AND POST SEPTEMBER 11, 2001

In the Western world, modern tourism security has two distinct historical periods. The first historical period was prior to September 11, 2001.

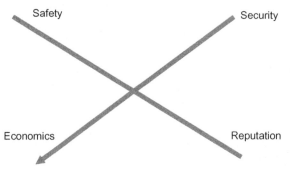

Figure 1.2 The relationships between safety, security, economics, and reputation.

As has been noted, this period was marked by several historical trends within tourism:

- There was no clear distinction made between acts of terrorism and criminal acts. Terrorism was treated as if it were a criminal act rather than an act of war.
- Most tourism professionals underplayed the importance of tourism security. Agents were kept out of sight or given uniforms that blended in with the locale's décor.
- Police and tourism officials often had no (or a minimal amount of) collaboration. Both sides of the public security/tourism line tended to know little about each other.
- There was often a pseudo-hostile environment between public safety agencies and tourism professionals.
- Public safety officials and tourism officials did not share a common vocabulary.

A few examples serve to illustrate these trends. If we look at the United States, the attitudes listed above prevailed despite the fact that many destinations and locales, such as Florida, had received a great deal of undeserved negative publicity in the 1990s, due to the unfortunate murders of, and assaults on, several foreign tourists. In many other nations around the world, the level of awareness was even lower. Tourism professionals even admitted that their industry required a safe and secure environment in which to thrive, but they often chose to look the other way. Furthermore, prior to 9/11, few U.S. police departments were aware of their responsibilities toward the tourism industry. Many police departments took pride in the fact that they treated tourists just like anyone else and had no special policies for tourists or police trained in tourism security. The idea that tourists or tourist facilities, such as hotels, were a high-risk group, that local police might need special training in working with a location's out-of-town guests, or that the industry needed special protection were simply either unknown to most U.S. police departments or had not entered the realm of consciousness.

This first historical period came to a sudden closure on September 11, 2001, when the forced grounding of air traffic around the world meant that travel and tourism had come to an almost sudden and total halt. September 11, 2001, changed the course of travel and tourism forever, and it forced tourism professionals to realize that without tourism surety, no amount of marketing would save their industry. While many tourism professionals did not consider tourism security to be essential prior to 9/11, after that time, the industry radically changed its position.

TOURISM SAFETY, SECURITY, AND SURETY IN THE POST-9/11 WORLD

Although many disciplines make a clear distinction between security and safety, tourism scientists and professionals tend not to. The reason is simple: a ruined vacation is a ruined vacation, and the fixing of blame is therefore a secondary activity. Another reason for this merging is that there are no clear and precise definitions of safety and security. Practitioners often view security as the act of protection of a person, place, thing, reputation, or economy against someone (or someone's tool) that seeks to harm. They typically define safety as the protecting of people (or places, things, reputations, or economies) against unintended consequences of an involuntary nature. From the perspective of the travel and tourism industry, both a safety and a security mishap can destroy not only a vacation, but also the industry. It is for this reason that the two are combined into the term "tourism surety."

Although we use terms such as "tourism safety," "security," or "surety," in reality there is no such thing as total travel (tourism) security/safety. A good rule of thumb is to remember that everything made by human beings can also be harmed or destroyed by human beings. Also, there is never 100% total security. Accordingly, security, or tourism surety, is a game of risk management. The job of the tourism professional is to limit the risk to manageable levels. This is another reason why we use the term "surety," which is a term borrowed from the insurance industry. Surety refers to a lowering of the probability that a negative event will occur. Surety focuses on improvement rather than perfection because it takes into account that risk is prevalent in everyday life. Since few people work according to strict academic guidelines, this book uses the terms "surety," "security," and "safety" interchangeably.

AN OVERVIEW OF TOURISM SURETY: THE PRE-9/11 YEARS

In the first part of this chapter, we saw how travel and tourism professionals treated issues of tourism surety (security). Now, we return to the early years and see how police and other security agencies treated the topic. It is in these earlier years that the basic principles of tourism surety were first established.

In the 1990s, the idea that tourism security was important and required a partnership with other security professionals, such as hotel security departments, had only just started to enter into the collective psyche of the travel and tourism industry. Tourism textbooks treated the subject in a superficial manner, criminology texts ignored the topic completely, and there was little separate theory to support or guide police as to why they should even be concerned with another facet of their profession.

During the 1990s, even major U.S. tourism centers, such as Las Vegas and Honolulu, had done little to study the problem. Until 1990, there was no such thing as a tourism security conference. The first such conference was held in Las Vegas in the early 1990s. As stated before, the industry was still fearful of speaking openly about security, so this inaugural conference was called the "Las Vegas Tourism Safety Seminar." The conference leaders chose the words *seminar* and *safety* (instead of *security*) so as to not scare people or call too much attention to the issue of tourism safety. As late as the 1990s, no police academy provided police officers with any special tourism training, and few police departments were even aware that the topic existed.

In 1992, several foreign tourists were murdered in Miami, and the media turned these deaths into a cause. Soon, Florida tourism officials were on the defensive. From the perspective of history, these incidents in Florida were incredibly important, not because a great number of people were injured, but because the negative publicity that Florida received made police departments sensitive to a whole new area of policing and the fact that new methods and units would need to be established. Perhaps for this reason, several police agencies in the early 1990s began to see the need for what was then called "tourism safety." Among the pioneering departments were the Orange County (Orlando, Florida) Sheriff's office, which developed a tourism task force lead by Detective Ray Wood; Clark County's Metro (Las Vegas, Nevada), whose Sheriff Jerry Kelley asked his detective Curtis Williams to develop a task force; and Honolulu, Hawaii, whose Captain Karl Godsey worked with local tourism officials to develop what eventually came to be known as "the Aloha patrol." By the end of the decade, other cities, such as Miami (Florida), New Orleans (Louisiana), New York City, Detroit (Michigan), and Anaheim (California), had also established some form of special tourism safety unit.

As the importance of tourism spread throughout the United States, the idea of tourism policing also spread. For example, Texas A&M University's extension program asked me to develop a course for Texas communities in tourism safety, and it noted that tourism policing also aided police departments in related issues, such as:

- Customer service
- Ethnic diversity
- Cultural awareness
- Community policing

In the latter part of the decade, special police courses also began in less major tourism-oriented areas such as Long Beach (Washington), College Station (Texas), and Charleston (South Carolina). While these latter communities were not major tourism centers, tourism still played a significant part in their local economy. The field also continued to grow when the United States Bureau of Reclamation asked me to develop a groundbreaking tourism safety course for all of its facilities.

Starting in 1990, a series of tourism safety conferences began. The earliest ones were held in Las Vegas and Orlando. During the latter half of the decade, under the leadership of Don Ahl of the Las Vegas Convention and Visitors Authority and I, the Las Vegas seminar has turned into a national seminar on tourism safety. It has also fostered a number of local spin-off seminars in such cities as Detroit, Honolulu, and Anaheim. Today, these seminars have become part of both the Spanish- and English-speaking worlds, with sessions in places such as the Dominican Republic, Panama, Colombia, and Aruba. Although each individual seminar often reflects specific local or national needs, there are a number of topics that unite these assemblies:

- The idea that tourism security is composed of multicomponents and is multifaceted
- The need for tourism security officials to explain to the industry that every security decision is, in the end, a business decision
- Tourism security is a highly complex profession that requires a tremendous amount of knowledge in many diverse areas, such as
  - Language skills
  - Intercultural communication skills
  - Sensitivity training
  - Gender roles
  - Listening skills
  - Anger management

Tourism security professionals are increasingly aware of the high level of professionalism exhibited by those who would seek to take advantage of tourists and the tourism industry itself. Although many visitors assume that tourism criminals (and/or terrorists who act against the tourism industry) are amateurs, the reality is that these criminals have become adept in sophisticated technology, and they study their victims (i.e., businesses, locales, or people) with high levels of precision.

Then, during the 1990s, there was a slow development of the general principles of tourism safety. In 1996, the International Association of Chiefs of Police (located in Arlington, Virginia) established its first course in tourism safety, and in 1998, George Washington University launched its first course in tourism safety via the Internet. In 1999, Orange County, Florida, attempted to establish a conference of major tourism cities. Some of the established doctrines included:

- Local police departments cannot assume that visitors will use the highest level of common sense when it comes to their own safety. Police departments and hotel/attraction security professionals will have to do what the visitor will not.
- Crimes committed against visitors cost the industry and local communities millions of dollars. Plus, these crimes can ruin a locale's reputation for many years.
- Tourism protection requires partnerships. These partnerships include many aspects of the security and safety industries, government agencies, hotel managers, and tourism offices.
- The tourism industry needs the help of universities to understand and find solutions to the problems concerning visitor safety.
- Tourism security and safety must be handled on a regional, state, and national basis.
- Wherever there is tourism, there is a major need for tourism security and tourism-oriented policing/protection services training.
- Recognize that tourism is a significant item on the crime prevention and community safety agenda that has been slow to arrive in most countries.

THE POST-9/11 PERIOD

Soon after the attacks of September 11, 2001, it was not uncommon to hear people use the phrase "9/11 changed everything." The numbers 9 and 11 have now become a new noun, 9/11, and to a greater extent reflect a new era of travel hassles and fear. September 11, 2001, may be considered the date when the travel and tourism industry lost its innocence. Along with much of the world's economy, the travel and tourism industry suffered. To illustrate, in the city of Las Vegas, well over 10% of the tourism workforce (hotels, valets, etc.) lost their jobs within hours of the attack. Tourism professionals, who had avoided speaking about tourism security issues, now began to wonder if they might have been incorrect. Police officers were revered as heroes, while the public, which had been antimilitary due to the Vietnam War, now began to embrace the military. In the days immediately following 9/11, tourism officials throughout the world knew that they were in a fight for the very survival of their industry.

Moreover, the tourism industry faced another difficulty. The public now demanded what the tourism industry could not deliver: total security. Security professionals understood that no person or agency could ever guarantee 100% security. The trouble was that the public and the media refused to accept this fact. Instead of viewing successes, tourism had to deal with a media that chose to sensationalize every act or threat against tourism. This new form of "yellow-journalism by perception" created a new problem, the perception that travel was more dangerous than it really was. The travel and tourism industry now had to face three separate enemies: the terrorist who sought to destroy tourism, the criminal who sought to take advantage of the industry and its clients, and the media that inadvertently became an ally to the industry's enemies.

More than a decade has passed since 9/11 became a household term. We often forget that in the years immediately following 9/11, the public begged for tighter airport security, "foreign" biological substances were found on airplanes, and fear manifested in the form of believing post office deliveries contained anthrax. At the dawn of the new millennium, newspapers reported, on an almost daily basis, threats by terrorist groups against transportation companies and prominent locations. Due to the shock of how vulnerable it was, the tourism industry began to see the world through different eyes, and tourism security evolved from hidden necessity to marketing tool. Tourism professionals realized they needed a great deal more than just cosmetic changes to beat the threats against their industry; they also needed cooperation from allies outside of the industry. Travel and tourism leaders turned to governmental agencies and to both public and private security for help. For example, in the United States immediately following 9/11, then President George W. Bush, along with several Hollywood stars, made a series of television adds encouraging the public to return to the world of travel. It was at this time (e.g., 2002) that the Department of Homeland Security was born. The Department's official website notes:

> Eleven days after the September 11, 2001, terrorist attacks, Pennsylvania Governor Tom Ridge was appointed as the first Director of the Office of Homeland Security in the White House. The office oversaw and coordinated a comprehensive national strategy to safeguard the country against terrorism and respond to any future attacks.
>
> With the passage of the Homeland Security Act by Congress in November 2002, the Department of Homeland Security formally came into being

as a stand-alone, Cabinet-level department to further coordinate and unify national homeland security efforts, opening its doors on March 1, 2003. (Department of Homeland Security, 2002, *Department Creation section*).

The old paradigm of hiding security professionals was no longer valid. Eventually, visible security was not only in vogue, but it was understood to be a tourism-marketing tool. In a like manner, the tourism industry and local police departments realized that they could no longer afford to ignore each other and have a serious incident arise. It became clear to both travel and tourism officials and police departments that the best way to recover from terrorism was to prevent it. Industry and political leaders realized that it was only through vigilance, interagency cooperation, and a serious commitment to security that they would regain the public's trust.[1]

After 9/11, tourism officials soon became intimately involved in national and international security issues. This involvement, however, was not a mere "love fest." Tourism officials soon realized that governmental changes, such as the creation of the TSA in the United States, often were cosmetic rather than substantive. Furthermore, many of these changes added a new "hassle factor" that turned travel from a pleasure into a chore. Additionally, a number of high-profile mistakes were made by less well-trained "air security personnel," which caused the public to rapidly lose confidence in government-run tourism security programs. It was also during the post-9/11 period that tourism security conferences went from small conclaves or seminars to large conferences. At the same time, universities, such as George Washington University in Washington, D.C., began to offer courses and/or lecture series in tourism security and safety.

TOPPs: THE FIRST DEFENSE AGAINST TOURISM CRIMES

Many communities have established special police units to aid in the tourism industry. The most common term in the English language to describe these units is "TOPPs," which is an acronym standing for *tourism-oriented policing/ protection services*. In Spanish the word is often translated as "*seguridad turística*" or "*politur*" (a composite word of the two Spanish words *policía* and *turismo*).

---

[1] See articles such as "Tourism in Crisis: Managing the Effects of Terrorism" (Sönmez, Apostolopoulos, & Tarlow); "Providing Safety for Tourists: A Study of a Selected Sample of Tourist Destinations in the United States and Brazil" (Tarlow & Santana, *Journal of Travel Research*, May 2002; 40(4), 424–431); and "Making Tourists Feel Safe: Whose Responsibility Is It?" (Pizam, Tarlow, & Bloom).

No matter what these officers are called, they share certain similarities. Although TOPPs units reflect local conditions, they tend to emphasize at least the following topics:
- Tourism's economic impact on the community
- Law enforcement's role in the special needs of specific demographic groups
- Law enforcement and customer service
- Crimes of distraction
- Terrorism
- Crime prevention through environmental design
- Media relations
- Foreign language skills
- Anger management
- Transportation security issues
- Tourism crowd control issues

TOPPs units differentiate themselves from typical law enforcement by how they judge success. Classical police departments judge success by the number of crimes solved. From this perspective, policing tends to be more reactive than proactive. TOPPs units, on the other hand, are encouraged to count success not by the number of crimes solved but rather by the number of crimes prevented. Because travel and tourism is a composite industry, TOPPs units must reflect the industry's varied nature. Although no two TOPPs units are alike, most of them have to deal with at least six major tourism areas. These are:

- *Visitor Protection.* Tourism surety assumes that security professionals and police will need to know how to protect visitors from themselves, from locals, from other visitors, and even from less than honest staff members. Tourism security and safety experts should consider the needs of less-seen employees, such as cleaning staff and hotel engineers, and they must seek to ensure that site environments are both attractive and as secure/safe as possible.
- *Protection of Staff.* It is essential that the industry demonstrate to its employees that it cares about its staff. Travel and tourism is a service-oriented industry, so it cannot afford low employee morale. When staff members work in crime-ridden environments or are subjected to multiple forms of harassment, morale soon begins to drop, and then the customer receives lower levels of service. Tourism is a high-pressure industry and it is all too easy for staff members to be abused or for tempers to flare, which leads to a hostile work situation.

- *Site Protection.* It is the responsibility of tourism surety specialists to protect tourism sites. The term "site" is used loosely and can refer to any physical place, from a place of lodging to an attraction or monument. Site protection must take into account both the person who seeks to do harm to the site, as well as the careless traveler. For example, vacationers may simply forget to care for furniture, appliances, or equipment.
- *Ecological Management.* Closely related to, yet distinct from, site security is the protection of the area's ecology. In this text, ecology not only refers to the physical environment, but to the cultural environment also. No tourism entity lives in a vacuum. The care of a locale's streets, lawns, and internal environment has a major impact on tourism surety. It behooves specialists in tourism surety to protect the cultural ecology of an area. Strong cultures tend to produce safe places. On the other hand, when cultures begin to decay, crime levels tend to rise. Protecting the cultural ecology, along with the physical ecology, of a locale is a major preventative step that tourism surety professionals can do to lower crime rates and to ensure a safer and more secure environment.
- *Economic Protection.* Tourism is a major generator of income on both national and local levels. Consequently, it is open to attack from various sources. For example, terrorists may see a tourism site as an ideal opportunity to create economic havoc. In opposition to terrorists, criminals often do not wish to destroy a tourism locale; instead, they view that locale as an ideal "fishing" ground to harvest an abundance of riches. A philosophical question that has still not been resolved is, Do law enforcement agents and tourism security professionals have a special role in protecting the economic viability of a locale so as to provide tourism with extra levels of protection?
- *Reputation Protection.* We only need to read a newspaper to realize that crimes and acts of terrorism against tourism entities receive a great deal of media attention. The classical method of simply denying that there is a problem is no longer valid and can undercut a tourism locale's promotional efforts. For example, the Natalie Holloway case in Aruba in 2005 cost the island not only millions of dollars in lost tourism revenue, but also prestige and reputation. When there is a lapse in tourism security, the effect is long term. Some of the consequences to a locale's reputation may include the locale's moving from upper- to lower-class clientele, the need to drop prices, the general deterioration of the site, and the need for a major marketing effort to counteract the negative reputation.

SUMMARY

Travel and tourism have undergone historic changes. In this chapter, we see an overview of travel and tourism and the interacting role that safety, security, and surety has played in one of the world's largest industries. The chapter emphasizes the concept of leisure and shows how our modern concept is based on a Biblical premise, of rest on the seventh day. The chapter touches upon public perceptions of tourism security and safety and reality and it emphasizes the difficulties faced by a security professional, whether in the private or public sector. The chapter also underlines the financial and social challenges that face the tourism security practitioner.

REFERENCES

Merriam-Webster's Collegiate Dictionary (10 ed.) (1993). Springfield, MA: Merriam-Webster.

2013 tourism highlights (2013). *World Tourism Organization*. Retrieved from http://dtxtq4w60xqpw.cloudfront.net/sites/all/files/pdf/unwto_highlights13_en_hr.pdf.

Brazil: Foreign tourist raped on Rio de Janeiro minibus (2013). *BBC News*. Retrieved from http://www.bbc.co.uk/news/world-latin-america-21990788.

Choy, D., Gee, Y., & Makens, J. (1989). *The travel industry* (2nd ed.). New York, NY: Van Nostrand-Reinhold.

Creation of the Department of Homeland Security (2002). *United States Department of Homeland Security*. Retrieved from http://www.dhs.gov/creation-department-homeland-security.

Goeldner, C., & McIntosh, R. (1990). *Tourism principles, practices and philosophies* (6th ed.). Hoboken, NJ: John Willey & Sons, Inc.

International tourism, number of arrivals (2013). *The World Bank*. Retrieved from http://data.worldbank.org/indicator/ST.INT.ARVL.

Pattinson, D. (1985). Preface. In *The tourism system: an introductory text Robert Christie Mill and Alastair M. Morrison* (p. xvi). Upper Saddle River, NJ: Prentice Hall.

Tarlow, P. E. (2001). Tourism safety and security. In T. Jamal, & M. Robinson (Eds.), *The SAGE handbook of tourism studies* (p. 466). Los Angeles, CA: Sage.

World Tourism Organization (2012). *UNWTO*. Retrieved from http://www2.unwto.org.

CHAPTER 2

The Relationship between Tourism Security and the Economy

PART 1: HOW SECURITY, OR THE LACK OF SECURITY, IMPACTS THE TOURISM INDUSTRY'S ECONOMY

Chicago is one of the great U.S. cities, famous for its Magnificent Mile, beautiful lakefront, many museums, and fine dining. Chicago attracts both leisure and business travelers, and it has a thriving convention business. Unfortunately, Chicago also has its darker side. In the 1920s, this city was home to illegal establishments to consume alcoholic beverages, called speak-easies, and was famous for its gangster, rum-runner culture. The entertainment industry has enshrined the city's sordid past with the play *Chicago*. There is no doubt that Chicago's dark past has become part of its tourism product. There are different definitions for the term "dark tourism." Baran (2012), writing in an article for *Travel Weekly*, notes: "It can be morbid. It's always a bit voyeuristic. But it seems like a fundamental human urge. Like drivers slowing to gawk at a gruesome accident, tourists often feel a profound need to see the aftermath of disaster and devastation wherever in the world they strike. The result is a form of travel increasingly coming to be known as 'dark tourism'" (para. 1–2).

Dark tourism then is a place where death and destruction have turned into tourism attractions. These "places that silently speak out to us" may be cemeteries, places where crimes have been committed, and/or reminders of a past best forgotten. As Baran (2012) writes: "From ground zero in New York and Katrina's destructive force in New Orleans to the Auschwitz concentration camp in Poland and the Killing Fields in Cambodia, witnessing places where horrific deaths have occurred has for many become an integral part of experiencing a destination" (para. 3).

Within dark tourism we find a range of options. Thus, it should come as no surprise that Chicago's checkered past can serve as a tourism draw. Recently, Chicago's violent past turned into its violent present. Although most of Chicago's current inflation in crime (2012–2013) has nothing to do with bootlegging, and as of the writing of this chapter, the violence has not touched the city's tourism districts, there is the fear that the city's negative crime wave may be impacting the city's tourism industry. In fact, Bergen (2012) wrote the following in the *Chicago Tribune*:

> Chicago's extensive efforts to reinvigorate its convention and tourism industries could be damaged unless the city quickly defuses the violent crime wave that has exploded in its neighborhoods and nicked the downtown, the city's top convention and tourism official said Wednesday.
>
> "We hope this sunsets quickly because all the good work we're doing regionally, nationally and internationally, if this is not contained in a reasonable period of time, it will have an impact," Don Welsh, president and chief executive of Choose Chicago, said in a morning meeting with the Chicago Tribune's editorial board.
>
> **(Business section, p. 1)**

The impact of Welch's words was felt immediately. The next day the *Huffington Post* noted that Welsh had had to retract his words, claiming that they were taken out of context, due to a deluge of inquiries regarding Chicago safety. The following day, the *Huffington Post* wrote:

> Welsh then revealed that his office has been receiving inquiries from meeting planners questioning whether the Second City is a safe destination, particularly as reports of so-called "mob-style" attacks in and near the city's Magnificent Mile shopping district and the city's surging homicide rate have gone national.
>
> Welsh later Wednesday claimed in an interview with the Chicago Sun-Times that his comments were "taken out of context," though he did acknowledge that Choose Chicago has fielded "five or six" calls over a period of just over a month from meeting planners anxious about crime in the city.
>
> "They're asking if these issues are taking place in the downtown area or near McCormick Place and the answer we've given them is an emphatic, 'No,'" Welsh told the Sun-Times.
>
> Welsh went on to call a "mob-style" attack near Michigan Avenue last month an "isolated incident" and maintained that Chicago is "the safest big city in the world." Last week, 11 youths attacked a man leaving the Fourth of July fireworks show in the city's River North neighborhood.
>
> "The shootings we have seen have been almost 100% isolated to neighborhoods outside the downtown core of Chicago where tourists and visitors from around the world frequent," Welsh told the paper.
>
> **("Chicago crime impacting tourism?," para. 3–7)**

The Chicago example is not unique. For example, in the early part of 2013, Las Vegas found itself in the ironic situation that its crime rate had fallen but due to a few highly publicized crimes, people's confidence in their safety had also fallen. For example, one headline from the *Las Vegas Sun* stated that "Las Vegas seen as dangerous even as crime drops" (Dreier, 2013). The article goes on to state that the perception of crime is enough to keep people away, thereby transforming a negative perception into a negative economy. Vacations have traditionally been a means by which people attempt to escape from the stress and rigors of everyday life. However, what once served as a way to repair body and soul has now become a new area for victimization. The perception that travel may result in bodily harm, loss of property, or even death is a threat to one of the country's largest industries. Events such as the bombing of New York's World Trade Center, the Los Angeles riots with its subsequent loss of billions of dollars, and attacks on foreign tourists in various locations throughout the United States have once again made travel/visitor officials realize how sensitive their industry's economy is to security issues.

Questions of violence directly impact the travel industry's ability to promote a safe and worry-free experience and can result in major economic losses. Vacationers traditionally have viewed their trips as an escape from the world's problems and from the worries of everyday life. While on tour, the last thing vacationers want to be concerned about is being a victim of crime. Business travelers, being more cognizant of safety issues, may also shy away from high-risk locales. Although no locale can provide a perfect security environment, by developing a cooperative relationship between the law enforcement and tourism industries, the risk factor of private security concerns can be substantially reduced. This new relationship is a means for law enforcement to emphasize its commitment to public service and demonstrate its importance to a community's economic viability.

Consequently, toward the end of 2008 major tourism centers and small towns felt an economic meltdown whose impact has lasted for at least 5 years after. The economic meltdown was also a sign that tourism is/was very much connected to the global economy. In this new world, no industry, nation, or economy is an island unto itself. Tourism is, to a great extent, in the forefront of these economic changes and challenges. How the travel and tourism industry adapts to this new environment teaches us a great deal about what may lie ahead.

The relationship between tourism security and economics is essential. This is especially true during periods when the economy is weak and people may fear to spend expendable income on what they perceive to be a luxury commodity. To begin to understand these issues, we need to ask, "Whose security?" Do we mean the security of:
• the local community caused by an increase in acts of violence due to economic constrictions;
• the tourist community faced with greater threats by the locals;
• the middle and upper classes of a community;

- the poorer and disenfranchised classes;
- specific districts, such as a downtown areas, that possibly see greater levels of crime as tourism constricts in those neighborhoods?

Such questions, especially in challenging economic cycles, are critical as the allocation of resources often depends on our sociogeographic definition of what constitutes a tourism crime. Table 2.1 demonstrates the advantages and disadvantages of resource allocation and some of what it may signify for a hypothetical tourism locale.

Table 2.2 provides a sense of who wins and who loses during challenging economic periods.

Economic difficulties within a tourism locale may inspire at least four categories of potential crimes:

Table 2.1 Advantages and Disadvantages of Resource Allocation

Group	Advantages	Disadvantages
Total community	Safe city Higher level of economic growth Positive environmental impact Higher tax revenue	Major investment Requires tight coordination between the political, judicial, and police Political price to pay in the beginning
Tourism sectors	Easier to control Less expensive Creates an illusion of safety	Must keep tourists in "ghetto" Criminals will slip into the tourist zone Media problems
Wealthier areas of town	Easy to patrol Less expensive than total city The middle and upper classes tend to vote and control the political arena	Ghettos and segregation form along neighborhood lines Criminals will slip into the upper-class zones Media problems
Poor and disenfranchised	Gives them a chance to raise their level of life All people deserve protection May lower crime throughout the city Permits concentration of police in highest crime areas	Expensive Political problems from both poor and middle class Police may fall into reactive patterns of solving crimes rather than preventing crimes

Table 2.2 Winners and Losers During Challenging Economic Periods

Whose challenge	Winners	Losers
Tourists	Those from more affluent areas may see locale as now affordable	Tourists from weaker economies will have to be more careful or will travel less
Tourism industry	Better service must be given and innovations and creativity will be needed	A lot of people may lose their jobs, adding to the unemployment base and possible crime by those who know tourism best
The local population	Less crowded streets May have more opportunities to use local facilities Prices may fall	Possible hike in taxes Less money for city services when they are needed most May lose jobs, causing some to turn to crime

1. Crimes by locals against tourists
2. Crimes by tourists against locals
3. Crimes by locals against other locals that create a negative image
4. Crimes by tourists against other tourists

To complicate our problem further, the challenges faced by the tourism industry are not only different from those being faced by the local population, but they may also be in conflict with the local population's needs. From the perspective of the traveler, periods of economic decline may present both advantages and disadvantages.

This chapter looks at the interrelationship between tourism security and economics from a double perspective. The first part of the chapter looks at how security or the lack of security impacts the tourism industry's economy. The second half of the chapter looks at how tourism security must face the issues of shrinking budgets and how security personnel must do more with less.

Assumptions about Crime and Economic Viability

Before either of these two major themes can be addressed, we must first look at some assumptions within the world of crime and terrorism and question if these assumptions are valid or not.

The first assumption that must be examined is that terrorism is a form of crime. Although it is beyond the scope of this book to enter into the many reasons for criminal and terrorist acts, for the most part, and from the perspective of tourism, this book rejects this assumption. The one area where the issue of crime and terrorism do merge is in the illegal drug trade. In this case, terrorists often engage in the selling of illegal narcotics for the purposes of raising money for terrorism acts. However, in most other cases, we distinguish crime issues from terrorism issues. The reason for this distinction is that crime issues are often tied to a successful tourism industry. In other words, tourism criminals need tourists if they are to have a steady supply of victims. Furthermore, from the tourism perspective, there are two types of criminal acts that impact tourism. As noted, one side of the crime issue is crimes committed against tourists, and these are specific crimes that target visitors. From the criminal's perspective, these people have a parasitic business relationship with the tourism industry; that is to say that without tourists/visitors, there can be no crimes against tourists. From this perspective, the criminal needs the tourism industry to succeed. In simple terms, where there are no tourists there can be no tourism crimes. On the other side of the criminal coin are *collateral crimes*. These are local crimes that have nothing to do directly with tourism, but spill over into the tourism industry. This spillover effect may either be due to a tourist or visitor being in the wrong place at the wrong time, or the crime giving the impression that a locale is not safe and thus discouraging visitor or convention business.

Terrorism presents the tourism official and security specialist with a different situation. Terrorism is often interlocked with the desire to destroy a local economy. Tourism is a big business. An attack on a tourism industry can cause loss of life and negative publicity; in addition, it can provoke a major economic downturn. "Terrorists are not out for profits, but for a cause. As such they seek the macro destruction of the tourism industry as a way to hurt or destroy a particular nation's economy. Terrorists rarely seek profit, but instead determine success by the quantity of dead bodies and by the loss of economic opportunities" (Tarlow, 2005a; 2005b, p. 39). Terrorists may cause either direct or indirect damage to a tourism industry, but in all cases, terrorists will judge the economic downturn caused by their actions to be a success. Table 2.3 then places these four different actions into perspective.

The second major assumption that must be addressed is the belief that declining economies produce an increase in crime (and perhaps in terrorism). This assumption is based on a theoretical Marxist perspective. Marxism divides the world into good and bad and tends to see the proletariat as good and the bourgeois as bad. Thus, classical Marxist theory tends to justify certain criminal acts as necessary in order for inherently good members of the proletariat to survive in economically hard times. From this perspective,

Table 2.3 Effects of Acts of Crime Versus Acts of Terrorism on Tourism

Tourism crime	Hurts individual tourist but not aimed at industry as a whole
Local crimes with tourism collateral damage	Not aimed at tourist or visitor. The victim was merely in the wrong place at the wrong time
Direct terrorist attack	Aimed at tourism industry for the purpose of causing economic pain, negative publicity, and death
Terrorist attack at nontourism site	Negative economic fallout along with negative publicity

people do not steal due to a lack of morality (often defined by Marxists as bourgeois morality), but rather for the need to survive. Chambliss, Mankoff, Pearce, and Snider (2000) summarize the Marxist theory on crime (a perspective often assumed to be true by a large proportion of the media) as "The idea that the poor are driven to commit crime strongly underpins the theories of those criminologists who have taken Marx's work further..." (Basic Beliefs section, para. 1).

Marxists assume that deviance is caused by economic disparity within a society. This unequal distribution of goods and wealth produces jealousy or envy resulting in crime. Thus, the criminal is not at fault, but rather the capitalist who provokes the criminal with an ostentatious show of wealth. Furthermore, the Marxist argues that crime arises due to people being forced into demeaning work that exacerbates the already unstable economic situation. Marxists further argue that laws are promulgated to serve the ruling class, so even when a member of the ruling class breaks the law, he or she has good access to a lawyer (e.g., "money buys protection"). Marxist analysis then leads to the assumption that tourism is dependent on those classes that have expendable income. To have expendable income means that the visitor is not part of the proletariat and therefore may have provoked the crime of which he or she is the victim.

The belief that tourism crimes rise during difficult economic times may well be predicated on a "Robin Hood" scenario. In this scenario, good poor people are driven to crimes due to the ostentatious behavior of rich tourists. Yet, one's proclivity toward crime may well be determined more by morals than by economics. There are few people who cannot think of "good" poor people who simply do not rob, and of "bad" rich people who do rob. Ethics may be a far greater determining factor in our tendency to commit crimes than is the size of our bank account.

To a certain extent, the same concept is found in classical literature. For example, the "Robin Hood" syndrome of the "good guy" who steals from the rich to give to the poor is found in much of Western literature. It is assumed in this scenario that the poor are "good" and the rich are "bad." Furthermore, Spanish literature reflects this same notion in the "Picarro." In the sixteenth-century Spanish picaresque novel *Lazarillo de Tormes*, the hero stops just short of illegal behavior. The novel presents the *"picarro"* (loosely translated as "rogue") in endearing terms, leading the antihero to become the hero. American cinema is also not stranger to this glorification of the criminal as a man of the people. In the movie *Ocean's Eleven*, the villain is the casino owner, while the thieves are presented as the heroes.

The *New York Times* reflected this Marxist viewpoint in an article titled "Keeping Wary Eye on Crime as Economy Sinks." Despite the fact that the article quotes New York City Police Commissioner Ray Kelly as saying, "he did not subscribe to the idea that there was a strong connection between a city's financial fortunes and its safety," the article begins with the words: "It is the question on the minds of New Yorkers, once they stop pondering the fate of their 401(k)'s: If the city's economy sinks to depths not seen in decades, will crime return with a vengeance?" (Baker & Hauser, 2008, para. 1). The article's theme is that there is a relationship between a tumbling economy and rising crime rates.

The causality of crime then is intertwined with economics and tourism. For example, in the classic book *The Theory of the Leisure Class*, Thorstein Veblen (1963) writes: "It has already been remarked that the term 'leisure' as used here does not connote indolence or quiescence. What it connotes is nonproductive consumption of time. Time is consumed nonproductively (1) from a sense of the unworthiness of productive work and (2) as an evidence of pecuniary ability to afford a life of idleness" (p. 46). Mills, writing about Veblen, quotes Veblen as stating, "the accumulation of wealth at the upper end of the pecuniary scale implies privation at the lower end of the scale." Veblen tended to assume that the pie was a certain size, and that the wealthy class withdraws from the lower class "as much as it may of the means of substance. . ." (p. xiv). The same point is made many years later when Eric P. Baumer and Richard Rosenfeld from the College of Criminology and Criminal Justice at Florida State University wrote:

> The most recent of these economic downturns has stimulated renewed interest in, and speculation about, a possible link between economic conditions and crime rates. Numerous media reports in the first months of the most recent recession suggested possible links between increased crime rates and the foreclosure crisis, rising unemployment, mass layoffs, and depressed wages. Many accounts speculated

*that it was just a matter of time before those adverse conditions would yield
a significant crime wave.*

(Baumer, Rosenfeld, & Wolff, 2010, p. 2)

Tarlow has summarized this perspective in a paper delivered in Kalmar,
Sweden:

1. Economic declines lead to higher levels of frustration and desperation by
   the local population.
2. Economic declines lead to greater competition for customers. Such competition may lead to falling of prices and rising expectations by tourists,
   which creates higher levels of frustration.
3. Periods of economic decline may mean less governmental help for local
   tourism industries, thus creating industry contractions, unemployment,
   and downward wage spirals.
4. Periods of economic decline may result in greater levels of sensationalism
   within the media resulting in copycatting and a desensitizing of the public to acts of violence. (Tarlow, 2000, p. 142)

There is, however, a large body of evidence that contradicts the Marxist
perspective on crime. For example, Plumer (2010), writing in *The New
Republic*, noted:

> In December 2008, just a few months after the U.S. financial system imploded, New
> York City was hit by a flurry of bank robberies. On the Monday before New Year's,
> four banks were attacked in an hour-and-a-half; one daytime raid took place just
> steps from the Lincoln Center in downtown Manhattan. The week before, San
> Diego had seen four bank holdups in a single day. Criminologists wondered if
> the holiday spree was the first sign of a looming crime wave in recession-battered
> America. Take an uptick in poverty and economic misery, toss in budget cuts to
> police departments across the country, and that should be a blueprint for
> chaos—right?
>
> Except, as it turns out, the exact opposite occurred. According to FBI statistics,
> crime rates went down across the board in 2009. Way down. Murder, rape, robbery,
> assault, auto theft—plummeted, one and all. Then, this week, the FBI released pre-
> liminary data for the first 6 months of 2010, and again the same pattern emerged.
> Violent crimes and property crimes alike have been falling in every region of the
> country...

(para. 1–2)

A British study published in May 2009, titled "Crime and the Economy," by
the Police Federations of England and Wales, seems to both contradict
and support the Marxist perspective. The report notes that household consumption is recognized as the principal economic indicator of economic

well-being. However, previous research has noted complexity in the relationship between crime and consumption. In particular, consumption growth has been found to have two principal effects on property crime:

- A growth in consumption increases the number and value of goods available for theft. It is argued that crime increases as the number of opportunities for crime increases. An economic theory of crime suggests that the increase in the stock of goods in society will tend to increase the incentive to commit crime, otherwise known as the "opportunity effect."
- Consumption growth indicates increased expectations of lifetime income. The increased expectation of lawful income will reduce the temptation of illegitimate activity. This is referred to as the "motivation effect."

The opportunity effect is a long-term influence that is positively correlated with crime, while the motivation effect is more short term and has a negative correlation with crime. Thus, in years when people increase their spending by very small amounts or reduce it altogether, notably when the economy is in recession, property crime tends to grow relatively quickly. In contrast, during years when people rapidly increase their expenditure, property crime tends to grow less rapidly or even fall (Plumer, 2010).

The third assumption is that tourism produces crime due to the social inequality between tourists and many locals or people who are working in the tourism industry. This third assumption also has a Marxist tinge to it. It argues that visitors tend to show off their wealth, which produces a sense of jealousy or anger that results in some forms of crime. Thus, Muehsam and Tarlow have written: "Periods of economic decline, then, may also signify periods in which there is a merging of the Robin Hood hypothesis with the assumptions of pure conflict theory creating a postmodernist cacophony of moral inequity. This proposition is even pertinent when one chooses to view the tourism industry as nothing more than the merging of Marxian thought with Veblen's ideas" (Muehsam & Tarlow, 1996, p. 15). In such a scenario, tourism becomes especially open to an ethical malaise for the following reasons:

- By its nature, tourism must be multicultural and "open" to conflicting ideas.
- As noted above, tourists have no sense of place.
- Tourists may be confused as to local mores.
- Victimizers of tourists, especially during periods of economic decline, may see themselves as heroes helping to redistribute wealth.

- As we move from a world of physical-facing to cyber-facing, the victim becomes even more anonymous.

(Tarlow, 2000)

The assumption that tourists are often responsible for their own victimization can be clearly seen in an article published in the *Annals of Tourism Research* by Meda Chesney-Lind and Ian Lind (1986). The authors note that tourists possess characteristics that produce crime. Among these are that tourists (1) carry large sums of money; (2) have desired items such as jewelry and cameras; (3) are often in anomic states (they pay little attention to where they leave their valuables); (4) participate in activities where crime is high (such a nightclubs); and (5) travel to areas of the locale in which they are unfamiliar. The authors then go on to state, "They may also engage in behaviors in these settings that they would not consider at home, such as buying drugs and 'picking up' prostitutes or strangers. Indeed, Uzzell (1984:97) has suggested that risk-taking behavior is an important element of fantasy and escape, which are central to the vacation experience" (p. 179). Two other reasons that tourists generate crimes against themselves may be differentiation in dress from the local population and/or loud use of a foreign language or accent. When tourists fail to recognize or respond to local customs, locals often perceive them as aggressive and/or insensitive to the feelings of others. For example, a *New York Times* article quotes a young Hawaiian: "We never go to the beach where tourists are, because they make you feel like animals in a zoo" (Trumbull, 1980). A review of the literature from that period makes it clear that crimes against tourists are to a great extent the tourist's own fault. Although no author came out and stated that hypothesis with such bluntness, the literature of the 1980s indicated that the tourist had it coming to him or her and that tourism may also be responsible to some extent for a greater level of crime against the local population. Lind and Lind (1986) note, "In addition, there is a limited amount of evidence to suggest that tourism might lead to increased rates of crimes in which residents, remains at least some residual effect on local residents. At a minimum, cases of 'mistaken identity' surely take place, and it seems likely that persons who enter criminal careers through offenses rather than visitors, are the primary victims." (p. 177).

It is interesting to note that the early studies of crimes against tourists assumed that the fault lay with the visitor and thus reflected a pseudo-Marxian outlook in which the victim was blamed for bringing on the crime.

A review of the literature then indicates that there is a division between scholars who believe crime increases during periods of economic decline and those who argue against such a theory. In a like manner, there are those who

Table 2.4 Two Views of Economies and Crime

	Marxist view	Conservative view
Strong economy	Expected lower levels of crime	More consumer goods available raising higher crime possibilities
Weak economy	Crime increase due to greater needs and desperation	Crime decreases as people put more emphasis on seeking work
Tourism in strong economy	Bourgeois has control of the situation	Greater economic strength creates greater leisure activity opportunities
Tourism in weak economy	Tourists provoke jealousy	Tourism produces economic opportunity

see the visitor as being responsible for his or her own victimization and those who reject the self-victimizing theory. Table 2.4 demonstrates the interaction between these two diverse sets of assumptions.

How Security or the Lack of Security Impacts the Tourism Industry's Economy

As mentioned previously, the various terms "tourism security," "safety," "surety," and even "tourism well-being" are often used in an interchangeable manner. The reason for this is that a tourism mishap can result not only in a ruined vacation, but also in loss of reputation and the potential harm to (or even destruction of) a local tourism or visitor industry. From the client's perspective, a robbery or a major health problem can rob the victim of his or her treasured vacation memories. In all cases, these "mishaps" can cause serious reputational harm, especially if they become part of a vicious cycle or spread via word-of-mouth or the Internet. Due to numerous Websites in which visitors can post and share their experiences with the world, the concept of the isolated incident in tourism no longer exists. In a paper delivered in Innsbruck, Austria, by Baggio, Milano, and Piattelli (2011), the authors note that:

As stated ten years ago by the Cluetrain Manifesto (Locke et al., 2000: xxiii): "people in networked markets have figured out that they get far better information and support from one another than from vendors." In the Web 2.0 era, the boundaries between information producers and users are blurred, and the usual concepts of authority and control are radically changed. Among the other consequences, marketing approaches aiming at improving online reputation are being greatly affected. Brand awareness, one of the objectives of classical marketing practices transforms into brand engagement, the purpose of Marketing 2.0. This engagement is created by the perceptions, attitudes, and behaviors of those with whom the different companies and organizations are communicating. More importantly, especially for tourism, it passes necessarily through the experience (direct or indirect) a customer gains

(Weinberger, 2007). (p. 3)

Baggio et al. (2011) further note the importance of personal reporting (versus the industry's reporting) in the world of social media when they state:

These positions, however, create a tension between demand (tourists, travelers, visitors) and supply (tourism businesses and organizations). As well reported by Xiang and Gretzel (2010: 186): "social media Websites are 'ubiquitous' in online travel information search in that they occur everywhere [. . .] no matter what search keywords a traveler uses. Certain social media Websites [. . .], which can be considered more comprehensive and travel-specific sites, are becoming increasingly popular and are likely to evolve into primary online travel information sources [. . .]. The results confirm that tourism marketers can no longer ignore the role of social media in distributing travel-related information without risking to become irrelevant."

(p. 5)

From an economic perspective, the industry and the industry's marketers no longer control tourism marketing. Perspective clients are as or more likely to consult social media as they are to consult what the industry says about itself. This tendency means that any negative incident, whether it be a crime, an act of terrorism, an epidemic to an outbreak of food poisoning in local restaurants, and so on, will be known throughout the world almost instantly.

We can then look at the economic impact of a tourism mishap from the perspective of:
- Crime and violence
- Safety issues
- Terrorism
- Natural disaster

It should be noted that three of the four tourism crises sited above are manmade, while the fourth one, natural disasters, has both a human and a nonhuman component.

The Impact of Crime and Violence on Tourism

Across the Rio Grande River from the Texas border city of Laredo is the Mexican city of Nuevo Laredo. Nuevo Laredo was once a bustling city with its main tourism street, Guerrero, almost butting up to the U.S.–Mexican border. The border was nothing more than a simple transit point until gang and narcotic violence became a way of life. Visitors would cross the border into Mexico with ease in order to spend a few hours shopping for souvenirs and handicrafts, or they would go for an evening out. Mexican citizens were also able to cross the border, and they went shopping in the United States and returned to Mexico with almost no hassle. However, due to the onset of violence in Nuevo Laredo, everything has changed. Now, visitors and locals no longer cross the border. Guerrero Street, which was once filled with visitors, is practically empty of tourists, and its once-thriving nightlife has all but disappeared.

Perhaps no nation's reputation in recent years has suffered as much as that of Mexico. From a tourism perspective, Mexico has everything: spectacular beaches, mountain resorts, great cities and museums, internationally acclaimed gastronomies, historic relics, and modern architecture. Unfortunately, Mexico also has a significant problem with violence. The nation has suffered from what has become a never-ending intercartel warfare resulting in the deaths of over 66,000 people. The cartel gang violence has spilled over into other forms of violence, such as robbery, bribery, and the all too famous "*mordida*." To clarify, a *mordida* is a police shakedown in which a local police authority demands money to "forgive" a crime that was never committed. The violence has impacted northern Mexico, where a large part of its tourism business has died, along with the nation's entire reputation. Thus, every negative event that takes place in any part of Mexico now becomes a negative headline. For example, even a small-town newspaper, such as the *Bryan (Texas) Eagle*, provides headlines when something happens in any part of Mexico. In February 2013, six women were raped in the city of Acapulco. This unfortunate and tragic incident was reported by the *Eagle* with the following words: "The tourism world turned its eyes on Mexico after six Spanish women were raped by masked gunman during a vacation on the long troubled Pacific coast resort of Acapulco" (Ramos & Stevenson, 2013, para. 1). The report then went on to state: "the question now is whether the attack will affect other resorts as Mexico prepares for its annual spring break onslaught and peak season" (p. A10). The article alludes to violence stemming from Acapulco beginning in 2009, and it notes that the city has never recovered from the 18 murders that took place near Acapulco's Flamingo Hotel.

The article highlights the importance of safety and security for a tourism industry. If we read the article carefully, a number of subthemes emerge. Among these are:

• Acts of violent crime can have long-term and lasting effects.
• Visitors tend to stay away from places that they do not consider to be safe.

- The media does not often distinguish geographic locations within political or national borders. So, in our example, Mexico (a very large country) is contaminated by headlines that lump the entire nation together. In reality other parts of Mexico may be perfectly safe, but these safe locations must still deal with the negative fallout and perceptions stemming from violence within Mexico's national borders.
- The further away we are from a place, the worse the incident may appear to be. In reality crimes of sexual assault occur throughout the world, but once a particular crime enters into the media, it takes on a life that is almost independent of the event.
- People tend to be less forgiving of a locale that suffers from an act of violence than of other tragic events such as acts of nature.

Crime, of course, is not a Mexican problem. Tourism officials are well aware that once it enters the media, crime can have a highly destructive impact on a local tourism industry. To illustrate, Jamaica's tourism minister, who is well aware of his nation's crime problem, spoke at the Jamaica Hotel and Tourist Association (JHTA) 47th Annual General Meeting about crime's negative impact on his country in February 2013:

> *"Crime, in my mind is the single most debilitating factor, the one area that is worrying to me beyond anything else, and I must tell you that the fuel crisis is not as worrying to me as crime. The turmoil in the aviation industry is not as worrying to me as crime. . ." Meanwhile, President of the JHTA Wayne Cummings echoed similar sentiments and deep concern about the negative effects of crime on the tourist industry.*
>
> *"I don't care which Commissioner you have, I don't care which Minister of National Security you get, even though both are important, if Jamaicans don't decide to take back Jamaica (from the criminals), then tourism, manufacturing, and other such industries are doomed. . ."*
>
> **("Crime hurting Jamaica tourism," 2008, para. 2 and 6)**

We see another example of the impact of crime especially when it is combined with less than hospitable customer service in the case of Venezuela. The Venezuelan newspaper *El Universal* reported the dearth of tourists to the country, asking the question: "Where are the tourists?" The article notes how a lack of security, combined with a sense of inhospitality, has done a great amount of harm to the country. *El Universal* concludes that among the factors having done the most harm to the country is its being ranked as an insecure nation. It states:

> *We are well aware of the frequent kidnappings, the violence and crime that has plagued Venezuela during the last decade and that this has now become*

a frequent international topic of conversation and (this lack of security) has its con-sequences. However, these dangers, as bad as they are, are not sufficient to explain how a country with so many advantages has succeeded in winning the dubious honor (of lack of security). Indeed among those few countries even more insecure than Venezuela, Honduras and Sierra Leone, almost all are considered to be more hospitable than Venezuela.

(Rodríguez, 2013, para. 4)[1]

The article pointed to the fact that a tourism industry without customer service and good security will soon wither.

Measuring Crime's Impact

Crimes against tourists have a negative impact on the industry. Measuring exactly how many people choose to stay away from a location due to crime is never easy to measure. This fact is noted in a 2008 United Nations Economic Commission for Latin America and the Caribbean (ECLAC) document about the Caribbean that states:

Definitions of crime vary significantly among countries. The joint report of the UNODC and the Latin America and the Caribbean Region of the World Bank notes that "even for what seems like an easily defined offense such as murder, definitions vary widely, and crimes like burglary, robbery and sexual offenses are defined very differently across jurisdictions."

("Exploring policy linkages between poverty," 2008, p. 6)

The reasons for this are numerous:

1. Crime figures are not standardized. What may be a crime in one location is not necessarily a crime in another location. "Personalized" acts such as drug usage and prostitution differ from one locale to another. Thus, in some locations, prostitution is considered to be a major crime, while in others, prostitution is legal or it is still illegal but tolerated.

2. Tourists and visitors often do not report crimes. The reasons for this non-reportage are numerous. Included in the list is the fact that many visitors do not realize that they have been victims of crime; they simply assume that they have lost an article or money. Additionally, many visitors do not believe that reporting a crime is worthwhile. They assume that either the police can (or will) do nothing, or by the time something might be done, the visitors will have left the locale. Visitors also may not know how to report a crime. Police stations are often hard to find, or not in visitor-frequented neighborhoods, and if the tourist is from abroad, he

---

[1] Author's translation of the Spanish. The full and original Spanish text can be found at: http://www.eluniversal.com/opinion/130322/donde-estan-los-turistas.

or she may not be able to fill out the necessary paperwork in an under-
standable language.

3. There are reported crimes that are "self-generated." Often, reported
crimes are nothing more than fraudulent ways to obtain insurance on
an object that a visitor may wish to replace. Thus, cameras often become
"stolen" as a means to purchase a new camera.

4. The tourism industry does not encourage people to report crimes. What
this means is that often it is to the advantage of the local hotel, restaurant,
or attraction to work out a private deal with the visitor rather than have
the crime reported to the police. From a business perspective such a policy may make sense, but the result of such "agreements" is that all tourism
crime statistics are suspect.

A review of the academic literature demonstrates that there are multiple
modes of measurement used in determining crime rates. In the same way
that it is almost impossible to measure crime due to lack of standardized data,
the cost of crime (its economic consequences) is also highly difficult to determine. To elaborate, the World Health Organization (2004) draws a distinction between direct costs (medical, legal, policing, prisons, foster care, and
private security) and indirect costs (lost earnings and time, lower human capital, lower productivity, lower investment, psychological costs, and other
nonmonetary costs). Other scholars use more complex methodologies.
For example, some students of tourism divide the cost of crimes against tourism by their various costs. Among these costs we can include:

- *Direct costs*: the value of all goods and services used to prevent violence or
offer treatment to its victims or perpetrators.
- *Nonmonetary costs*: higher mortality and morbidity rates that result in pain,
suffering, and death, but do not necessarily result in either expenditures
on health care or in easily quantifiable economic losses.
- *Economic multiplier effects*: impacts on human capital, labor force participa-
tion, lower wages and incomes, savings, and macroeconomic growth.
- *Social multiplier effects*: erosion of social capital, intergenerational transmission of violence, and lower quality of life.

("Socioeconomic costs of crime," n.d., p. 1)

PART 2: HOW TOURISM SECURITY MUST FACE THE ISSUES OF SHRINKING BUDGETS AND HOW SECURITY PERSONNEL MUST DO MORE WITH LESS

Tourism security professionals, like other forms of security and law enforcement professionals, often complain about the fact that their profession all too

often suffers from low status, poor equipment, and too few people being asked to do too many tasks. There are multiple reasons for this problem.

If the event never occurs, then often administrators question the need for risk management. If the event does occur, then the risk has clearly not been mitigated. Thus, the risk manager is placed in the precarious situation that success means a lowering of resources and potential salary loss, while failure means that he or she is not doing his or her job well. The outside observer can recognize this "damned if I do/damned if I don't" scenario simply by viewing the high rate of turnover for hotel security managers. These men and women are often blamed for being too successful and are therefore prone to job elimination, or they are blamed for events that take place beyond their control. This unstable model tends to produce high rates of frustration and attrition among risk managers. Often tourism risk managers may go by other names. To illustrate, a wedding is an event and often a tourism generator. Wedding planners do not call themselves risk managers, but in reality they are risk management specialists. The one difference being that their risk ends after the wedding reception comes to its conclusion, while in the world of tourism, the risk lasts as long as that part of the tourism industry remains in business. From an economic perspective, the crisis manager has a much easier job. Table 2.5 delineates the differences and challenges between crisis and risk management.

As noted in the first part of this chapter, tourism and the economy are intertwined. Tourism is highly sensitive to the economy's undulations since it is an industry based on disposable income. In a like manner, those working in tourism security are vulnerable to a tourism economy, both its changes and challenges. These economic changes have more consequences than what is initially expected. For example, criminals such as distraction artists (pickpockets, baggage thieves, shoplifters) tend to have a parasitic relationship with tourism (Tarlow, 2005a; 2005b, p. 79). A lack of tourists means that these criminals have fewer victims, so they are impacted by an economic recession. While it is a common assumption that crime rises during down periods, there may be good reasons to assume the opposite. Not only are there fewer visitors, and thus fewer victims, but also many people tend to take extra precautions during poor economic periods, which offers better passive resistance.

Given this difficult situation, tourism security specialists must prove themselves on a daily basis. Unfortunately, the following headline is all too rare: "Kashmir enjoys spike in tourism due to reduced violence" (Das, 2012). The article goes on to state, "With extremism on the wane, the number of visitors has been on the rise over the past two years" (para. 1).

Table 2.5 Some Basic Differences Between Crisis and Risk Management

	Risk	Crisis
Surety of occurrence	Uses a statistical system	Is a known tourism event
Goal of management	To stop the tourism prior to occurrence	To minimize the damage once tourism has taken place
Type of preparation to combat risk that can be used	Probability studies Knowledge of past tourism Tracking systems Learning from others	Specific information such as medical, psychological, or crime Developing a what-if attitude
Training needed	Assume crises and find ways to prevent them	Assume crises and practice reacting to them
Reactive or proactive	Proactive	Reactive, thorough training can be proactive toward the reactive
Types of victim	Anyone, maybe visitor or staff	Can be visitors, staff members, or site
Publicity	Goal is to prevent publicity by acting to create nontourism	Goal is to limit the public relations damage that may occur
Some common problems	Poor building maintenance Poor food quality Poor lighting Fear of terrorism Fear of a crime occurring	Rude visitor Sick person Robbery Threat to staff Bomb scare Lack of language skills

Source: EDIT Program, University of Hawaii (2006)

Although this success story is not unique, the reporting of such successes rarely enters into the media. There are several reasons for this lack of reporting:

- Media is a business, and those involved in it believe that tragedies and dark stories increase viewer or listenership.
- It is easier to write about and report a negative happening than it is to report about a success.
- Failure and tragedy are believed to be more interesting reads.

Faced with such difficulties tourism security professionals, whether they are from the private sector or the public sector, need to find ways to explain what they do, what the probability of success is, and why the media and outside administrators often confuse probability of success with possibility of success. To begin to understand how to initiate dialogue with tourism managers and government agencies, it is helpful to understand the concerns of the people whom the security professional is serving. In reality, there are a number of publics that must be served. Among these are:

- The tourism industry's leaders and administrators
- The general public
- The media
- Government officials

Listed below are several issues of concern to the tourism industry. These issues offer law enforcement administrators the means to which they can start a dialogue with their tourism counterparts.

- Issues of room invasion
- Issues of negative publicity and media response
- Issues of acts of terrorism
- Issues of gang violence
- Issues of sexual tourism
- Issues of prostitution and sexual slavery

Tourism security officials need to emphasize in a calm, businesslike manner that a tourism industry cannot long survive in an environment that is perceived to be unstable or precarious. Tourism security professionals then play a vital role in making tourists feel safe. Convention and visitor's bureaus or national (or provincial) tourism offices are keenly aware that a pleasure visitor need not come to his or her community. For example, some American cities face a complex security situation. High crime rates, especially at night, keep visitors and locals alike from frequenting downtown establishments. Good working relations with both law enforcement and private security officials can help to lessen risks. Here are some suggestions on how law enforcement agencies can help to reduce a visitor's vulnerability to crime.

Tourism Security Marketing Tip!

Offer to incorporate your agency into your community's tourist force. Like the English "bobbies" or the Royal Canadian Mounted Police, a police force can do double duty. Design in conjunction with your community's tourist industry an "officer-friendly" program. Initiate a program where police "park, walk, and talk" to strangers especially in tourist quarters, thereby making the police approachable. Promote the service side of policing by developing a positive police attitude toward tourism. Encourage your police officers to go beyond their job description as providers of security. Additionally, a service-oriented police force can become a source of information for tourists and goodwill ambassadors for a community. Ask tourist officials to provide your department with event information. Up-to-date information not only allows security agencies to do their job better but also integrates officers into the tourist community.

Then, tourism security professionals need to market themselves to their four constituencies. Below are several ideas on how security professionals can win over at least some of their various constituencies.

- Offer special tourist training for your police force.

- A law enforcement officer can be an asset to any community's tourist industry. Developing a special training program for your community's police will sensitize them on tourism's importance. This program ought to include the economic and social impact of tourism on its community, a hospitality program on how to handle strangers, and an information packet on the tourist facilities and attractions within the community. Make sure that officers have some idea as to the demographic makeup of their community's tourist population, and what special needs these visitors may have. For example, communities that have high levels of elderly visitors may need extra traffic police and additional signage. Cities that attract large numbers of foreign visitors may desire to offer their law enforcement officers special language training courses.

- Use tourism information services as an implicit anticrime tool. Even in cities with high crime rates, crime tends to be highly concentrated in small geographic regions. Use tourist information services, and especially city tour maps, to direct tourists along the safest and best-lit routes between attractions. Develop time-oriented maps that indicate what times of the day particular intersections, roads, or areas should be avoided. Whenever possible, seek the transportation department's indications of road repairs or detours, and then indicate alternate routes.

- Encourage tourism offices to publicize public transportation options. Bus schedules should be well publicized and accurate. Waiting at bus stops can be dangerous and can make a tourist vulnerable to crime. Public transportation stops should be well lit with emergency phones in close proximity. Explain to tourist officials that publicized bus schedules allow tourists to avoid being in an unprotected area for a protracted amount of time. To minimize the likelihood that a visitor will be stranded, emphasize the last scheduled pickup at major tourist attractions. Work with tourist officials to get bus companies to coordinate their runs with local attractions.

- Be aware that tourism officials traditionally have viewed a police presence as a double-edged sword. Work with tourist officials to determine the right mix of uniform and plainclothes officers need. A visible police force can serve as a "psychological" security blanket. On the other hand, too large a presence can make a tourist wonder why such a large force is needed, and ask if he or she should be worried. By working together, tourist officials and police departments can determine the number of officers needed to maintain safe tourist areas without producing anxiety. Remind tourism officials in a gentle manner that police departments do not have unlimited budgets. If more officers are needed in a particular area, ask that tourist officials cooperate with the local police department to see that proper funding is included in the police's budget.

- Have a plan of action to deal with tourists who are victimized by crime. Even in the safest of places a crime can occur. This is the moment to give the tourist all the "TLC" possible. An officer's actions can create a situation where the victimized tourist leaves with a positive attitude about the locale's hospitality rather than as a vocal critic of that city.

- Terrorism is a possibility everywhere. In the world of tourism, there is no place that is immune from terrorism. Tourism officials and police departments need to develop plans to protect iconic places with minimal damage to their architectural integrity. For example, concrete barriers can keep a car at a safe distance from a building, but it can destroy a building's architectural tone. Use beautification methods, such as flowers, to camouflage these barriers, or convert these barriers into concrete works of art. Be careful to ensure that landscaping does not create an opportunity for criminals to lay-in-wait. Encourage the use of state-of-the-art surveillance cameras to watch for possible problems, and record them should they occur.

Festivals

Festivals and mega-events, such as the Olympic games, bring a great deal of money to a community, but they require careful planning and security expenses. These events demonstrate the need for cooperative efforts between the law enforcement and tourism industries. Perhaps no area of tourism creates greater security headaches than festivals and large events, such as the World Cup. The festival's multiple entrance points, volunteer staffs, and nonspecialized location create an unstructured atmosphere in which security people must operate. Festivals and major events are open to both criminals of opportunity and to terrorists. Furthermore, to complicate the security situation, the festival's multiple access points facilitate easy entrance and escape routes. However, by cooperating, these two industries can lessen the potential risks.

- Offer to meet with festival representatives at the earliest stages of planning. Offer your department's expertise in such areas as planning for

traffic flow, parking, and pedestrian access points. Work with festival officials to confront specific security concerns.
- Work with tourist officials to confront specific monetary concerns. Inform tourist officials that police departments have specific restrictions on the number of hours a police officer can work on- or off-duty. Commit these officers as quickly as possible to ensure their presence. Discuss budgetary problems early, and determine out of which budget these police officers will be paid.

Although no locale can totally eliminate all forms of crime, being aware of potential problems and developing good relations with local tourism officials can help to create an environment to which visitors will want to return. To help determine your own strategy, we present the following ideas and possible future trends.

- Remember that we no longer live in a one-country world. No matter what nation you may be living in, the local market will not be enough to sustain your growth. Even small towns will find it necessary to become part of the global market. This means that it will be necessary for local banks to change currency, restaurants to offer menus in various languages, traffic and road signs to be internationalized, and police departments to learn how to deal with a myriad of cultures and languages.
- Do not think only in short intervals. For example, even though the price of fuel continues to rise and fall, it is bound to go up in the long term. During less costly periods, use the reprieve to develop alternative forms of transportation. Communities that are totally dependent on self-driven means of transportation may have much greater difficulties in attracting visitors in the next few decades. Creative thinking will be necessary as not every community can produce an instant public transportation system.
- Learn to watch trends and then incorporate them into your business model. Travel and tourism, for the most part, are expendable products. So, it behooves travel and tourism professionals to watch cost of credit, to understand how the foreign exchange markets work, and where unemployment is headed in your major markets. In today's interconnected world, news sources are essential. Read at least three newspapers a day from various parts of the world and from places that constitute your current major markets.
- Be flexible. What was or has always been may not be the same in the future. For example, if your tourism industry or business traditionally drew from place X, and that locale is expected to go through a major

economic downturn, be prepared to switch markets or products rapidly. Every tourism community should now have an economic watchdog committee that analyzes the current situation and makes recommendations on how to adapt to a rapidly changing world. The less assets that you need to care for, such as buildings, vehicles, etc., the better off you may be especially in a restricting world economy.

- Think small as well as big. All too often tourism industries suffer because they spend so much time on catching the big fish, they lose the small fish. Remember, in challenging economic times, there are less big fish to catch. Thus, try to consider smaller conventions instead of only seeking larger ones. The basic principle is some profit is better than no profit.

- Look at both macro and micro economic trends. Because tourism is a big business composed of many small businesses, it is essential for tourism professionals to integrate macro trends into their business plan. For example, how will new car sales impact your tourism industry? What happens if this current crisis is only the first of two or three waves of crises? How will aging populations in developed countries impact tourism? Which nations have expanding economies and where are economies contracting? All these are essential questions that must be updated on a regular basis.

- Look at successful models around the world. All too often tourism officials have a highly parochial view of their industry. Seek out and communicate with colleagues from different parts of the world and look at their best practices. Where have they succeeded and failed? Think how you may be able to adapt or modify other people's ideas so that they meet the needs of your local situation. Then, ask yourself some essential questions, such as: Is my business model flexible enough to withstand rapid changes? How stable is my current supply chain? For instance, If you are a hotel and the blanket factory goes bankrupt, are there other sources available? If you are a locale based around a single attraction, what happens if that attraction closes? Finally, do you know your business partners and how you can work with them to face an ever more challenging world?

- Adapt your marketing efforts to a globalized industry. Tourism and travel professionals may need to consider major overhauls of their world-market advertising. Magazine and local television ads may need to be replaced with innovative web strategies. A monolingual Website may become a thing of the past, and new direct marketing procedures will become essential. Remember that in an interconnected world, you are no longer just compared with your neighbors. No matter where you are located, your community and/or business will be judged on an international scale. Think through what makes you unique and what is special about your community or business.

REFERENCES

Baggio, R., Milano, R., & Piattelli, R. (2011). The effects of online social media on tourism websites. *18th International Conference on Information Technology and Travel & Tourism.* Retrieved from http://www.iby.it/turismo/papers/baggio_socialmedia.pdf.

Baker, A., & Hauser, C. (2008). Keeping wary eye on crime as economy sinks. *The New York Times.* Retrieved from http://www.nytimes.com/2008/10/10/nyregion/10crime.html?pagewanted=all&_r=2&amp.

Baran, M. (2012). Dark tourism. *Travel Weekly.* Retrieved from http://www.travelweekly.com/Travel-News/Tour-Operators/Dark-tourism/.

Baumer, E. P., Rosenfeld, R., & Wolff, K. T. (2010). Are the criminogenic consequences of economic downturns conditional? Assessing potential moderators of the link between adverse economic conditions and crime rates. Retrieved from http://www.criminology.fsu.edu/p/pdf/Recession%20and%20Crime.pdf.

Bergen, K. (2012). City's tourism could be collateral damage if spike in violence continues, says Don Welsh, president and CEO of Choose Chicago. *Chicago Tribune.* Retrieved from http://articles.chicagotribune.com/2012-07-12/business/ct-biz-0712-convention-buro-20120712_1_bruce-rauner-tourism-don-welsh.

Chambliss, W., Mankoff, M., Pearce, F., & Snider, L. (2000). *Traditional Marxist perspectives on crime.* Retrieved from http://www.sociology.org.uk/pcdevmx.pdf.

Chesney-Lind, M., & Lind, I. (1986). Visitors as victims: Crimes against tourists in Hawaii. Reprinted from the *Annals of Tourism Research, 13*(2), 167–191, with permission from Elsevier. http://www.sciencedirect.com/science/Journal/01607383.

Chicago crime impacting tourism? City tourism official suggests so, then backs down (2012). *Huffington Post.* Retrieved from http://www.huffingtonpost.com/2012/07/12/chicago-crime-impacting-t_n_1668106.html?.

Crime hurting Jamaica tourism (2008). *Caribbean 360.* Retrieved from http://www.caribbean360.com/index.php/news/13435.html#ixzz2KKUf3Mif.

Das, C. (2012). Kashmir enjoys spike in tourism due to reduced violence. *Khabar South Asia.* Retrieved from http://khabarsouthasia.com/en_GB/articles/apwi/articles/features/2012/03/20/feature-01.

Dreier, H. (2013, February 25). Las Vegas seen as dangerous even as crime drops. *Las Vegas Sun.* Retrieved from http://www.lasvegassun.com/news/2013/feb/25/las-vegas-seen-dangerous-even-crime-drops/.

Exploring policy linkages between poverty, crime and violence: A look at three Caribbean states (2008). *Economics Commission for Latin American and the Caribbean.* Retrieved from http://www.eclac.org/publicaciones/xml/2/33252/l.172.pdf.

Locke, C., Levine, C., Searls, D., & Weinberger, D. (2000). *The cluetrain manifesto: The end of business as usual.* Cambridge, MA: Perseus Publishings.

Muehsam, M., & Tarlow, P. E. (1996). Theoretical aspects of crime as they impact the tourism industry. In A. Pizam, & Y. Mansfeld (Eds.), *Tourism, crime and international security issues.* Chichester, UK: John Wiley & Sons.

Plumer, B. (2010). Crime conundrum. *New Republic.* Retrieved from http://www.newrepublic.com/article/80316/relationship-poverty-crime-rates-economic-conditions#.

Ramos, B., & Stevenson, M. (2013). Acapulco rape case overshadows peak tourist season. *Yahoo News*. Retrieved from http://news.yahoo.com/acapulco-rape-case-overshadows-peak-tourist-season-001515646--finance.html.

Rodríguez, D. L. (2013). ¿Dónde están los turistas? *El Universal*. Retrieved from http://www.eluniversal.com/opinion/130322/donde-estan-los-turistas.

Socioeconomic costs of crime (n.d.). *World Bank*. Retrieved from http://siteresources.worldbank.org/INTHAITI/Resources/CaribbeanC&VChapter4.pdf.

Tarlow, P. E. (2000). Creating safe and secure communities in economically challenging times. *Tourism Economics*, *6*(2), 139–149.

Tarlow, P. E. (2005a). Terrorism and tourism. In J. Wilks, D. Pendergast, & P. Leggat (Eds.), *Tourism in turbulent times* (pp. 79–92). Oxford, UK: Elsevier Inc.

Tarlow, P. E. (2005b). A social theory of terrorism and tourism. In Y. Mansfeld, & A. Pizam (Eds.), *Tourism security and safety* (pp. 33–47). Oxford, UK: Elsevier Inc.

Trumbull, R. (1980). Hawaii acts to curb crimes against visitors. *The New York Times*, Section 10:XX1.

Veblen, T. (1963). *The theory of the leisure class* (7th ed.). New York: Mentor Books, New American Library.

Weinberger, D. (2007). *Everything is miscellaneous: The power of the new digital disorder*. New York, NY: Times Books.

Xiang, Z., & Gretzel, U. (2010). Role of social media in online travel information search. *Tourism Management*, *31*(2), 179–188.

CHAPTER 3

Hotel and Motel Security

Figure 3.1 Grand Hyatt hotel, Gold Coast, Australia.

PLACES OF LODGING IN THE TOURISM HISTORY

Along with restaurants (food consumption) and attractions, places of lodging, such as hotels and motels, form one of tourism's three major pillars (Figure 3.1). When people participate in tourism, they expect a reason to be at an attraction, a restaurant, and an establishment that functions as their home away from home. Places of lodging play such a critical role in tourism that many definitions of tourism include them as an integral part of the definition.

Since the conception of travel, visitors have needed a place to lodge during their journey. Although the need existed, the idea of the modern hotel, however, did not exist. Instead, most people stayed with family or friends. In ancient Rome, there were taverns that accepted guests, as well as institutions known as "mansios" where imperial messengers could eat, change horses, and sleep, and some of these mansios also allowed other patrons.

Tourism Security

Guest and lodging personnel safety and security is an ongoing concern throughout the world. At first thought, most guests tend to think more about other items, such as room rate, comfort, location, and access, than they do about security. Yet, when there is a security or safety mishap, it is security that gains negative attention, and it may even cause a major lawsuit. When a traveler chooses a place of lodging, the traveler assumes that he or she is under the protection of the chosen place of lodging and the hotelier (or motel operator) has done everything foreseeable to ensure his or her safety. Security can impact the hotel's reputation and viability; lack of security may be a strong reason for a guest choosing not to visit the hotel again. Places of lodging then have a business, moral, and legal obligation to take every possible measure to ensure guest safety and security. How to provide this security without undue guest inconvenience has been a major issue in tourism for decades. For example, in 1999, the television program *Dateline NBC* ran a full program dealing with the issue of motel security. About 2 years later, a follow-up program was aired on the issue of hotel security. Hotels were originally places of lodging that contained multiple floors and offered additional services. Motels were places of lodging that tended to be one or two floors at the most, had outside room entrances, and were merely places to sleep with easy off-road access. The word itself is most likely derived from a combination of *motor* and *hotel*. In the late twentieth century, many former motels have taken on the appearance of hotels, so the terms are much more loosely defined. Therefore, this book uses the following three terms[1]:

- Low-rise places of lodging with exterior room entrances (entrances off the parking lot).
- High-rise places of lodging with interior room entrances (entrances from a hallway within the building).
- Other places of lodging such as bed 'n breakfasts that may be homes or other structures converted into a less formal form of lodging.

HOTEL SECURITY: THE OVERVIEW

In Chapter 1 we discussed how many tourism professionals fear the question of security. What is true of the industry as a whole is also true of the lodging industry. Indeed, many hotel managers falsely believe that these topics will frighten customers; there are still too many tourism and lodging professionals

---

[1] Although cruise ships are in reality floating resort hotels, cruises are separately addressed in Chapter 6.

who hesitate to speak about tourism/lodging security and safety issues. Often, risk management and security department members report feeling underappreciated and overworked.

However, there is nothing that can destroy the reputation of a lodging establishment more effectively than a lack of security or safety. In reality, there is no such thing as total travel (tourism) security or safety, but there is still many options the lodging industry can undertake to promote a safe and secure visit. Below is a checklist of some things lodging establishments need to consider, no matter their type, size, or location.

- Clarity of communication between staff and guests
- Clarity of communication between staff members
- Delivery procedures
- Entrance security
- Evacuation procedures
- Fire prevention
- Health regulations
- Issues of lighting
- Neighborhood in which the lodging establishment is located
- Relationship with local law enforcement and security agencies
- Staff background checks and clearances
- Types of guests that tend to frequent the lodging establishment and their special security needs
- Types of locks on doors and windows
- Unruly or difficult guests, and/or guests who become ill.

Lodging security seeks to provide a safe and secure environment for those who stay and work in locations that provide overnight stays. Another way to analyze lodging is if the facility is merely for sleeping or if the lodging establishment also provides other physical facilities, such as restaurants, meeting spaces, and a convention center. Each one of these additional facilities complicates the security director's job and provides him or her with additional challenges.

COMMON PROBLEMS

Traditionally we divide lodging security into three separate large categories and then subdivide these categories into numerous subcategories. The three major categories are (1) care of the guest, (2) care of the staff, and (3) care of the physical site. We can also argue that there is a fourth category: care of the place of lodging's reputation. Yet, success in the first three categories ensures success in the fourth. In all cases, hosts must be aware of the fact that they are dealing with a highly transient clientele, many of whom may never return.

Accordingly, all lodging establishments share some common problems. For example, Tarlow (2007) has written:

> Places of lodging and their guests suffer from reciprocal ignorance. That is to say personnel tend to know very little about the guests' personal history and guests tend to know nothing about the personal history of those who have access to their rooms. To make matters even more complicated, in large places of lodging, such as major hotels, the staff rarely knows who is or is not a guest at the place of lodging. In the case of a motel, rooms may have direct access to the street, so a person may never need to pass through a lobby.
>
> **(p. 455)**

HOTEL CHALLENGES

There is no one universal definition of what a hotel is. Hotels[2] tend to be multistoried edifices. Hotels can be purely geared toward sleeping, or they may contain a variety of additional facilities such as convention centers, swimming pools, health spas, restaurants, casinos, and shopping centers. Each one of these additional features represents a new risk for the hotel along with additional challenges for the hotel's security staff.

The mixing of hotel guests with clientele of conventions, restaurants, and shopping centers presents the security staff with major identification problems. In the cases of trade shows or merchandise markets being held within the hotel's convention center, the security staff must also deal with the protection of exhibitor goods, as well as the problem of pilferage.

MOTEL CHALLENGES

Although many motels are sleep-oriented establishments, they may also be connected to a restaurant. Motels are often built on the premise of easy access. This easy access provides convenience for guests, but it could become a security nightmare. Rooms are usually on the ground level or one level up. Many motels do not have a lobby and guests have direct access to their rooms. Although direct access makes it easy for motel guests to unload

---

[2] The author recognizes that some hotels are residential hotels with long-term guests. For purposes of simplicity this chapter assumes that guests are short term and function more as transient visitors than as permanent residents. There is now a growing trend of mixing transient hotels with condominiums and thus creating a whole new host of security challenges.

and reload baggage, direct room access also means that the motel's staff has no idea when someone enters or leaves a room, who might be observing a room, or when a thief may be stalking a room.

BED 'N BREAKFAST (B&B) CHALLENGES

These places of lodging are often found within private homes, or they are private homes that have been converted into business establishments. B&Bs are built on the principle of trust. Room keys are often primitive at best, and there is rarely any form of sophisticated security equipment. Some bed 'n breakfasts even resemble early boarding houses with shared bathrooms. Because B&Bs are often built around charm and romance, some guests treat them as if they were visiting a friend's home, bringing expensive or emotionally laden personal items. It should be noted, however, that many bed 'n breakfast rooms have poor levels of security. Front doors are often left open, which make B&Bs perfect targets for crimes of opportunity.

CAMPGROUNDS AND OTHER LODGING CHALLENGES

Another form of lodging that is not often considered is a campground. These lodging institutions may provide tents or just drinking water and sanitation facilities. Often, these highly informal locations are under the protection of park rangers, and due to budgetary restraints, park rangers have been replaced by off-duty police officers. Some of the security challenges that occur are sexual assault; lack of places to lock valuables; entering of vehicles with the intent to steal or rob; and exposure to weather, potential fire hazards, and insects and wild animals (Table 3.1).

LODGING SECURITY IN A CONSISTENTLY CHANGING WORLD

Ecclesiastes wrote that there is nothing new under the sun. If Ecclesiastes was referring to the fact that evil seems to never go out of style, then he was correct. While "evil" in the form of crime and terrorism may not change over time, the techniques and instruments of crime do.

Although lodging security has been around for quite some time, the face of hotel/motel security has changed radically; in every generation, new challenges have developed. In the 1980s and 1990s, lodging security emphasized such problems as room invasions, issues of prostitution, theft by other guests and employees, questions of sexual assault, and issues of pilferage. The dawn of the new millennium added the fear of terrorism to issues that the security

Table 3.1 Some common and unique problems in places of lodging

	Hotels	Motels	Bed 'n' breakfasts
Primary types of keys used	Standard or electronic	Standard or electronic	Standard or electronic
Security of room	Ranges from good to poor	Ranges from good to poor	Tends to be poor
Conventions at the place of lodging	High probability	Low probability	No
Staff knows guests	Usually does not	Usually not	Yes
Location well-known	Yes	Yes	Often no
Security staff on premises	Yes in the larger hotels	Rarely	Never
Staff trained in matters of security	Often	Rarely	Almost never
Secure parking	Often	Often	Almost never
Large numbers of people staying at place of lodging	Yes	Yes	No
Secure access to room	Often	At times	Rarely
Lobby	Yes	Often	Parlor may serve as lobby during awake hours

Source: (Tarlow 2007, p. 456)

professional had to face. The twenty-first century's second decade may be called the "age of electronic security." For example, Patrick Mayock, writing in the professional journal *Hotel News Now* in January 2012, noted that we have entered an age in which IT has become both a blessing and a curse. Mayock (2012) quoted Anthony Roman, saying:

> In general most mobile devices that are used for business remain unprotected, including lack of any password, let alone a complex password.... Rarely do we find that any business using smart mobile technology has any encryption on it whatsoever. Even less than that do we find that there are written policies and procedures relative to the securing and protection of mobile devices, technology and the information continued within them.
>
> *(IT section, para. 2)*

Another twenty-first century problem is the fact that we now have grown accustomed to terrorism. Simply put, it is hard to maintain a state of diligence when terrorists can simply outwait the industry. A third major threat today is what the industry calls "skimmers." Skimmers are devices that "catch" credit card numbers when a consumer uses his or her card to pay for a purchase. The skimmer problem as a form of identity theft is a major threat to anyone who travels. Mayock (2012) quoted Chad Callaghan, security consultant for the America Hotel and Lodging Association, in stating: "Skimmers typically require an 'inside man' or worker who swipes a credit card through a device before processing the payment. These are usually not hardened criminals, they're just 'opportunists'" (Skimmers section, para. 3).

The final twenty-first century security problem is liability and insurance fraud. Although these two problems do not immediately impact the consumer, they raise the cost of doing business considerably, so they indirectly impact the price of lodging. These issues, Roman notes, extend from small claims due to a minor injury to significant criminal acts. For example, a major lawsuit was filed when a stalker violated the privacy of then ESPN reporter Erin Andrews by filming her changing in her guestroom through a peephole. Mayock (2012) once again quoted Callaghan: "Whether frivolous or not, such cases are costly because they have to be defended" (Liability and Insurance Fraud section, para. 6).

It should be noted that the problems of the past have not disappeared. Although not lodging industry specific, some of these problems are:

- Child trafficking/protection of children
- Antibiotic-resistant pandemic potential
- Crazed gun or knife murderers
- Death and/or dying due to natural causes or suicide
- Hostage situations
- Kidnapping and hostage situations
- In-room alcohol or drug abuse
- Food poisoning at restaurants connected with places of lodging
- High degrees of noise that impact other guests (e.g., running through halls, children jumping on beds)
- Illegal drug usage
- Illegal meetings (mafia, terrorists, etc.)
- Illegal sexual activity and issues of sadomasochism
- Illegal use of equipment that may result in fires or other hazards
- Lack of safety concerns such as smoking in bed
- Loud parties
- Room invasions by criminals
- Sexual assault

Stealing of guest property by those working in or outside of the place of lodging is an ongoing problem that security officers must address on a routine basis. Thus, the classic problems as stated above continue even when new problems continue to arise.

One of the difficulties in lodging security is that there are numerous forms of lodging and each requires its own form of security. Table 3.2 gives an overview of some of the types of lodging and their individual challenges.

No matter the type of lodging establishment, there are certain principles that remain constant. Among these basic dos and don'ts are:

- Never forget that places of lodging are part of the local environment. Never separate the security found inside of an attraction or place of lodging from the environment in which it is located. Hoteliers, managers, and guesthouse providers need to be keenly aware of the crime issues that are found in the location in which their business is situated. For example, if a hotel is located in an area that attracts the homeless, then that fact must be taken into the overall security plan. The key concept here is that lodging security does not stop at a business's doorsteps.
- Places of lodging with low levels of good customer service often tend to be the least safe places in which to stay. Tourism hospitality businesses that provide poor customer service send out a message that they do not care about the well-being of their guests. In contrast, places of lodging in which the staff tends to care about its guests and safety is a high

Table 3.2 Types of Public Lodging and Some Security Challenges

Type of lodging	Positive	Negative
Interior-entrance hotel	Traffic control by front desk Often higher floors are accessible only by elevator Often full services within the hotel	Personnel dependent Evacuation may be difficult
Exterior-entrance motel	Easy access Easy evacuation Parking close to hotel room	Rooms open to invasion Front desk has little control People can enter and leave motel without being detected
Bed 'n breakfast	Produce homey feelings Cleaning personnel are often the owners	Often front doors left open Personal rooms often lack sturdy locks
Open air (campgrounds)	Highly informal Sense of social cohesion often exists within the social context	No real protection against other people and animals Open to weather problems

priority are usually safer. Creating an environment of caring is the first step toward good guest safety and security procedures.

- It is essential that in non-family-run places of lodging that the management knows who is working at the establishment. Administrators should perform background clearance. It is essential to remember that many lodging staff members have free access to guests' rooms, and they often know when the guests are not there. In larger hotels, security personnel often complain that they have no knowledge as to who has access to a guest's room and whether staff members have a previous criminal past. Take simple precautions such as requiring that employees be regularly tested for substance abuse. The security staff should also possess a copy of each employee's photo ID, and they should know which keys each employee has in his or her possession.
- Understand that many guests neither read the safety material that has been provided for them nor will they remember what the material says in times of emergency. When designing a hotel/motel security program, develop it in such a way as to assume that the management cannot depend on the guests to think for themselves, especially in times of crisis.
- Make sure that your staff is well trained in tourism security protection and they receive regular security updates. If your guests tend to use multiple languages, then know upon whom to call during times of crisis. All too often, security fails simply because the staff cannot communicate with the people it is serving. Whenever possible, make sure that hotel staff is certified in its security knowledge by an independent agency.
- Remember to protect your guests and staff first, and then protect your property. It is the responsibility of lodging professionals to protect both their guests and property. In an age of terrorism, we must not only protect our site, but also take into account the careless traveler. These people are not terrorists, but they can cost a place of lodging a great deal of money. For example, vacationers may simply forget to care for furniture, appliances, or equipment. Hotel security must take into account the needs of the cleaning staff and hotel engineers and seek to ensure that site environment is both attractive and as secure/safe as possible.
- In locations frequented by international travelers, make sure that security agents are well trained in guests' customs and the cultural habits of the hotel. For example, some cultures tend to be more trusting than others, while others may have distinct patterns for what is acceptable or not for female guests. It is essential that management develop security patterns that meet the local environment, as well as the cultural needs of the hotel's guests.

- Develop a relationship between the hotel's security staff and local law enforcement agencies. The local police department should not have to learn where things are in a hotel after an incident has taken place. Regular walk-throughs and meetings can save both time and lives and reduce what might have been a major incident into a minor one.
- Obtain the best equipment for guest protection that your business can afford. While not all properties need metal detectors, there are a number of less obvious improvements that can be made. Among these include proper windows, alarming for exit doors, upgraded key systems, and stringent controls on who may dispense keys. Review key return policy, ensure security cameras create "safe areas" where guests can go in case they feel uncomfortable on an elevator, and do regular reviews of equipment to decide if any changes are necessary. In an age of terrorism, hotels need to protect those locations where trash is disposed and make sure that all parking lots are well lit.
- Work with specialists to determine what is required to upgrade facilities. Small establishments often argue that they cannot afford to pay for expert advice. Many law enforcement agencies, however, are more than willing to provide free on-site inspections and help to develop security plans. For example, check the hotel's air ventilation system on a regular basis and make sure that all fire exits are clear of debris. Hoteliers and lodging providers need to ask themselves if guests could be evacuated from the establishment's roof in case of an emergency. The staff needs to have a backup plan in case there is an electrical blackout; the plan needs to include an evacuation method that will work without electricity. This means that guests may have to be evacuated without lights and informed of the situation without a loudspeaker system. Furthermore, in a world of international tourism, hotels need to have a plan to communicate with their guests who speak a foreign language. Giving orders in a language that is not understood is not useful.
- Security and safety also include items such as food and drink. Whenever food and drink are served, safety is an issue that must never be overlooked. Food safety means much more than simply refrigerating the mayonnaise. It means making sure that food preparation areas are secure and that there is a close working relationship between your security department and your food preparation services. It also means having a policy so that employees who are sick do not prepare food for others. Food safety in today's world also means that background checks need to be performed on all employees who handle food and that these employees are trained in pertinent aspects of hotel security.

THE ROLE OF THE SECURITY OFFICER

For many of the reasons stated above many large hotels have full-time security officers or staffs. Security officers, sometimes called risk management specialists so as to avoid the name security officer, are usually tasked with the overall responsibility of guests. In reality, all employees should share in this responsibility, but the security officer is considered the security and safety specialist, as well as the chief motivator. Hotel security departments are also responsible for the hotel's property, its goods, and the well-being of its employees. There is no specific style for the hotel security staff. The types of security used and the equipment selected depends on several factors. Included in these are the hotel's budgetary restraints, geography, type of guests it attracts, and locale in which it is located. For example, casinos tend to utilize a large amount of closed-circuit cameras, while beach resorts may rely heavily on people, such as lifeguards. Also, hotel security personnel are the first responders. Therefore, they must be trained in everything from fire prevention to first aid and medical emergencies.

Lodging security officers often fall into two broad categories. The first category can be called the professionalized long-term officer. These people are true specialists in lodging security, and they may be members of the hotel's senior staff. Their work is less physical than it is mental, and they are responsible for deciding what equipment is needed and what policies should be implemented. The second category can be described as the front-line security personnel. People working in this part of security must deal with a multiplicity of tasks. For example, it is the front-line security professional with which guests often interact. Their jobs usually consist of tasks, such as patrolling the grounds of the hotel or motel, checking stairwells, and ensuring that locks are in working order. The front-line security professional acts as the eyes and ears of the hotel's security office and management. Although in most cases it is not the front-line security professional's task to determine which equipment will be purchased, it is their responsibility to monitor closed-circuit cameras and use other forms of security devices, such as alarm systems.

In many cases, front-line security professionals must provide a sense of security; in addition, they should attend to guests when there is a complaint, such as too much noise coming from another room or in cases of emergency. For example, if a guest were to not leave his or her room for an inordinate amount of time, it would fall upon the front-line security professional to enter the room to determine if the guest is fine or if a medical or physical problem has occurred. A third task for the front-line security professional is to provide escorts. Escorts may be needed when guests are intoxicated and cannot find their way safely to their room or when a guest feels uncomfortable. For example, single female travelers are often advised to seek an escort to their room if they arrive late at night and must use an outside entrance.

Another aspect of the hotel security officer's work is his or her psychological ability to prevent negative incidents. Successful security directors should have a working knowledge of their local legal system. It is a good idea to have a group of experts who are backing up the security director. Among the experts that a security director will want on his or her team are a lawyer and an expert in property management. No one person can keep pace with all of the changes in the modern world and for this reason, security experts need to rely on team members for expert and up-to-date advice.

Because all places of lodging share the tourism industry's desire to avoid incidents, the security officer's number one task may be to prevent an incident from occurring. For this reason, security officers need to be extremely good listeners, and they should know how to abate a customer's anger, whether this anger is aimed at the hotel's staff or at another guest staying at the hotel.

Not all places of lodging can afford full-time security and risk management staffs. So, smaller or less wealthy properties may choose to employ off-duty police officers, former police officers, or other security professionals. Although these officers are trained to respond to physical complaints, such as disorderly conduct or questions of thievery, they are not hotel security specialists. Many of these people come from diverse corporate or public cultures, so they should be retrained in the use of verbal defense and customer service. It is also important to remind off-duty officers and retirees that although this may be a second job for them, from the perspective of guests, their security has to be the officer's primary job. Thus, when seeking a security person, it is best to seek people who are good listeners and who understand the corporate culture. Prevention and a proactive policy are always advisable in tourism over reactive policies. Seek people with as many skills as possible rather than emphasizing only the job's security aspects. It is essential that they hire people who do not see their job as an entranceway into police work. When hiring a security professional, be sure to explain to them that there are many differences between the role of a police officer and a security manager. Those individuals who see hotel security as nothing more than a stepping-stone into police work tend not to do a good job.

A third option is a combination of off-duty or retired police and a smaller full-time staff. The former can deal with such issues as payroll protection and preventing unauthorized entrances and exits, and the latter can deal with policy and psychological issues. Remember, the off-duty police officer has the advantage that he or she has the power of arrest and does not need to wait for the police to come in cases of legal emergencies.

Security officers often complain that they are considered a "necessary evil." Hotel managers sometimes see security officers as adding nothing to the bottom line; they are merely an additional expense that must be borne. There are times when hotel general managers fail to heed warnings or make mistakes in regard to security. Just as there are constants in the realm of lodging security, there are also common oversights in lodging security. A few of these common mistakes are:

1. Poorly considered reductions in the number of security personnel. This is a common mistake based on the fact that security is often seen as an added extra. Often, managers are willing to risk their reputation and their business on the hope that nothing will occur. In statistical theory, this is called a type-4 error. Simply put, the event may be unlikely to occur, but if it does occur, the consequences would be grave.

2. Failing to pay careful enough attention to risk management plans or not having a plan. The problem with risk management is that if nothing happens, management may say the plan was not needed. Yet, if something does happen, then the response is that the risk management plan did not stop the event. This type of teleological thinking only leads to lawsuits or worse.

3. Failing to provide adequate lighting in such places as parking lots. This lack of lighting becomes an invitation for crime and is a perfect example of the fact that tragedy can often be prevented with minimal expense and adequate foresight.

4. Lack of post-employment training. Security is part of a dynamic and changing world. All professionals need to review their techniques and knowledge base and then learn how to deal with ever changing threats and problems.

5. Ignoring the need to protect one's data from cyber attacks and not having data at an off-site location. The cyber problem is a growing one. Cyber attacks may occur either for reasons of theft or as pure annoyances. No matter what the reason, most businesses are vulnerable to a cyber attack, so there is a need to constantly backup data and hold the backups at off-site locations.

6. Allowing fitness centers to be unmanned and unmonitored. Although most places of lodging have signs that read "Use at one's own risk," these

signs do not provide adequate legal protection and leave the hotel open to negative publicity. It is beyond a reasonable expectation to expect a property to employ fitness center staff, but there should be means to communicate with the front desk in case of emergency.

7. Not having conducted adequate background checks on all staff members. Often hotel and/or motel management hires people with little or no knowledge of the employee's background. Given that staff members have keys to other people's rooms, and are often left alone in them, it is essential for management to have some idea as to whom it is giving room entrance permission.

8. Failing to run equipment tests in real time to detect the state of all security equipment. The best security equipment in the world provides little help if it does not work properly. Equipment may break down due to the following issues: longevity, weather, or mechanical error. Even the best equipment must be checked on a regular basis. (Barber, 2004)

DEALING WITH THE SPECIFICS OF LODGING SECURITY

All places of lodging exist for one reason. They are businesses, and no business survives if it does not bring in more money. Monetary inflow must be greater than monetary outflow or the business will fail. Thus, the interconnection between personal and physical security and economic security is ever present.

Although the economic–security threat to the lodging industry is not physical, it is just as, or even more, dangerous. Once people begin to shy away from a specific locale, the business's survival is questionable. This challenge is especially true in periods of economic uncertainty and for businesses that depend on disposable income.

Places of lodging need to be realistic with their security. They do not want to panic their clientele, nor do they want to give them a false sense of security. When developing a security plan, step back for a few moments and think about your own establishment's challenges. What are some possible solutions that will permit a particular business to overcome these challenges? Remember, the best way to solve big problems is to break them down into smaller and more manageable problems. Many lodging managers face the issue of time frames. Hotel and motel owners, as well as customers, want immediate results. Nevertheless, these results are often impossible to deliver immediately.

Whether the lodging's management likes it or not, it must take the media into account. It should realize that the media plays a major role in the establishment's economic security. In most cases, the media will tend to follow the principle of "If it bleeds, it leads." This attitude means that security personnel must be cognizant that a security mishap could become a news item that may have a devastating impact on the lodging establishment's economic security and viability. Therefore, it is essential that security people not only learn how to separate facts from "analytical fictions," but also understand how the media works in order to develop good media relations. Security professionals dare not forget that the news media is hampered by their need to provide 24-hour coverage and attract viewers' attention.

Other factors that security personnel and professionals should take into consideration are the fact that travel and tourism are component industries, and that hotels are part of a larger industry. This reality means that the travel and tourism industry touches every aspect of tourism business life. What happens in a place of lodging vibrates throughout the tourism industry. For example, if a community loses restaurants, then that loss will impact the number of people staying in town, which may hurt local hotels. If hotels are not occupied, not only will lodging tax revenues decrease, but this decrease will also impact a wide variety of business owners. Tourism and travel will need to practice collective survival. The power of clustering to increase business will become an important trend.

Because places of lodging are part of a larger entity, that is, the community in which they are located and the community's tourism industry, lodging security professionals must participate with their colleagues as part of broad-based community teams. It is essential to develop good communications between places of lodging. Fax or email or text networks can be used to warn other establishments of a problem. Networking with the local police department is also essential. The worst thing is for a police, fire, or first-aid department to have to learn where things are located in a building during a crisis. Instead, make sure that first responders know the floor plans, where circuit breakers are located, and how to access other essential devices. It is also a good idea for general managers and security professionals to network with a wide range of local political and financial specialists. These people can best support the security professional's work if they understand the reasons behind a professional's actions.

Train yourself in the art of out-of–the-box thinking. Do not wait for a crisis to try to figure out ways to do more with less. Consider ways to connect your product development to your marketing. Make sure that your security staff provides tourism essentials, such as information on how to find local attractions, streets that are best to be avoided, and at what times to be off the streets.

Remember, most hotels are not islands unto themselves. Beautification projects add value to your lodging product, and they provide an uplifting environment, which lowers the proclivity toward crime. In the world of tourism and lodging management, everyone has to learn to work together. This means that all hotel employees need to be part of a single team, and members of the community, from the police to sanitation workers, need to see security as their responsibility.

Even the smartest specialists are not always right. To paraphrase an old adage, "The road to hell is often paved with good intentions." Listen to the best advice, but at the same time, even the best make mistakes. Security is not an exact science, and no one is always right. Listen to expert opinions, but never forget that the final decision is yours in the end. If your gut tells you that something is not right, then simply do not go forward. So, once you have done your research, listen to your gut. It may be giving you the best advice of all.

PLANNING LODGING SECURITY

Let us assume that you are starting a new job as a security professional at a major international hotel. As in any other lodging security position, your establishment will have both its own particularities and its commonalities with all other security positions. You settle in at your desk, look at the walls, and ask yourself, "Now what?" What are the essential questions that you would ask yourself?

Perhaps to begin you would start by asking four essential questions:
1. Where is my hotel vulnerable?
2. What are the greatest security exposures at your facility?
3. What areas do you believe to be safest in your hotel?
4. What areas are the least secure?

Being a professional, you should realize that 100% safety can never be achieved. Even if it were possible, you would never have the necessary resources to assure total security. Instead, lodging security, like other forms of security, is a "game" of risk management. We attempt to make educated guesses on where our greatest vulnerabilities lie and then prioritize.

Security is not only an "artistic" science, but it also has its political side. Thus, on the first day on the job, your second task is to realize that without political support, your work can never be successful. For this reason, you might ask yourself some political questions that will determine who is your ally and who wishes you were not there. Does your general manager support you or did corporate headquarters send you to the hotel against their will? Who on the hotel staff would oppose you and how much influence does your opposition have?

Although these questions may, at first, seem to be irrelevant to the job of a security professional, reality tells us that no professional works in a vacuum. To quote an old saying: "Politics is all about the realm of the possible." So, in order to succeed, you need the support of your colleagues. If you do not have their support, then before doing anything else, work to gain their support and understanding. In all forms of tourism security the psychological is as important as the physical.

To gain your colleagues' support, make sure that people understand what you do and who you are. This type of support can be garnered by simple actions. For example, take the time to display degrees and professional certifications. Then, assuming you have a professional security team, assess the team. How many team members do you have? Are they full time or part time? What problems do they have? Good security begins with good listening and observation. The security professional needs to listen to his or her colleagues and observe their problems.

It is imperative that as the head person in security, you know as much about the hotel's staff as possible. What background checks have been performed on the staff? Are there events in their personal histories about which you need to be aware? To better understand the people with whom you are working, consider the following:

- Is it already part of the corporate culture that all employees be regularly tested for substance abuse?
- Who on the staff has received a course on security awareness training?
- How are employees regularly reminded about hotel safety and security measures?
- Are hotel employees required to demonstrate proficiency with your security and safety procedures manual?
- Are hotel employees trained in crisis response?
- Do all of the hotel's employees, including cleaning personnel, have the opportunity to interact with local law enforcement?
- How well will your colleagues be able to handle a crisis situation, especially if you are off the property?

Do your colleagues possess any useful talents? Do you have colleagues who speak more than one language? What negatives must you face? For example, does the hotel employ people who come to work with resentments or bring their problems from home to work? Every workplace has at least a few employees who have special challenges. The best way to start creating a secure hotel environment is to know what those challenges are.

It is also important to know how much the hotel's staff knows about security issues. Do you know what is the amount of time that each staff member has been working for the hotel? Determine if the staff has been trained and tested on your hotel's security policies. How are staff members identified? Do they have special passes besides uniforms? Do staff members have access to every part of the hotel or are there restrictions? Does every staff member have a master key and, if so, why? If not, why do some people have master keys and others do not? What is the policy and procedures for staff termination and departures? Are there employees who have been accused of a theft against a hotel guest, found innocent, and are still working for the hotel? Is there a list of staff members who have been fired? Is there a written record of why these people have been fired?

In a like manner, it would be imperative to know what equipment you have and what equipment you will need to order. It should be emphasized that not every hotel needs every piece of equipment. Remember, the best equipment is only as good as the people who operate it. Taking this provision into account, good security does need good equipment because it provides your security personnel with the proper tools, and it makes a statement that management views them as serious professionals. Before assessing what equipment you need, first assess what equipment you have. Do you have:

- Metal detectors?
- X-ray machines on property?
- Bulletproof or locked windows overlooking sensitive areas?
- Alarmed exit doors?
- A key system that meets your needs?
- A system of key control?
- Security cameras that work?

Also you will want to know:

- Are the security cameras watched in real time, or do they record incidents for later viewing?
- How much of the property is monitored by cameras?
- Where are your "blind spots"?
- Are there cameras in the elevators?

The hotel's physical security is multifaceted and deals with a wide variety of additional issues, such as when is it proper and not proper to use closed-circuit TV cameras? Should you use exterior and interior intrusion sensors? What type of alarm system management, access control, and, in cases of more upscale properties, executive protection will you choose to use and on what will you be basing your decision? In a hotel, even simple security matters may have larger consequences. For example, most security experts agree that the more lighting the better, but the amount of lighting needs to be balanced with other issues, such as the type of ambiance that the hotel wishes to create, or even which types of lighting highlight flaws in personal appearance.

As part of a security assessment, you should want to know what is on the premises, what your challenges are going to be, and what problem areas can be postponed for a later time. Developing your priorities is essential. Table 3.3 should help you make some key decisions regarding your premises' evaluation. Fill in each box with numbers from 1 to 10 with 1 being the least important (you can live with it at least until other areas are repaired) and 10 being the most important (do it/fix it now). Then, add the numbers so as to have a priority calculation. Remember, while all items listed below are important, there will never be enough time and money to do everything all at once.

WORKING WITH OTHERS

No one in the world of security can do everything by him- or herself. We all need others to help us with both physical knowledge and job specialization. As a result, it is important that security specialists know whom they can count on within their community. Ask yourself such questions as:

- Do I have a regularly updated list of specialists in town? The list should contain first responders, law enforcement officers, legal experts, medical personnel, etc. Do you have an updated emergency contact list?
- How often do they meet with your security team?
- How often do people tend to leave this job for another?

It is essential that at least two people from your security team meet with first responders on a regular basis. The reason for this is that it deals with the important security concept of redundancy.

The Rule of Redundancy: Redundancy is the notion that we can never depend on one person or system, and so we use backups or secondary people or systems to ensure that in case of an emergency there is a second person or system that can also do the job.

It is a good idea to invite the hotel's general manager to some of the meetings. His or her attendance will ensure better communications and

Table 3.3 Priority Calculator

Item/locale	Life-threatening?	Required under law?	Cost to benefit?	Publicity due to failure	Numerical total
Fire exits					
Guards at exits					
Restaurant/bar cleanliness					
Secured air vents					
Roof access by security					
Roof access by others					
Roof secured area					
Helicopter access in case of emergency					
Emergency power supply					
Emergency lighting system					
Quality of fire system					
PA communication system					
Multilingual communication system					
Parking lot lighting					
Parking lot secured					
Weather protection against hurricanes or tornados					
After-hours security in parking lots					
Safe deposit boxes in guests' rooms					
Secure Internet access					
Dumpsters and trash secured					
Other					

a better understanding of the challenges that must be met on a regular basis by the security team.

The hotel's security team should also have some contact with foreign representatives, hospital management, and members of the local medical establishment.

The Rule of Changeability: Both hotel staff and emergency management tend to have high turnover rates. That means that interinstitutional relationships need to be renewed constantly. The rule of redundancy must also be observed. This means that due to changeability it is essential that at least two people know every job and know how to operate each piece of equipment.

Words of Caution: Never fail to consider both the rules of redundancy and changeability (see below) in all of your security personnel plans.

AROUND THE HOTEL

Hotels are often considered social systems. Each part of the hotel interacts with each one of its other parts, and a change in one part impacts all other parts.

FRONT DESK AND LOBBY AREA

Perhaps no one part of a hotel is as important as the front desk. This is the location where guests are greeted and bid farewell, and it is the hotel's front line of security. The hotel's front desk area and reception locale is the place where people gather, luggage is sometimes left unattended, and people tend to let their guards down. The bombings of two hotels in Kenya in November 2002 should serve as a reminder that the lobby and front desk area can be targets for a terrorist attack. This part of the hotel has several security challenges, among them:

1. Awareness of front-line personnel (people working at the front desk) to potential threats: How vigilant are those working at the front desk to potential problems?
2. The physical safety and security of the lobby: Are guests and hotel staff protected while in an exposed area? How easily can these people call for help, should the need arise?
3. The baggage/storage area. This area is often in close proximity to the lobby. Bags are normally held for guests without inspection, so personnel does not know what these bags contain.

FRONT DESK PERSONNEL

Most front desk people are trained to smile. Yet, anyone who has ever observed front desk associates knows that they do not have an easy job. Even in large hotels, these employees do a great deal more than merely provide room keys to incoming guests. It is often the same person who is manning the phones, helping people with both check-in and check-out procedures, and dealing with particular guest's issues and problems, especially those that may occur in a guest's room. Usually, front desk personnel are so busy that they barely notice the guest's appearance. Adding to this difficult scenario, front desk personnel often work long shifts, so by the end of their shift, they are simply worn out. Consequently, people who are overworked are often the ones managing a hotel's first line of defense.

From a security perspective, it is imperative to consider a variety of matters, most importantly the number of hours that this person is on duty and if is there an adequate number of people manning the front desk, especially during peak check-in and check-out times.

When it comes to protecting the premises, the front desk personnel should always be trained to:

- Ask for a government-issued identification document during guest registration.
- Make a copy of the guest's identification card and hold it for the length of his or her stay.
- Shred all of the copies of the guest's identification upon the guest's departure.
- Insist that the guest always use his or her legal name.
- Note suspicious behavior and have a system of reporting this behavior immediately.
- Other than petty cash, place additional cash, as well as credit card numbers, in a safe place that is not in public view.
- Beware of the storage areas. The luggage and storage areas are a clear potential hazard. Most hotels insist that guests check out of their rooms around 12:00 P.M. The problem with this scenario is that many flights do not leave until later in the day. The solution has been to allow guests to store their luggage. This policy, however, has created several new difficulties. Among these are:
  - The hotel may have no way of knowing what is in checked luggage.
  - Most people storing the luggage have no way of identifying suspicious luggage or packages. Hotels need to develop policies as to

how long luggage is allowed to be stored, and what to do with the luggage should it be in storage for more than the permitted time.

When it comes to protecting the guest, the front desk personnel should complete the following tasks:

- Never announcing out loud a guest's room number.
- Never giving out a guest's personal information.
- Being mindful not to send a single female traveler to a room that may be hidden from view.
- Sending a hotel staff person to see the guest safely to her room if there is no room alternative.
- Ensuring guests are escorted to their rooms if the staff is adequate. Hotel staff should inspect all rooms, making sure that the telephone and lights are in working order and the room has been properly serviced.
- Safeguarding and noting the well-being of persons with special physical needs, such as those who are blind or deaf.
- Having a way to inform and protect special-needs guests in case of emergencies such as a fire.
- Providing guests with local information in case of emergency, such as police, local consulates, and medical services.
- Shredding all of a guest's information upon the guest's check-out from the premises.
- Asking guests upon check-out if they noted any security problems or mishaps.

ROOMS AND HALLWAYS

Most people assume that they are safe in the privacy of their rooms. However, this assumption is not always accurate, so the security person must be careful to look at issues of both safety and security. From the safety side of the equation, bathtubs and showers may be especially challenging. If the bathroom has a "slippery" tile floor, then a guest could easily fall upon leaving the shower or bath. Some tubs are so high that climbing out may become a challenge. Another place where safety needs to be examined carefully is that of windows, balconies, and ledges. Windows should be double-locked and built in a manner that prevents a child from climbing up to the ledge and then falling. Balcony walls should not only impede potential falls, but they must be built in such a way that prohibits intruders from climbing onto the balcony. Often, it is easy to travel from one balcony to the next, which means that unlocked balcony doors offer free access to the room.

Within the room itself, electrical outlets should be constructed so that guests are not climbing under furniture and light switches are easily accessible.

To ensure room security, all doors should have a deadbolt lock and full latches. Unfortunately, there is no lock that cannot be broken or outsmarted. As far back as 1999, NBC's *Dateline* reported that electronic locks could be decoded. Since then, there have been a series of reports indicating that an unbreakable lock does not exist. The December 14, 2012, edition of *USA Today* reported that hotels are now taking the lock situation seriously:

> To comply with its "duty of care" responsibility, a hotel in this situation should disclose the fact to customers and encourage them to take secondary measures, such as using the in-room safe and applying their door's safety latch, says Barth, president of HospitalityLawyer.com. He also says travelers should first check those safety latches to make sure they are in good working condition.
>
> "The issue here is that hotels that have Onity lock systems are aware of this flaw, so do they have a duty to warn their guests?," he says. "Most hotels so far have taken the position that they're not going to tell guests but encourage them to be sure to use the security bar."
>
> **("Hotels fixing flaw," 2012, Travelers Told to Take Precautions section, para. 2-3)**

The hotel security staff also needs to develop policies regarding hallways. Are they monitored and if so is the monitoring active or passive? Is anyone allowed into the elevator? Are there ways for guests to seek help should there be a mishap not only in the elevator but also in the hallways?

FOOD AND BEVERAGES

Hotels have a wide range of food and beverage services. These services range from merely providing vending machines to full-scale restaurants. Many hotels offer a variety of restaurants, and they also provide room service, including some that offer a full menu 24 hours a day, along with catering services for conventions and conferences. Note that the issue of food preparation is not addressed in this chapter. The safety and security professional also needs to know that the food preparation and storage areas are secure. It is essential to do a background inspection on food handlers. Also, medical checks and policies need to be put into place concerning working while sick. For example, a sick food preparer may not want to lose a day's pay, so they come to work with a contagious infection.

In a like manner, banquet staff banquet staff should not have any communicative diseases or any open wounds. The surety professional needs to ask questions such as, Who hired the wait and cooking staff? Are part-time staff members required to complete security awareness training prior to working at the hotel?

THE OUTSIDE PUBLIC AREAS

Hotel security does not stop at the hotel's walls. Many hotels have gardens, walking trails, swimming pools, tennis courts and other outdoor sporting areas, and beaches. These areas are as much a part of the hotel as anything inside the hotel. Once again, the security professional staff should consider the guests' and employee's safety and security along with the protection of the hotel's property.

Police officers and security specialists have used a variety of methods not only to protect guests who are on the hotel property, but outside of the hotel itself. Security is often broken down into passive methods, such as the proper use of lighting, and active methods, such as regular walking patrols. A non-invasive passive method called CPTED (crime prevention through environmental design) has the advantage of protecting people while also enhancing the property's beauty. The theory behind CPTED, and other forms of security through beautification, is that the environment often influences us, as well as the actions we chose to take. CPTED creates criminal-unfriendly environments through the use of low bushes and flowers that allow security guards to have a clear vision of the area to be protected. Often, CPTED is reduced to four simple principles. These principles are:

1. Create situations in which the criminal knows that he or she can be seen. A good example is the proper use of lighting.
2. The control of accesses by environmental design, for example, the placement of walkways that guide people to safe areas while making entrance for intruders difficult
3. Creating clear distinctions between public and private areas. This distinction is used to delineate no-go areas from welcome areas and to discourage trespassing.
4. Property maintenance and proper upkeep. Criminologists have long held that a rundown appearance leads to higher levels of crime. By cutting grass, fixing broken windows, and raking leaves, the location is given a sense of being cared for and discourages crime. ("Crime Prevention through Environmental Design," 2005)

CPTED tries to incorporate the locale's ambiance into its strategies for physical security. Thus, it looks at issues such as:

- Is there natural surveillance?
- Are windows strategically placed?
- Do the windows provide access points to the property's exterior?
- What can the security professional see and not see from his or her window?
- What areas provide cover for ambushes?

POOL AND ATHLETIC SAFETY

Swimming pools, and other athletic areas, are a guest's delight and a risk manager's nightmare. For example, no matter how well protected the pool may be, the fear of a guest drowning is ever present. However, hotel surety staffs can do a great deal to ensure the maximum amount of safety.

Most communities have regulations regarding swimming pools. Before developing any policy, review the legal restrictions and rules dealing with all aspects of swimming pools and then enforce these codes. Yet, these codes may not always be sufficient, so it behooves the security agent to know the industry's standard of care. Finally, each location has its own particular needs and idiosyncrasies. No two locales are exactly alike and security should be built around the locale's particular needs.

Needless to say, hotels must develop guidelines, such as when a lifeguard is on duty, when the pool is open to the public, and how access to the pool is limited when the pool is not open. Most hotels have a "no child without adult" supervision policy and the term "child" must be clearly specified. Glass containers should never be allowed in places where people go barefoot. Are emergency numbers posted in a place where all can see them? Is there telephone communication from the pool or beach?

Other things that must be considered are the level of chlorine or other chemicals that are used. It is a good idea to remember that there are people who are chlorine sensitive. In a like manner, public toilets and showers are breeding grounds for germs. How often are they cleaned, and what type of sanitizer does your hotel use?

Finally, never forget that we live in a litigious society. Good security means that it is our responsibility to protect the hotel's guests, as well as the hotel from lawsuits. It is essential to have written policies along with clear-cut methods to ensure several situations, such as driving safety, sunstroke on the tennis courts, insurance against claims against personnel belongings, etc. Always check equipment and make sure that an equipment flaw will not lead to a guest's injury or worse. It is the responsibility of the security staff to know the industry standards of care and to abide by them.

OTHER AREAS IN THE HOTEL

A part of hotels that is often overlooked is the area where packages are received and shipped out. These areas may be anything from loading docks to a mailroom. The receiving and dispatch zone is the area through which the hotel's supplies travel. Some of these materials may range from food to special flowers. No matter the receiving area, be sure that it is secure. As a result, there needs to be random searches of delivery vehicles. Drivers or delivery persons should be identified as working for that company, and a hotel's staff member should check all incoming and outgoing packages. Security staff should have a suspicious package policy in place. If the hotel has people working in the shipping and receiving department, then these people should be trained in the identifying and handling of suspicious packages.

OUTSOURCING

Many hotels need to outsource. Outsourcing may be the hiring of specialized contractors, such as electricians or plumbers, or the need for specialized dry cleaning services. It is essential to know something about these people, especially if they are performing their work on the hotel's property. At times, these "outside employees" handle sensitive equipment. They may have access to computerized records or they may be the valets parking cars. In all cases, it is essential that the hotel's security staff knows who they are, and if the person performing the service is who he or she says. In a like manner it is important to know not just their job description but to what parts of the property these people will have access. For example, what type of training do valets receive? Does the hotel valet check identification when given the claim to a car? Do valet service providers know what to do in case of a suspicious person or package? Are valet service providers encouraged to check trunks when given the vehicle?

What is essential here is that the security team develops and practices policies dealing with each auxiliary service provider, which may range from the person taking coats at the hotel's restaurant or convention center, to the person who organizes the hotel's lost and found. In all cases, the hotel security staff must have developed a set of written guidelines. Train people in these guidelines and check to make sure that these guidelines are put into practice.

PROTECTING THE HOTEL'S STAFF

Hotels should not only protect their guests from dishonest employees or those who may seek to do harm, but also their employees from dishonest guests.

Hotel employees may be subjected to a series of challenges. These security and safety challenges can range from simply being the object of verbal abuse, to being physically or sexually assaulted. The employee needs to be protected from physical assaults and exposure to a range of potentially infectious diseases, including the common cold, major illnesses, or a potential pandemic. Hotel staff members are also required to work with their colleagues; consequently, there is the continuous potential for workplace violence. This is especially true in high-stress, customer service positions, such as those in a hotel. At times, hotel guests can be demanding. So those working in hotels must depend on their colleagues while dealing with difficult people. Furthermore, people who work in entry-level hotel jobs may be new to the United States, so their command of the English language may be poor. It is essential that security personnel establish both training sessions and policies for their employees. For example, chambermaids should never allow a person to enter the room they are cleaning. The practice of allowing chambermaids to clean four rooms at a time with the door open is not safe for the employee or the hotel's guests.

Here are a few of the physical problems facing chambermaids:
- Germ-infested rooms
- Potential for blood left on sheets or other parts of the room
- Potential for being cut
- Guests who abuse, insult, or assault

It is for this reason that all employees should be trained in recognizing violent traits in employees or guests. The list below provides some of the basic traits employees should be made aware of:
- Threats or acts of intimidation against a colleague or employee
- Showing off a weapon at inappropriate times
- Demonstrating paranoid behavior (the world is against me)

- Being overly righteous ("I'm good; you're not")
- Act of regularly blaming others for one's mistakes
- Poor interaction with others; tendency toward depression and/or isolation
- Rapid decline in performance for no apparent reason
- Holding grudges, especially against those who criticize one's work
- Obsessive involvement with one's job, often accompanied by uneven job performance
- Unwanted romantic obsession with a coworker
- Expressions of extreme desperation due to family, financial, or personal problem(s)
- Personal history of violence
- Consistently speaking about workplace violence
- Demonstrating an extreme interest in the use of nonhunting weapons, that is, automatic or semiautomatic weapons
- Disregard for the safety of coworkers
- Excessive attendance/tardiness or forgetfulness (when combined with a trait above)

SHOULD AN EMPLOYEE OR GUEST BECOME VIOLENT

The following are ideas that law/security enforcement may want to stress to workers in the visitor industry.

- Isolate the violent individual as quickly as possible.
- Many visitor officials do not want the presence of law enforcement known even when an "action" is occurring. Do your job, but be sensitive to other people's needs.
- Each situation is unique, think before you act.
- Stay calm and take immediate action to protect the other employees and guests.
- Teach visitor employees how to sound alarms and to alert coworkers.
- Stress that you protect life first and only then property or money. Things can be recovered, a life cannot!
- Nonsecurity personnel should not try to disarm a person.
- Suggest counseling for the victims.
- Ask what the security professional department can do to help in the post-violence recovery phase.

REFERENCES

Barber, D. S., Esq. (2004, July). 10 safety mistakes hotel managers make and how to avoid them. Retrieved from http://www.slideshare.net/palpoelsayed/10-safety-mistakes-hotel-managers-make.

Crime prevention through environmental design. (2005). *CPTED Security*. Retrieved from http://cptedsecurity.com/cpted_design_guidelines.htm.

Hotels fixing flaw that made room locks vulnerable to hackers. (2012, December 14). *USA Today*. Retrieved from http://www.usatoday.com/story/hotelcheckin/2012/12/14/hotels-fixing-flaw-that-made-room-locks-vulnerable-to-hackers/1769081/.

Mayock, P. (2012, January 4). 5 pressing hotel security concerns for 2012. *Hotel News Now*. Retrieved from http://www.hotelnewsnow.com/Article/7229/5-pressing-hotel-security-concerns-for-2012.

Tarlow, P. (2007). In J. Fay (Ed.), *Encyclopedia of Security Management* (2nd ed.). Boston, MA: Elsevier B.V.

Your hotel room may not be as secure as you think. (2012, December 13). *ITS Tactical*. Retrieved from http://www.itstactical.com/digicom/security/your-hotel-room-may-not-be-as-secure-as-you-think/.

CHAPTER 4

Risk and Crisis Management

INTRODUCTION

On the third Monday of every April, the city of Boston, Massachusetts, holds its traditional marathon. April 15, 2013 would seem to have been just another Monday in Boston. The day dawned without any bad expectations, but suddenly, toward the marathon's end, a day of sport became a day of tragedy. Struck by two bombs, allegedly planted by two brothers in an act of terrorism, three people lost their lives and almost 200 people were injured, with some even losing limbs. The events of that day caused the city of Boston to virtually shut down. Hundreds of thousands of people's lives were impacted, and the city of Boston, along with the state of Massachusetts, lost millions of dollars in sales and tax revenue.

The 2013 Boston Marathon tragedy is a significant lesson in tourism risk management. It teaches us the importance of risk management and its limitations. The tragedy also reminds us about the consequence of having a crisis plan to handle a situation when a risk becomes a reality, and a risk management plan must become a crisis management plan.

Of course, Boston is not the only city to hold major sporting events. Sports tourism and event tourism are big businesses. For example, the city of Rio de Janeiro, Brazil, will soon be hosting some of the world's largest events, most notably the FIFA World Cup in 2014 and the Olympic Summer Games in 2016. These events will attract thousands of people from around the world, while millions more will watch from the comfort of their homes. What happens in Rio during these events will be broadcast across the globe. Risk, however, does not only refer to tourism events. All tourism carries elements of risk, from transportation, to hotel safety and security, to alcohol consumption.

This chapter deals with two essential topics within tourism security and safety: that of risk and crisis management. There is also a special section dealing with the risk/crisis continuum and how it pertains to terrorism and tourism.

RISK MANAGEMENT

One noteworthy problem with the term "risk management" is that it lacks a common definition. One reason for this lack of commonality is that the term "risk" has different meanings in a variety of fields. For example, if we consider the concept of risk simply in the field of finance, then we soon discover it covers a wide variety of subfields. Note that the Northrup Grunmann Group lists the following forms of financial risk:

- Market risk: The risk that the value of your investment will decline as a result of market conditions. This type of risk is primarily associated with stocks. You might buy the stock of a promising or successful company only to have its market value fall with a generally falling stock market.
- Interest rate risk: The risk caused by changes in the general level of interest rates in the marketplace. This type of risk is most apparent in the bond market because bonds are issued at specific interest rates. Generally, a rise in interest rates will cause a decline in market prices of existing bonds, while a decline in interest rates tends to cause bond prices to rise. For example, say you buy a 30-year bond today with a 6% annual yield. If interest rates rise, a new 30-year bond may be issued with an 8% annual yield. The price of your bond drops because investors aren't willing to pay full value for a bond that yields less than the current rate of interest.
- Inflation or purchasing power risk: The risk that the return on your investment will fail to outpace inflation. This type of risk is most closely associated with cash/stable value investments. Thus, although you may think a traditional bank savings account is relatively risk free, you actually could be losing purchasing power unless the interest rate on the account exceeds the current rate of inflation.
- Business risk: This is the risk that issuers of an investment may run into financial difficulties and not be able to live up to market expectations. For example, a company's profits may be hurt by a lawsuit, a change in management, or some other event.
- Credit risk: For bonds, this is the risk that the issuer may default on periodic interest payments and/or the repayment of principal. For stocks, it is the risk that the company might reduce or eliminate dividend payments due to financial troubles.

When you invest internationally, you also face additional risks:

- Exchange rate risk: This is the risk that returns will be adversely affected by changes in the exchange rate.

- Country or political risk: This is the risk that arises in connection with uncertainty about a country's political environment and the stability of its economy. This risk is especially important in emerging markets. ("What are the different types of risk?", 2013)

Each one of these areas for risk has a specific meaning in the world of finance. We can say the same in most fields, and this multiplicity of meanings holds true in the worlds of tourism and event management.

WHY ANALYZING TOURISM RISKS IS DIFFICULT

Because tourism is a composite industry, tourism and events are open to a wide variety of risks. Yet, there is no one standard for determining overall risk. Instead, tourism is composed of a series of subevents or potentials, and each one has its own set of risks. For example, a tourism business must face the interaction of weather-related risk with a number of other semi-related risks. So, an outdoor event may have to deal with the risk of too much heat, which produces the additional medical risk of heat exhaustion. Below is a very short list of primary and secondary risks that different factions of the tourism industry face:

- Crime
- Fire
- Health concerns
- Terrorism
- Travel dilemmas
- Weather

Each one of these principal risks has numerous subrisks, each possibly interacting with one another. Within this perspective, a pure mathematical formula or quantitative breakdowns describing risk must be balanced with qualitative analysis. Even when we combine both the qualitative and quantitative analysis of risk, we still lack clear-cut delineations. To illustrate, the military's use of biochemicals, or other forms of terrorism, means that there is a strong possibility of crossovers between issues of health and security, which causes an interaction between these two types of risk.

In each of these cases, the tourism professional must be aware that the risk potential is ever ubiquitous. Brazilian scholar Gui Santana has noted that crises in the tourism industry can take many shapes and forms—from terrorism to sexual harassment, white-collar crime to civil disturbances, a jet crashing into a hotel to cash flow problems, guest injury to strikes, bribery to price fixing, noise to vandalism, guest misuse of facilities to technological change (Santana & Tarlow, 2002).

Tourism risk managers must be aware of not only a single crisis, but also any combination or crossovers of crises.

As in all fields, risk management is based on a series of assumptions. Risk management is stochastic (probabilistic) in nature. Below are some of the key assumptions that support the field:

- There is no person, place, thing, or event that is 100% free of risk. If human beings can design it, then there is a human being or group of human beings who can destroy or harm it.
- Risk management relies heavily on statistics by utilizing statistical data analysis. The better the data are, the lesser the chance of failure. Yet, no matter how good the data are, the element of surprise and failure is ever present.
- In the field of tourism risk management, the risk manager must be keenly aware that to travel is to be insecure. In today's world of travel, the traveler knows that he or she is often not in control.
- There are different levels of acceptable risk within the sociopsychological range of tourists and visitors. This means that certain people can accept a higher level of risk than others. How risk is managed depends as much on the clientele as on the risk itself.
- Many guests assume that they can leave their safety and security in the hands of the risk manager and/or security staff.
- As world tension mounts, the demand for risk management increases.
- In risk management, as in tourism, there is no distinction between security and safety. As will be seen later in this chapter, a failure in either category, or a crossover between categories, will result in a ruined vacation, or worse.
- The further we travel from a crisis, the worse the crisis seems. The further we are from a crisis, the longer it lasts in the collective memory. Thus, the protection of a tourism entity's reputation is essential.

CRISIS MANAGEMENT

Just as there is no one definition of risk management, there is no one definition for emergency and/or crisis management. We can say, however, that the two are interrelated. Risk management is always proactive. Crisis and emergency management are reactive by nature in that they react to a crisis rather than act to prevent it. David Bierman defines a tourism crisis as "a situation requiring radical management action in response to events beyond the internal control of the organization, necessitating urgent adaptation of marketing and operational practices to restore the confidence of employees, associated enterprises and consumers in the viability of the destination" (2003, p. 4).

It will soon be discussed that risk and crisis management may be defined as two sides of the same coin. Table 4.1 delineates some of the most important differences between risk and crisis management.

Thus, the best way to avoid a crisis or an emergency is through good risk management. Just as there are many forms of risk, there are multiple types of crises.

It is the risk manager's task to prevent a crisis from occurring. However even the best risk management cannot prevent all crises. It therefore behooves a risk manager to also understand the types of crises that may occur.

Unlike risk (an ever-present potential), crises only become crises when they are known and publicized. Below is a listing of some of the major tourism crisis categories:

- Any form of adversity
- International war and conflict
- Specific act of terrorism
- Crime wave or a well-publicized crime
- Natural disaster
- Health crisis
- Corruption and scandal

This list is far from inclusive and is meant only to provide ideas for the risk manager. It is the job of the risk manager to imagine the potential crisis that may impact his or her particular situation and then how he or she will transition from risk manager into crisis manager.

Crises can come in various forms. In the space below, list five of the most likely crises to impact your tourism location. Some examples may be (1) illnesses, (2) acts of violence, or (3) building crisis. Then, list one or two ways in which you are or should be prepared to face this crisis.

    1.
    2.
    3.
    4.
    5.

Table 4.1 Some Basic Differences between Crisis and Risk Management

	Risk	Crisis
Surety of occurrence	Uses a statistical system	Is a known event
Goal of management	To stop the event prior to occurrence	To minimize the damage once event has taken place
Type of preparation to combat risk that can be used	Probability studies Knowledge of past events Tracking systems Learning from others	Specific information such as medical, psychological, or crime Developing a what-if attitude
Training needed	Assume crises and find ways to prevent them	Assume crises and practice reacting to them
Reactive or proactive	Proactive	Reactive, though training can be proactive toward the reactive
Types of victim	Anyone, maybe visitors or staff	Can be visitors or staff members
Publicity	Goal is to prevent publicity by acting to create nonevents	Goal is to limit the public relations damage that may occur
Some common problems	Poor building maintenance Poor food quality Poor lighting Fear of terrorism Fear of a crime occurring	Rude visitor Sick person Robbery Threat to staff Bomb scare Lack of language skills
Statistical accuracy	Often very low; in many cases, the travel and tourism industry does everything possible to hide the information	Often very low; in many cases, the travel and tourism industry does everything possible to hide the information
Length of negative effects on the local tourism industry	In most cases, it is short term	In most cases, it is long term unless replaced by new positive image
Recovery strategies	• New marketing plans, assumes short-term memory of traveling public • Probability ideals: "Odds are it will not happen to you" Hide information as best as one can	• Showing of compassion • Need to admit the situation and demonstrate control • Higher levels of observed security Highly trained (in tourism, terrorism, and customer service) personnel

PERFORMING RISK MANAGEMENT

Risk management plans are developed from data that is collected. Whether you are the risk manager at a hotel, restaurant, attraction, or event, there are certain pieces of data that you must know in order to develop a risk management plan. Among these are:

- How many people come under your "protection"? There are several substantial differences for when there are 1,000 people versus 10 or 20 people who need to be given immediate care. Even in a hotel, there is the number of people who are staying in the hotel as guests, as well as the people attending some of the hotel's secondary components, such as its restaurant, convention center, parking spaces, etc.
- Where are the building's strengths and weaknesses? How many ingresses and egresses are there? What is the building's construction, and can it withstand physical problems such as earthquakes or hurricanes?
- What is the demographic makeup of the people you are serving? The type of person who you serve is a major part of risk management. A senior citizens' convention may have different health needs compared to college spring break. As such, the types of populations served impacts every part of your risk management plan. Also, it is essential to know if you serve different population cohorts on a continual basis.

What You Need to Know as a Risk Manager

It is almost impossible for human beings to divide their personality from the jobs they are doing. Therefore, it is essential to know what your personality strengths and weakness are. Which issues push your buttons, which ones are easier to deal with, and which issues are you simply better off just walking away from? Because tourism risk management deals with people, it is important to realize that we all deal with certain personalities better compared to other personality types. As a risk (and/or crisis) manager, it is essential that you know which personality types provoke you or cause you to think in a less than professional manner? With what personality types are you compatible, and with which types do you not work well? Take the time to assess the following:

- Your personal strengths and weaknesses
- What your boss, the public, and the media expect of you
- The assumptions you make about your staff

A RISK MANAGEMENT MODEL

There are multiple equations employed for risk management. Each one has its own strengths and limitations. The model found below is one of many. What makes this model work is that it is simple and it can be updated easily. The model assumes three major concepts about risk:

1. There is no such thing as a 100% risk-free environment.
2. The risk manager will never truly have a sufficient number of resources for risk to be eliminated.
3. The risk manager then must determine what is an acceptable risk and what is not.

Below is a five-step plan on how to determine risk for your tourism entity. There are no right answers here, only guidelines to help you determine what your risks are and how deep their consequences may be for your particular tourism business.

Step 1

In step 1, list every possible risk that your event or locale may have to face. Some examples are:

- Stolen car
- Murder
- Riot
- Gang violence
- Crime of distraction
- Sexual assault
- Vandalism
- "Con" game
- Prostitution or public nudity
- Purchases of illegal drugs
- Natural disaster
- Food poisoning

Note that you might consider some of the items above as irrelevant to your situation, but you should still list them anyway. There may actually be more relevance than you first believed, and if there is no relevance, then you can eliminate the issue.

Step 2

Divide the listed possible risks, that is, things that can go wrong, into one of four categories:

Table 4.2 Determining Which Type of Risk You Have

Risk	Type 1	Type 2	Type 3	Type 4
	High risk–high consequence	High risk–low consequence	Low risk–high consequence	Low risk–low consequence

- Category 1: Likely to happen and the consequences are grave
- Category 2: Unlikely to occur, but should the risk materialize, the consequences would be grave
- Category 3: Likely to occur but the consequences are not grave
- Category 4: Unlikely to occur, but should the risk materialize, the consequences would not be grave

You can place these in boxes such as in Table 4.2.

Step 3

Rank the incidents receiving your highest priority as category 1, followed by category 2, category 3, and finally category 4. In reality, category 4 is a totally acceptable risk; using resources to protect your property against a category 4 would be a waste of resources.

Step 4

Tourism is as much about perceptions as it is about realities. For this reason, the tourism risk manager must always consider negative publicity as a risk factor. Once the categories above are established, then they must be measured against the ever-present risk of negative publicity.

Classify each risk stated in step 3 along the following lines:
- Likely to create a great deal of ongoing negative publicity
- Likely to create a great deal of negative publicity of a short duration
- Likely to create some ongoing negative publicity
- Likely to create minimal amounts of negative publicity of a short duration

Step 5

Negative tourism events tend to have "after-lives." In some cases, good marketing efforts are successful in restoring the tourism location's reputation, so the public tends to forget about the negative event fairly quickly. In other cases, the negative event takes on a life unto itself, becoming a part of public memory. Thus, risk in tourism must be seen not only as the potential for a negative event to occur, but also the length of time that it lives in the public's memory. For example, except those people who are directly impacted by the tragedy, negative events that are acts of nature tend, in general, to be forgotten rather quickly. On the other hand, events that are deliberate acts usually last for a greater amount of time in the public's memory.

Determine if a particular act is one that will reside in the public's memory for a short or long duration. The longer the duration is, then the greater the risk. To accomplish this task, create a 1–10 index, with 1 being the lowest and 10 being the highest, then rank each one of the sample questions below.

1. Is this tragedy man-made?
2. Is the risk of a tourism tragedy an issue of weather?
3. Is your location easily accessible to the media?
4. Are there national or international correspondents located in your area?
5. Is your area a center of economic activity?
6. Is there a risk of multiple deaths that will be reported?
7. Do you have a national or international icon in close proximity?

Add your scores and divide by seven. The higher the score is, the greater the risk of tourism tragedy after-life.

Moreover, William Foos (Source: From speech given at Las Vegas international Tourism Safety and Security Conference, May 2013) has developed a series of risk analysis steps that include:

- Step 1: Define your tourism assets (both tangible and intangible)
- Step 2: Define consequences and establish benchmarks. Among these are consequences to life, property, reputation, and legal liabilities
- Step 3: Rate the consequences of the risk vis-à-vis your assets, services, reputation, etc.
- Step 4: Identify your business's vulnerabilities
- Step 5: Develop countermeasures to the threat
- Step 6: Determine opportunities within the threat
- Step 7: Evaluate the risks from a qualitative perspective
- Step 8: Perform a quantitative evaluation of the risks from both a safety and security perspective
- Step 9: Rank the risk factors
- Step 10: Deal with the risks according to the risk level or ranking

RISK MANAGEMENT GUIDELINES

Every risk manager needs to have a stated set of guidelines. The following self-analysis is not meant to be exhaustive, but, rather, it allows you to begin thinking about the questions that you need to ask. Never begin a risk management plan without asking yourself the following:

- Do you know your vulnerabilities?
- Do you have a full set of plans that cover what to do before, during, and after a crisis?
- Have you set up a team to develop crisis plans?
- Does your plan distinguish between natural, criminal, fire, and terrorism crises?
- Have you developed a plan that has immediate action steps and unique considerations for such travel and tourism crises as:
  - Airplane crash?
  - Act of terrorism at a hotel?
  - A biochemical attack?
  - Civil unrest?
  - Earthquake?
  - Fire?
  - Flood?
  - High-profile kidnapping?
- How will you be notified of a crisis?
- How will you notify others?
- Is there a plan to take immediate action?
- Is there a tourism crisis team in place?
- Is there a plan to deal with special tourism needs, such as foreign-language issues, notification of relatives abroad, and shipment of bodies to a foreign destination?
- Have you developed a set of crisis guidelines and reviewed them with every employee? Do you have guidelines to cover almost every aspect of the guest's visit, including security? Look at these details:
  - Type of lighting used in parking lots and along paths
  - Policies concerning single women travelers and/or travelers who need extra security
  - Employee background checks
  - Special security instructions for those working at ticket booths and entrances to festivals
  - What to do should a crime or accident take place
- Do a regular review of fire safety procedures. For example, it is important for all employees to know what to do in case of a fire. Some of the issues that should be touched upon include:

- Smoke. Many employees know that smoke doesn't necessarily mean there is a major fire. Their prime objective should be to evacuate the site or isolate the fire at the first sign of smoke. Smoke accumulates at the ceiling. If exit signs are at the ceiling, then will they be seen during a fire? Do employees know that fresh air for breathing is near the floor?
- Panic. How to handle panic and how not to panic. People who panic rarely save themselves or others. The more information that a guest or employee has, the less likely they are to panic.
- Exits. Make sure guests and employees know where the exits are located. This is especially important in enclosed visitor or information center areas. We can almost be sure that the exit will be needed when the guest is least prepared. It is important that multilingual signage provides evacuation instructions.
- Have visible guards. Contrary to what some tourism professionals may believe, professional security guards are greatly appreciated because they make guests feel secure. This sense of security is especially true for female guests and visitors from foreign lands. If trained properly, then professional security guards do not hurt profits, and they can add to a locale's bottom line. Festival managers should always do a spot-check of their guards to make sure that they are well trained and not asleep on the job.
- Do a full background check on the criminal history of all employees. Find out if a person has an arrest record.
- Get to know the people who work at local police departments and hospitals. Often, police and medical officers can point out errors and easy ways to correct problems. It is much cheaper to avoid a crisis than have to deal with the crisis after it has occurred.
- Have a clear policy regarding types of keys and who controls them.

ALCOHOL AND DRUGS AND TOURISM RISK

An area of tourism risk management that permeates through many parts of the tourism industry is the abuse of alcoholic beverages and illegal drugs. These substances can lead to another series of problems ranging from sexual assault to death at the wheel. Therefore, it is essential for the tourism risk manager to know the local laws and the establishment's policies concerning alcohol and drug usage. In most places, the law handles most of your drug policies, but alcohol is a different matter. Here are some guidelines to consider when developing a policy regarding alcohol.

- Is food always served with liquor? If not, why not?
- What types of foods are served? Do you emphasize high-protein foods?
- What do you do if someone becomes intoxicated?
- How do you stop brawls or physical violence?
- Are glass objects allowed to be used?
- Are all your bartenders licensed and vetted?
- Do you have as a standard policy that all alcoholic incidents are to be documented?

Developing a Tourism Risk Management Plan in an Age of Crime, Gangs, and Terrorism

The job of a risk manager in tourism is not easy. Most tourism-oriented risk managers must deal with issues of safety and security, or a combination of both. There are issues of fire and smoke safety, food safety, and issues of crime, such as robbery and assault. In an age of terrorism, these two fields tend to merge. For example, the risk manager will need to know if a food-poisoning incident came about due to tainted food or an act of terror. Are drug sales merely an illegal act, or is the sale of drugs a way to fund an act of terrorism? This merging of the criminal with the political means that risk managers' jobs are even more challenging than they were in the past. Despite these challenges, there are certain basic principles that underlie all tourism-oriented risk management plans. Among these are:

- Nothing in this world is totally free of risk. Like most of the public, tourists, industry leaders, the media, and tourism business stakeholders all want to believe the tourism industry can be made 100% risk free. The reality, however, is that we live with continuous risk, so there are no guarantees in life.
- Risk managers will never have enough manpower or money to prevent all risks from occurring. Tourism risk management must then be seen as a game of probabilities. Because no risk management plan can eliminate all risk, the only alternative is to decide what is and is not an acceptable risk. Acceptable risks are those that are considered the least probable of occurring, so they do not warrant resource expenditure.
- Tourism risk managers must deal with people who behave differently than when they are at home. Tourists are more likely to panic, they often have higher levels of anxiety, they have demonstrated lower levels of common sense, and they tend to enter into psychological anomic states. Consequently, the risk manager who works in the world of tourism must

consider a highly unstable public when developing an overall risk management plan.

- Risk managers in tourism must never forget that they have to handle risk while at the same time provide excellent customer service. Tourism is just an activity by choice. Even during terrorism incidents, visitors are still guests, and they consider themselves as such. This makes risk management all the more difficult because risk managers are well aware they cannot take precautions that drive away business.

- The risk manager must always be aware of world events, even when these events appear to be distant from where he or she may be working. In an interconnected world where the public is exposed to a continuous 24-hour news cycle, people in one part of the world could feel the tensions in another part of the world.

- Tourism centers are not isolated from the community. This means that the risk manager must worry about what occurs on his or her property, as well as what occurs throughout the community in which the tourism entity is located. Risk in tourism involves a great deal more than mere property protection. For example, issues of weather impact the entire community, along with illnesses ranging from influenzas to pandemics. The risk manager can never forget that the employees of a tourism business are part of the local community. What impacts the community also impacts the tourism entity's customers and staff.

- Risk management is also about the law of unintended consequences. To illustrate, electronics are wonderful, but they are only as good as the person operating them. With the rise of electronic and computerized technology, some risks are reduced, but at the same time, new risks develop. New forms of rationalizations do not mean less risk but merely different risks.

Some Examples of the Interaction Between Issues of Safety and Security in the World of Tourism

As noted previously, tourism risk managers must deal with the fact that there are numerous interactions between the local population and their client/guest population. In the post-9/11 world, the clear-cut distinctions between issues of safety and security have blended into new challenges. Below are just a few of the many security–safety blended challenges arising in the age of terrorism and tourism, as well as some of the necessary countermeasures.

DRUGS, TOURISM, AND TERRORISM

The world of drugs has become one of the great challenges for many individuals involved with tourism. There was once a time when tourism risk managers and law enforcement only had to deal with illegal drug use and the occasional drug dealer. This age of "comparative innocence" came to its conclusion when gangs entered into the illegal narcotics industry and began turf wars.

In the early years of the twenty-first century, the line between terrorism and crime became increasingly blurred. This blurring began to impact tourism when turf wars entered into the world of tourism, which occurred in a variety of ways. Among these were:

- The seeking of drugs by tourists. Tourists who believe that they are merely using an illegal substance may also be aiding and abetting worldwide terrorism.
- The destruction of tourism security due to violence stemming from those areas of the world dominated by drug trafficking. The violence often produces secondary impacts, including:
  - Loss of reputation due to violence in cartel-dominated areas
  - Lowering of customer service in cartel-dominated areas.
- The realization that risk managers do not know whether law enforcement officials and other first responders have been "bought" by the drug cartels. The Spanish saying "plata o plomo" means the police officer has been given a choice: either accept the money from the cartel and be "bought," or you and your family will become victims of violence. In places in which cartels have come to dominate society, it is no longer valid to assume that police officers and private security tourism experts have high degrees of integrity and are loyal to the rule of law and order.
- The potential lack of integrity causes tourism risk managers to assume that working with law enforcement adds risk rather than diminishes it.

Ways That the Illegal Drug Trade Present Challenges to Tourism Risk Managers

Locations where there is a high degree of illegal drugs tend to have security problems. Below is a listing of some of the negative results of illegal drugs on tourism centers, along with the additional risks they pose:

- Car burglaries or theft
- Kidnappings (especially business travelers held for ransom)

- Loss of tourism reputation resulting in the potential loss of travelers, which leads to lower room rates and the potential loss of foreign investors
- Potential for negative crime images that spread easily on the Internet and in social media
- Loss of confidence in protection services, and even in the government itself; higher levels of corruption translate into higher levels of risk that must be managed

THE RISK OF FOOD SAFETY IN TOURISM

Tourism depends on a safe and reliable food supply. Tourists and visitors cannot often go to local markets to buy food supplies, so they usually depend on restaurants or other public places to purchase food. This perhaps may be the reason that no industry in the world is as food dependent as tourism. Commercial eateries, whether they are street vendors or fine restaurants, are often the method by which most travelers eat. Food is not only an essential part of travel, but it is also one of its many pleasures. Travel affords the visitor new culinary opportunities. Food safety is much more than making sure that no one is poisoned. In this period of mass travel and tourism, food is an essential part of the total travel experience. Food is linked with a tourism experience's reputation, whether it is on an airline, on a cruise ship, at a convention, or at a public eating establishment.

Food supply chains in the modern world are highly complex systems. With such high levels of complexity, it should come as no surprise that there are food problems. These can range from outbreaks of salmonella to food contamination. Although tourism risk managers are not expected to be specialists in food safety or presentation, they do need to be aware that food safety issues are much more involved than making sure the mayonnaise is refrigerated. The U.S. Congressional Research Service (CRS) for the Library of Congress published a major paper on agro-terrorism. The CRS defined "agro-terrorism" as a subset of bioterrorism in which diseases are introduced into the food supply for the expressed purpose of creating mass fear, physical harm or death, and/or economic loss. In today's global economy, tourism entities import foods from around the world. This implies that an agro-terrorism attack on one continent can destroy a tourism industry on another continent.

In fact, food safety and tourism security have been linked for many decades. Even superficial studies of the food industry reveal that it is vulnerable on multiple levels. From food processing until its delivery to the table, food for human and animal consumption goes through a number of hands, machines, and processes. Tracing where food may have been contaminated is incredibly difficult. When we must distinguish between accidental food contamination and terrorist contamination geared toward a political purpose, the task becomes monumental. Restaurants are vulnerable for another reason: they are icons of their society. For example, it is almost impossible to separate a pizzeria from Italian culture or a croissant from French culture.

Restaurants and other eating establishments can be targeted for a number of reasons, but here are just a few:

- Most restaurant owners do not know their patrons. Thus, as public places, restaurants provide easy access and exit.
- Most restaurants in tourism areas have no idea where their clients are after they have left their premises. This lack of information means that it is difficult to track down when food poisoning occurs.
- Restaurants rarely keep records as to where participants live or how many came in a party.
- Restaurants sell "good times," which causes low vigilance.
- Most restaurants can easily be penetrated. Often back/side doors are left open and waiters and waitresses, working for tips, may not challenge a customer out of fear of losing income.

Therefore, risk managers need to be aware of the following:

- They have an idea as to which food can produce which illnesses. No one expects every person in travel and tourism to become an expert in all of the various food illnesses, but it is helpful to have a general idea of food safety.
- They take the time to know what the major food problems and potential crises are for their area. Each part of the world has special food safety needs and challenges. Often food safety issues are dependent on the type of food served, and where the food is obtained. Does their hotel, attraction, or restaurant use local produce, or does it import these fruits and vegetables from someplace else? What type of water supply is used in food irrigation? How good are the refrigerator containers that bring meats and fish to their locale?
- They must know who is working in the kitchen and what their state of health is. The safety of one's food is directly dependent on the health (both mental and physical) of those preparing the food that is served. It only takes one ill chef or food preparer to sicken many of the customers. Additionally, in an age of terrorism, food preparation areas invite terrorists to accomplish their primary goal of economic destruction

without being noticed. A risk manager must be sure that he or she has a full record of who is preparing food, what their backgrounds are, and continuous updates on the state of their health.

- In a like manner, waiters and waitresses are a key link in the tourism food chain. Who are the waiters and waitresses? Too many people in the tourism industry choose to ignore the safety and security issues that surround these essential links within the food service industry. Because the principal source of income for these people comes from tips, they often have no sick days, health insurance, or other social protection. Consequently, they will come to work even when they are sick. This implies that the public is placed at risk due to contaminated people handling their food. For example, it is essential for all food handlers to wash their hands often and maintain the highest levels of hygiene possible.

- Risk managers need to sensitize staff to food allergies. As stated previously, food can be contaminated through illnesses or a malevolent act. Yet, there are also a growing number of people suffering from food allergies or with special dietary needs. Unfortunately, too many staff either do not care or are ignorant of the fact that a mistake can be fatal. While no staff person can be expected to know every possible food allergy, it is essential that they be trained not to assume or guess. In case a customer indicates that he or she is allergic to a specific condiment or food substance, it is imperative that restaurants, hotels, and other food providers know how to obtain precise and accurate information.

- Risk managers must be sure that trash is deposited in a way that does not harm the environment. Food safety is not only about the quality of what is served and how, but also about the disposal methods for unused foods. Too often food is left outside in plastic bags that produce foul smells and are easily broken into by animals. Poor disposal techniques can lead to environmental hazards, eyesores for communities, and health hazards.

- If the tourism entity uses an outside catering service, then the risk manager must understand who and how that caterer operates. Many tourism events are catered affairs. However, people in the tourism industry often have no idea who works for their caterers, whom they employ, or what their backgrounds are. Caterers should come under the same scrutiny as hotels and restaurants.

FIRE AND TOURISM SAFETY

One of the great threats to any tourism entity, whether it is an attraction, hotel, or restaurant, is the issue of fire and fire safety. Visitors are notorious in being lax about fire and fire codes, and many tourists and visitors simply do not believe that a fire will impact their lives. Consequently, the denial of fire is one of the greatest risks that a risk manager has to confront.

Dr. Richard Feenstra is an expert on fire safety. He emphasizes the fact that risk managers need to work closely with the local fire department. For instance, referring to event management, Feenstra notes that when an event exceeds 300 people, a permit for temporary assembly is required in many U.S. locales. Cooking, fireworks, and even the simple use of candles may require an event planner to apply for a permit (Source: From Speech given at Third biannual Caribbean Tourism Security Conference, June 2012 and from 2012 personal interview).

Fire departments do more then merely put out fires. Fire departments are often the permit providers, so a mistake in one's permitting can result in denial of access, angry guests, and loss of money.

Risk managers must be constantly aware of the threat of fire, as well as the consequences of not following fire department rules. When it comes to fire prevention, consider the following:

- Have a full inspection by the local fire department and make sure that you meet all fire department regulations, codes, and/or ordinances.
- If you are holding an event, then submit a request for authorization as early as possible. The earlier the request is made, the better its chances with the bureaucratic procedures. Also, if something needs to be changed, then there is no last-minute crisis.
- Conduct an inspection before the fire inspector arrives. While the risk manager may not be aware of exactly when the inspector is going to arrive, it is a good idea to walk through the locale or event in order to check for the following: fire extinguishers are charged and have inspection tags, exits are not locked or blocked, exit signs are properly lit, there are no trip hazards, or if any other obvious safety concerns exist.
- Get agreements in writing. It is all too easy to misunderstand or mishear a fire inspector. The best way to avoid the risk of fire is to have the fire professional put everything in writing and then follow his instructions.
- Risk managers should never be afraid to admit that they do not know something. Most fire inspectors welcome honest questions. Although the risk manager is not expected to be an expert in everything, he or she is expected to contact and work with the people who have the expertise in a specific field. Most fire inspectors want to help, and they are happy to explain why a code or regulation is in place. If there is a

psychological breakdown between the risk manager and the expert, then it is the duty of the risk manager to find someone with whom he or she can develop a good working relationship.

- Know what the standards of care are, especially in deadly fields of endeavor such as fire safety. Risk is not only physical it is also legal. This means that a good risk manager knows the standards of care that are expected. A good risk manager not only consults a fire expert in the technicalities of something such as fire safety, but also a legal expert who can explain the legal issues involved.

TERRORISM AND TOURISM

As previously noted, risk management is a difficult term to define, and risk management in an age of terrorism is almost beyond the scope of definability. The term *terrorism* is not easy to define, and to complicate matters further: "There is no general consensus as to who is a terrorist or what the definition of terrorism is" (Tarlow, 2005a; 2005b, p. 79). Until now, no one has created a mathematical system that can accurately predict terrorist attacks. The somewhat random nature of terrorism attacks means that risk managers must consistently expect the unexpected. What we do know is that tourism has been a magnet for terrorist attacks. The reasons for tourism's attractiveness toward terrorism are numerous:

- Tourism provides soft targets. For example, few hotels make a person pass through a metal detector before entering, and many hotels were built in an age of innocence, in which the architectural goals were convenience and/or beauty, rather than security.
- Tourism provides opportunities for mass casualties. Given that tourist locations are often places of gathering with only a few people thinking about security issues, they provide excellent targets for terrorists who desire to murder or harm large numbers of people with relative ease.
- Tourism provides iconic settings. Icons are places that symbolize something within the local, national, or world community. For example, the Eiffel Tower is not only a symbol of Paris, but it is a structure that is part of the world's heritage. Any attack against an icon will receive a great deal of publicity, which puts fear into the hearts of many.
- Tourism is big business. Terrorists attempt to harm or murder innocents, and they seek to destroy economies. Because it is such a large industry,

the impact of tourism is felt within the total economy. In the case of 9/11, the attacks on the World Trade Center in New York caused millions of dollars' worth of loss not only for New York City, but also the global airlines industry, which came to a halt. Terrorists understand that airlines use large hubs; if a hub locale is attacked, then this will have repercussions on a worldwide basis.

- Attacks on tourism provide a great deal of publicity, and terrorism seeks publicity. Tourism centers are places where there is a great deal of media coverage. An attack against a tourism center creates an instant impact on the locale, which can lead to long-term perception consequences.
- Terrorists have the element of surprise in their favor. The risk manager has to outguess his opposition and be correct every time. The terrorist has the luxury to fail repeated times, but even his failure causes negative publicity, inconveniences, business disruptions, and forced additional expenditures or resources.
- Despite what the media may say, terrorists are not cowards. In all too many cases, terrorists believe that they are fighting for a righteous cause, and they are willing to lay down their lives for said beliefs.
- The risk manager must deal with the fact that terrorism may manifest itself in multiple formats, such as attack of food supplies, mass murder, or the introduction of drugs into a political body. In all cases, however, the terrorist hopes to gnaw away at a society with the hope of destroying its collective cohesiveness.
- Terrorists may target a wide variety of groups. Tourism is especially attractive because there is still a lingering belief that tourists are part of a leisure class that takes advantage of the working class. As such, there is often a reverse sense on the part of terrorists in which they see themselves as the true victims, while the victims of their attacks are somehow responsible for their own predicament. Terrorism then uses a form of victimization of the victim to justify its actions.
- Tourism represents many of the values that terrorism despises. Among these values are:
  - The fair and equal treatment of women.
  - The belief that a person should be judged by who he or she is and not by the group to which he or she belongs.
  - The belief that learning about other cultures and people is a positive endeavor and should be encouraged.

- The concept that the world is a better place when we celebrate our differences. Tourism is about the celebration of the other.
- There is nothing wrong with a business making money. Terrorists tend to think of money as "dirty" and capitalism as evil.
- It is important to find compromises to situations in which there are disagreements. Terrorism takes the opposite viewpoint and rejects the notion of compromise.

Tourism, almost by definition, is the opposite of terrorism. In fact, women hold major tourism positions throughout the world. The industry is based on individuals' experiences. It is the exact opposite of a xenophobic world in which the other is despised rather than celebrated.

TOURISM, TERRORISM, AND THE MEDIA

In the world of journalism, there is the saying, "If it bleeds it leads." If the media like a crime story, then terrorists provide the media with a world of intrigue from bloodshed to politics. Terrorist acts often seem designed for television, and terrorists, who are often incredibly media-savvy, find ways to provide the television cameras with as many visuals as possible.

Such problems become even more apparent when there is a great deal of publicity, such as that surrounding a major sporting, entertainment, or political event. For example, in April 2013 a tourist in the city of Rio de Janeiro suffered a brutal sexual assault ("American student was gang-raped," 2013). Although the police were able to apprehend the criminals almost immediately, the incident still created major headlines around the world, even though sexual assaults occur everywhere. The reasons for this hyped publicity had to do with Rio de Janeiro's hosting of the 2014 FIFA World Cup and the large number of reporters stationed in Rio. A simple rule of thumb is that the greater the number of journalists in a particular place, the higher the probability of negative incidents becoming major news stories. Terrorists are well aware of this fact, especially because journalists tend to report negative stories.

This means that risk managers must hinder acts of terrorism, while at the same time develop media plans to prevent journalists from unwittingly aiding terrorism in its attempt to destroy a local tourism industry. Below are some basic suggestions on dealing with the media before, during, and after an incident.

Before an Incident

- Develop relationships with people in the media. Know with whom you can count on and who seeks only the dramatic.
- Have a secure call number and place where the media can interview you. In the case of a terrorist attack, having a "safe" media location is essential.
- Develop a media chain of command. Know who will speak and who should refer journalists to others. Have one single message.
- Have a number of press release templates ready to go and make sure that these press releases are easy to read. If the media person cannot read or understand what you wrote, then the odds are that he or she will ignore it. Use a font size that is clear, avoid jargon and/or technical words, and underline or bullet your points.

During the Incident

In actual time, this stage is the shortest, but it is perhaps the most important. This is the time when the risk manager must show leadership, not panic. He or she should demonstrate knowledge of the plan in addition to professional flexibility. During the incident be sure to:

- Take careful notes. Reporters and management, both now and later on, will ask specific questions. The more accurate facts the risk manager has, the easier his or her life will be after the incident has come to its conclusion. Do not allow the confusion of the moment to blind you to what needs to be done
- Be polite but firm with reporters. If the risk/crisis manager cannot speak to media representatives during the incident, then he or she should explain that he or she will get back to the media as soon as it is known that lives are being cared for. During the incident, the risk/crisis manager's first priority is the safety of guests.
- When being interviewed, it is wise for the risk/crisis manager to offer the reporters a beverage because they work long hard days. It is ironic that in the hospitality industry, we often forget to be hospitable to those who report on our work. In the rare case that a reporter is hostile, a small human touch will usually soften their attitude toward you.
- Be brief. In most cases, a long explanation will be reduced to a single sound bite. For example, political candidates reduce messages to 90 seconds, with one or two phrases that can become a 10-second sound bite.

- Don't overload. It is rare that a reporter has the time to sort through a great deal of information. Most reporters have deadlines to meet. Keep your releases short and to the point.
- Be honest. The worst thing for anyone to do is to lie. It is perfectly acceptable to say you do not know, but whenever possible, follow up your "don't know" with a willingness to "find out." When a terrorist act occurs, the phrase "no comment" sounds as if you are covering up the truth.
- Be cooperative and smile. Never forget that the reporter has the last word. When dealing with a hostile reporter, do your best to win him or her over and turn an enemy into a friend. Never pass the reporter off to a superior. He or she may well resent your attitude and just use what material he or she already has.
- Be clear and specific. Assume the reporter and the public have little or no knowledge about what they are asking. Never use tourism jargon or acronyms such as convention and visitors bureau (CVB). State the entire word. By using clear precise nouns, you lessen the possibility that your answer can be taken out of context.
- Return all media phone calls. Even if you do not wish to speak to a reporter, eventually you are going to have to speak with that person because the reporter is still going to write the story even without hearing your side.
- Do not ask the reporter to let you check his or her story. Even if he or she agrees to your request, the odds are that "something" will happen, so you'll never see the story before it goes to print. The reporter may become defensive or angry, which will result in a bad situation being made to look much worse.

The Follow-up after the Incident

Risk/crisis managers are always caught in a significant conundrum. If nothing occurs, then their superiors want to know what they are getting for their money. Yet, if something does occur then these same managers want to know why the system has failed. If an incident takes place, then the risk manager realizes there will be an investigation as to what went wrong. In reality, 100% security is a fallacy. The hope is for the risk manager's report to identify weaknesses within the system rather than seeking a scapegoat. However, the risk manager should be prepared to protect him- or herself from being the scapegoat. Thus, he or she needs to review all notes; try to have as many complete answers as possible; and exude a nondefensive and cooperative attitude.

- Read what the reporters wrote. You may not like what you read, but you still need to do so. Even reading negative stories lets everyone know that you are not afraid to see the ways others view you.
- Maintain both a soft and hard copy of every article printed and/or a DVD of every newscast. This media library provides you with a database, and it indicates to the media that you take them seriously.
- When appropriate, provide compliments. Take the time to tell a reporter that he or she has done a good job on a story. Reporters are people too, and just like you, they also respond better to positive feedback.
- Be prepared to correct potential misinformation. Even the best reporters make mistakes. Letting reporters know that you are well aware of how accurate they have been demonstrates to the journalist that you take him or her seriously and that you expect accuracy in their news coverage.
- Invite reporters to return and show them how your recovery strategy has worked (is working). Above all, be positive. Part of every risk manager's job is to reduce the risk for next time.

FROM RISK MANAGEMENT TO CRISIS MANAGEMENT

Although it would be wonderful if risk management could be so successful that it eliminated the need for crisis management, the reality is that every person, thing, or business will eventually have to face a crisis at some point. Thus, risk managers must also be crisis managers. An ever-present risk is the inability of the risk manager to transition from risk to crisis management. To ease this transition, the risk-now-crisis manager must change his or her mindset. People involved in risk management are concerned with the need to predict and prevent a crisis. As such, the field of risk management is always oriented toward the future tense. Crisis management, on the other hand, is about what is occurring in the present and how to deal with an ongoing situation. These two disciplines merge when it comes to the post-crisis analysis where what happened in the past is analyzed so that preventative measures can be taken to avoid (or at least, lessen) the impact of a negative event in the future. Thus, there is a consistent merging of risk management with crisis management, and then back to risk management. The risk–crisis continuum then has three stages:

1. Prevent the negative event (risk management)
2. Deal with the negative event (crisis management)

3. Analyze and learn from the negative event (crisis management)
Stage 2 often has the least duration, but is the most critical. It is the one stage where there is no time to correct mistakes. The crisis manager may only have one chance to succeed.

To begin the transition process, the risk manager must be prepared to recognize that there is a crisis. Recognition and acceptance of a crisis is not easy. Humans psychologically tend to negate a negative event. This is known as the "this-cannot-be-happening" syndrome. The faster that the risk/crisis manager can react to the new and unfolding reality, the faster that he or she can begin to take the necessary measures to control and then overcome the crisis. The risk manager must be able to change from risk to crisis management almost instantaneously.

Once the crisis manager realizes that he or she is in the midst of a crisis, it is essential to decide the depth of the crisis based on a realistic assessment. Staying grounded in reality is essential because humans have a tendency either to over- or underreact to an ongoing crisis. Risk/crisis managers are human beings and denial and panic mechanisms often play a major role in the person's psychological stance during a crisis. Prior to the crisis, the risk manager should have developed a crisis management team. When the crisis is upon him or her, it is time to activate the team. Therefore, the crisis manager must know certain basic facts:

- Who is on the team?
- How does he or she communicate with team members?
- Is there a substitute person in case the team member is unavailable?
- How does the crisis manager communicate with his or her team members?
- What redundancy of addresses, telephone numbers, email addresses is there so a team member can easily obtain the information if access to the tourism site is not possible?

Because there may be more than one crisis occurring at any given time, the professional crisis manager must have a variety of people at his or her disposal. The crisis team(s) may consist of the following professionals:

- People from media and public relations
- Members of your marketing team
- Other members of the travel industry
- State and national tourism leadership, if available
- Local tourism and hospitality leaders
- Victim assistance units

Crisis Perceptions

Earlier we spoke of how important it is to understand and to take into account crisis perception because all crises have after-lives. In crisis management, we define a crisis after-life as the amount of time the media gives a particular event attention. A crisis may have a short or long period of media attention. Usually, the longer the crisis is a media focus, the more damage it does to the local tourism sector. Crises also have the ability to "expand." For example, instead of stating that there was a fire at a specific location, the media "expanded" the crisis to the entire community. This crisis expansion means that although other parts of the community are not in crisis, the media's imprecision of terminology may cause collateral damage that becomes a new risk crisis. Never forget that during a crisis, geographic confusions may occur. For example, if the media reports there are forest fires in a particular part of a state or province, then the public may assume that the whole state or province is on fire. Visitors are notoriously bad at realizing the geographic limits of a crisis. Instead, panic and geographic confusion often expand crises and make them worse than in reality.

Here are some general principles when handling a crisis:

- Never assume a crisis will not touch you. Perhaps the most important part of a crisis recovery plan is to have one in place prior to a crisis. While we can never predict the exact nature of a crisis before it occurs, flexible plans allow for a recovery starting point. The worst scenario is to realize that one is in the midst of a crisis without any plans on how to deal with it.

- Always see the crisis through the visitors' eyes. All too often people tend to assume that the outsider has the same knowledge base as that of the local person. Crises often seem worse and last longer from the outsiders' perspective than from the local person's perspective.

- Do not just throw money at a crisis. Often people deal with crises simply by spending money, especially on equipment. Good equipment has its role, but equipment without the human touch will only lead to another crisis. Never forget that *people* solve crises, not machines.

- Never use marketing/advertising as a cover-up or an excuse. The worst thing to do in a crisis is to lose the public's confidence. Be honest and work to solve the problem, not spin it. Excuses make no one happy except those that give them.

- No one has to visit your tourism locale, so once the media begins reporting that there is a crisis, visitors may quickly panic and begin to cancel trips. Often, it is the media that define a crisis as such. Have a plan in place so that correct information can be given to the media as quickly as possible.

CRISIS RECOVERY

Post-crisis recovery programs can never be based on one factor alone. The best recovery programs take into account a series of coordinated steps. Never depend on only one remedy to bring you toward recovery. Instead, coordinate your advertising and marketing campaign with your incentive program along with an improvement in service.[1] Here are several potential strategies to deal with the post-crisis aftermath:

- Ignore the crisis and hope that no one learns about it. This strategy assumes that the less said the better. In a minor crisis, it is often a successful strategy, or if the media is willing to aid the industry by not reporting an event. The strategy breaks down when the crisis becomes a media news item and the crisis management team allows an information vacuum to occur.
- In the case of a large region, the crisis management team may want to deemphasize one region, and instead place its marketing efforts on a non-impacted region. The problem with this technique is that in large areas, the impacted region loses twice, once from the crisis event and then by the diverting of visitors to other parts of the region or nation.
- Find industries that may be willing to partner with your community or region so as to encourage people to return. You may be able to speak to the hotel transportation or meetings and convention industries to create incentive programs that will help your community ease through the post-crisis period. For example, the airline industry may be willing to work with you to create special fares that encourage people to return to your community.
- Appeal to people's better nature: "We need you now!" President George W. Bush successfully used this technique after 9/11 when he asked people to resume travel as a patriotic duty. Yet, the system only works if there is an emotional tie between the locale and a specific public.
- Develop post-crisis incentives. Once you recognize a crisis has occurred, determine when you will be back in business, and begin rewarding people to visit the location. You can emphasize that during this recovery

---

[1] The following section is inspired by the work of Dr. Elie Cohen of Haifa University, Haifa, Israel.

Table 4.3 Types of Crisis and Their Consequences

Crimes committed by	Against whom	Some examples of	Goal of crime
Tourists	Other visitors or local population, or tourism personnel	Robbery, pickpockets	Usually economic or social gain
Locals	Visitors	Assaults, petty theft, con artists, crimes of distraction	Usually economic gain
Tourism industry	Visitors	Fraud, business misrepresentation	Economic

Source: Tarlow (2005a; 2005b, p. 96)

stage, there are great bargains, so it is the time to take advantage of these incentives. Emphasize the need for tourism employees to maintain both dignity and good service. The last thing a person on vacation wants to hear is how bad business is. Instead, emphasize the positive. State that you are pleased that the visitor has come to your business or community. After a crisis, do not frown, but smile!

- Invite magazines and other media people to write articles about your recovery. Make sure that you provide these people with accurate and up-to-date information. Offer the media representatives the opportunity to meet with local officials, and provide them with tours of the community. Then, seek ways to gain exposure for the local tourism community. Go on television, do radio pieces, invite the media to interview you as often as it likes. When speaking with the media in a post-crisis situation, always be positive, upbeat, and polite.

- In the case of politically independent regions, offer tax incentives and other forms of economic aid to allow local restaurants, hotels, and attractions to begin the recovery process.

Be sure to understand which techniques should be used for various types of crises. Is the crisis medical or health related? Is it the result of an act of nature? Was the crisis created through violence? Is the crisis ongoing or a one-time event? Is the crisis a media spectacle or something that will dissolve into the historic past in a relatively short period of time? The answers to these questions often help to indicate what type of crisis action and post-crisis recovery plan you wish to employ. For example, given that a crisis can be violence related, it is of value to know these differences in today's world (Table 4.3).

REFERENCES

American student was gang-raped for six hours in mini-bus by attackers in Rio as her helpless handcuffed boyfriend was forced to watch. (2013, April 3). *Mail Online*. Retrieved from http://www.dailymail.co.uk/news/article-2303255/Rio-gang-rape-American-tourist-attacked-3-men-SIX-HOURS-handcuffed-boyfriend-watched-on.html.

Beirman, D. (2003). *Restoring tourism destinations in crisis*. Okon, UK: Cabi Publishing.

Santana, G., & Tarlow, P. E. (2002). Providing safety for tourists: A study of a selected sample of tourism destinations in the United States and Brazil. *Journal of Travel Research*, *40*(4), 424–431.

Tarlow, P. E. (2005a). Terrorism and tourism. In J. Wilks, D. Pendergast, & P. Leggat (Eds.), *Tourism in turbulent times* (pp. 79–92). Oxford, UK: Elsevier Inc.

Tarlow, P. E. (2005b). Crime and tourism. In J. Wilks, D. Pendergast, & P. Leggat (Eds.), *Tourism in turbulent times* (pp. 93–105). Oxford, UK: Elsevier Inc.

What are the different types of risk? (2013). *Northrop Grumman*. Retrieved from http://benefits.northropgrumman.com/_layouts/NG.Ben/Pages/AnnouncementReader.aspx?w=B9F17B39-24B3-4958-A0EA-FE0C7835F43E&l=489D0D55-D3E7-4BB9-A8AD-FA1CC3D56EF1&i=31.

CHAPTER 5

Public Gathering Places

INTRODUCTION

One of Frank Sinatra's most famous songs referred to a man who was preparing to go to a casino, so he begged lady luck to be good to him as he entered the magical world of gaming. Casinos are built around the idea that skill plus luck will pay off in financial reward. No one knows for certain how to control "Lady Luck," or when she will shine upon a person's life. What we do know, however, is that casino security is not about luck, but rather hard work and careful planning. Casino security is a great deal more complicated than meets the eye. Casinos and gaming (the casino term for legalized gambling) can be found around the world. What used to exist in only a few locales is now a high-demand form of adult entertainment. With millions of people frequenting casinos, and billions of dollars changing hands, well-trained casino security specialists are needed to protect the gambling establishment and its patrons.

Casinos attract crime, which causes a constant challenge for casino security personnel. In a casino, we find a great deal of money on public display, a sense of entitlement, and a diverse population seeking a good time by often leaving common sense at the door. Furthermore, there is a whole class of people who seek to steal from a casino simply because it presents an exciting challenge to them, or they consider stealing to be part of the "game." Casinos have been home to some of the world's largest scandals and criminal acts. Even with large security staffs (some of the largest in the world of tourism), crimes still do occur. It is fascinating that about 50% of the reported crimes are thefts. Las Vegas Metro reports that there are relatively small amounts of violent crime at casinos; instead, casino crimes tend to center around disorderly conduct or recreational theft (thrill seekers). Because casinos tend to attract people whose inhibitions are lowered and anomic levels are high, some players may not keep track of their belongings. This anomic behavior, combined with a festive atmosphere, means that normal behavior is often replaced with a sense of "I found it, you lost it; too bad!" For the same reasons, casinos need to maintain an active lost and found department.

The major crimes committed in casinos are crimes of opportunity. Those crimes often consist of such acts as pickpocketing, walking off with another person's bag, or taking unguarded property. Casinos also attract people with serious gambling habits, or individuals who seek other "immoral acts." There are those who argue that casino crime is not merely related to what occurs inside of a casino, but also what occurs in the community in which the casino is located. This latter point has created a great deal of academic debate, which calls into question how much of the crime data are analyzed.

There is also a national debate about the spillover effect of casinos into the general population. Numerous academic studies have been conducted addressing the issue. The research, however, is inconclusive. For example, in a study conducted by Stitt, Giacopassi, and Nichols (2000) titled "The Effect of Casino Gambling on Crime in New Casino Jurisdictions," it was stated that:

> Part of the national debates surrounding casino gambling is whether crime increases as a result of the presence of casinos in the community. Casino supporters argue that casinos bring economic benefits to an area and point to Las Vegas, the world's "mecca" of casino gambling, as the prime example. Since 1980, Las Vegas has grown faster than any other city in America ... yet for many of those years Las Vegas ranked as one of America's safest cities.... The critics of casinos point to Atlantic City, its failed promise of economic rejuvenation, its crime rate that increased dramatically after casinos began operating there in 1978.
>
> **(Stitt, Giacopassi, & Nichols 2000, p. 1)**

The data are so inclusive because there are enough data points on both sides of the argument that a casino's impact on a local economy may be purely locally determined rather than casino driven. To elaborate, according to the March 22, 2013, *Concord (NH) Monitor*:

> While studies can be found that suggest that a casino has a limited effect on an area's crime rate, that was not the conclusion of the New Hampshire Gaming Study Commission, which estimated that opening a casino at Rockingham Park would result in an additional 1200 serious crimes per year in Salem and surrounding communities. Nor is Cooper's contention backed up by the most comprehensive analysis of the casino–crime relationship yet undertaken, a 19-year study of FBI statistics published in 2006 in The Review of Economics and Statistics.
>
> That study found that while crime can actually diminish for a few years after the opening of a casino, in just a few years it increases significantly as the crime and social ills that come with problem gambling increase. The study concluded, "Overall, 8.6 percent of property crime and 12.6 percent of violent crime in counties with a casino was due to the presence of the casino."
>
> **("Casino–crime link is well established," 2013)**

On the other side of the issue, Lance Tapley, a freelance investigative reporter based in Maine, writes the following in the *Crime Report*:

And pro-gambling forces argue that, statistically, reported crime increases around casinos are a result of bad number crunching. In calculating the crime rate of a casino town, they say, the number of visitors to the casino should be added to the number of local residents, which Grinols and Mustard didn't do. But if that's done, the crime rate—the number of crimes in a given area divided by the population (generally expressed as crimes per 100,000 people)—usually drops significantly. This accurately gauges "the risk of being victimized" for both groups, says Douglas Walker, an economist at the College of Charleston.

Complicating the professorial part of this debate, though, and provoking finger-pointing about bias, some academics take money from the gambling industry (like Walker) and others are out front with their religious perspective (like Grinols and Mustard, both active in the Association of Christian Economists).

Then there's the difficulty in singling out casinos as a factor in the overall crime picture. In Bangor, for example, law enforcement authorities and city officials attribute their rising crime rate to an increase in the number of methadone clinics as well as the worsening economy—not the local casino.

(Tapley, 2009, Gross Annual Wager section, para. 8–10)

The *Toronto Sun* seems to argue that crime is a multi-faceted phenomenon; casinos may or may not produce higher rates of crime due to a myriad of local sociological phenomena. Thus, in its comparison of Toronto and Singapore, the *Toronto Sun* notes that: "Most interestingly, the WSJ revealed 'the crime rate in Singapore fell 5.3% in 2011 from 2010 to a 20-year low, while casino-related crime—mainly cases of theft, cheating and counterfeiting—has remained stable at less than 2% of total crime in 2010 and 2011, according to police data'" (Kent, 2013, para. 9).

This brief glimpse of the academic discussion demonstrates just how difficult it is to determine a tourism crime rate of any form. Not only must the number of victims versus the population be calculated, but also the type of visitor and the length of stay. For example, one would expect a lower crime rate at a child-oriented amusement park than at a casino. In addition, visits to shopping malls are considerably shorter (and therefore, there is less time for individual assaults) than at a casino. The bottom line is that the crime data can often be manipulated so that it demonstrates what the researcher may consciously or even unconsciously desire.

Casino security officers in many ways resemble police officers. Like police officers, they wear badges and a specific uniform, they are expected to patrol and inspect the property, and they both deal with security and safety issues at the casino, primarily with guests who may be staying at a casino's hotel. Also, casino security officers must adhere to gaming regulations and laws. They must have the presence of mind to testify in court, as well as write detailed incident reports. In fact, the one difference between a casino security officer and a law enforcement official is that a security officer can hold a suspect, but he cannot issue an arrest.

Thus, casinos are a good example of how tourism security reflects the ideals of Talcott Parsons, in that every aspect of security interacts and is dependent on the other parts of the security system. As such, we can use casino security as a symbol for much of tourism security as a whole.

Casino security specialists should be mindful of the person who seeks to "cheat the house," and they must handle numerous other issues. To add to this phenomenon, casinos contain large amounts of money, which tempts or encourages people to find ways to illegally obtain it. Casino security professionals must deal with numerous security issues. Among these issues are:

- Pickpocketing
- Employee safety
- Employment theft
- Food and health issues in an enclosed location
- Issues of robbery and terrorism
- Identity theft
- Illegal card counting and other illegal plays
- Anger management
- Potential and actual suicides
- Armed robbery

Because governments highly regulate the casino industry, its security specialists must work closely with the many layers of law enforcement, whether it be local, state, or federal agencies. Not only must casino security specialists enforce the house rules, but they also need to be aware that breaking a local, state, and/or federal regulation may have dire consequences for the casino. In the post-9/11 world, it is imperative for casinos to worry about acts of terrorism and potential gang or organized crime affecting the world of legal gaming.

Casino specialists should work with governmental organizations, and it is crucial for them to be aware of homeland security issues, financial crimes, and social crimes, such as prostitution.

Despite all of the challenges that casino security personnel face, casinos are a growth industry. To elaborate, the Bureau of Labor Statistics predicts 34% job growth in casino security by the year 2016. This job growth reflects the fact that casinos have become big businesses, not only in places such as Nevada and New Jersey, but throughout much of the United States.

Casino security literally goes from the bottom up. Ed Grabianowski notes that: "Security starts on the floor of the casino, where casino employees keep their eyes on the games and the casino patrons to make sure everything goes as it should" (Grabianowski, 2007, Casino Security section, para. 2). However, security is based on a system of layers of concentric circles. Thus, security officers are not the only personnel who are watching players, but also dealers who are well trained in spotting people attempting to cheat the house. Added to this layer are casino managers and closed-circuit television (CCTV) cameras. Furthermore, Grabianowski notes that: "Each person (working) in the casino also has a 'higher-up' person tracking them, watching them as they work and noting how much money their tables are winning or losing" (Casino Security section, para. 2).

CCTV CAMERAS AT THE CASINO AND BEYOND

Perhaps the best-known places where CCTV cameras have proven highly useful is the world of casino gaming. CCTV cameras allow security personnel to determine who is cheating. Moreover, if a robbery should occur, then they can close the casino quickly while obtaining actual proof of who the culprit is. These cameras capture what is happening in real time; they allow casino personnel to monitor every aspect of what is happening on the casino floor. At casinos, cameras help to stop robberies and other scams, and they permit casino security personnel to determine who may or may not be cheating or trying to scam the casino.

From the world of casinos, the use of CCTV cameras has migrated to a multitude of other uses. These cameras are used in both the inside of specific spaces, or on the outside recording what occurs around outdoor spaces.

Though, the use of CCTV in a non-casino setting is not without controversy. Their use has provoked heated debates between security specialists, libertarians, politicians, and legal authorities. Traditionally the argument has centered on the need for security versus the need for privacy, along with how to balance both. There is no doubt that many tourism locales rely heavily on CCTV cameras. For example, airports, parking lots, hotel lobbies, and amusement parks all use these visual recording devices. However, they cannot be installed in many private locations, such as locker rooms or hotel bedrooms, and some security agents argue that they are merely reactive rather than proactive devices. To illustrate, there is no city on Earth that has more cameras than London, England. Yet, despite the prevalence of CCTV cameras, the cameras did not prevent the terrorist bombings there.

In reality, there are at least two different forms of CCTV cameras. On one hand, there are CCTV cameras that merely record. There is no one watching these cameras, but should an incident occur, there is a recording of the incident and possible proof of culpability. The second form of a CCTV camera is used in casinos. These cameras are constantly being monitored, and it is assumed that if something were to happen, then security would be able to respond immediately. Though, CCTV cameras still have their pros and cons. Below are just a few examples of the positives and negatives of this form of security device.

On the Pro Side

CCTV cameras:

- Provide a greater sense of security. The camera indicates that the tourism provider cares enough to spend money on his or her customers' security. Often, visitors feel better knowing that the tourism attraction, hotel, or transportation center is being monitored.
- The cameras may act as a criminal deterrent. While no camera acts as a total deterrent, the criminal does not know if the camera will record him or her and, therefore, he or she may shy away from that locale.
- May be a major deterrent in stopping internal theft or pilferage. Stores often lose a great deal of money from acts of pilferage, internal stealing, and employee theft. These cameras may be highly effective tools in limiting these problems.
- Provide conclusive evidence of a criminal. If the criminal is in the right position, then these cameras can be extremely helpful in obtaining a conviction.

On the Negative Side

It is essential that before installation the tourism entity consider:

- The setup and maintenance costs of the CCTV cameras are expensive. Even if the cameras are only passive instruments that will not be monitored, the costs of maintenance must be balanced against other costs. For example, would an additional security guard be more effective and provide greater protection?
- There may be issues regarding privacy rights. In most cases, public places are open to being video-recorded, but verify this with your lawyer (or legal team). Also, inform your marketers to muffle any unexpected publicity fallout.

- They may promote a sense of indifference in which people simply assume that the cameras will handle all security needs. There is at least a hypothetical chance that people who see these cameras may choose not to get involved if there are incidents.

To help you decide if and what type of CCTV camera works best for you, consider the following:

- If you are going to use CCTV cameras, then know what your objectives are. They are a major investment; make sure that you have clear and precise objectives. You should know exactly what you hope to achieve by placing these cameras in strategic locations.
- Make sure you know the limitations of the CCTV cameras. For example, if the crime takes place in a location that the camera is not recording, then it was basically of no use. Some cameras take clearer images than do others. If the image is not recognizable, then, once again, the camera created a false sense of security.
- Do not use dummy cameras. Perhaps the worst thing that you can do is to place nonworking cameras around your premises. These create a false sense of security, and in the end, they may lead to either a marketing disaster or a potential legal problem.
- If installing these cameras, then you need to make sure that you plan for both current and future needs. How easily can these cameras be upgraded? Do you have a plan should you need to change the cameras' placement and use? Also, ask if the cameras can be tampered with or what it would take to simply "disarm" the camera.
- Make sure you know the costs of replacing and repairing these cameras. Everything in this world will either need to be replaced or changed at some point. If you work with a reputable dealer, then these problems should be considered before purchasing cameras.

THE CASINO SECURITY PROFESSIONAL

Many people have the mistaken notion that being a casino security professional is not a complicated job or it requires minimal education. Yet, nothing could be further from the truth. Casino security is a highly professionalized profession and requires numerous skill sets.

A good security professional is first and foremost familiar with the basics of tourism security and the policies of his or her establishment. This means that the security professional must be able to handle a wide variety of customers, many of whom may exhibit, at times, less than acceptable social behavior. Communication and customer service skills must be utilized amidst a backdrop of a wide range of multicultural and ethical behaviors.

Having experience in customer service is essential, but it is not the totality of the officer's job. He or she must understand the psychology of the casino patron and his/her sociological patterns. At the same time, he or she must also know how to use a wide variety of equipment, tools, and even weapons.

Lastly, but perhaps as importantly, we live in a litigious society. Thus, it is essential for the casino security professional to be well aware of what he or she can and cannot do according to the law, as well as how to document an event. Documentation serves as an important method to review incidents, and it can be highly useful in cases when the courts become involved.

Background Checks

As has been stated, casino personnel are in close proximity to large quantities of money and to people whom it may be easy to take advantage. So, it is essential for those working in the casino industry, especially those who are employed in the area of casino security, to be of the highest moral quality.

In reality, no one ever fully knows another person, but personal histories (i.e., background checks) can at least reveal a great deal about what that person has done in the past. Because background checks are both timely and costly, it is best to do a trial run. Take the suggestions listed below and do a beta-test on yourself. That way you will have some idea as to what is missing and what changes you need to make in your examination of another person prior to investing a great deal of time and money.

Step 1: Is the Person Who He or She Says He or She Is?

Before beginning a background check, it is essential to make sure that the person is telling the truth about his personal history. In other words, begin your background check by making sure there is no fraud regarding the person's identity. In today's world, less than honest people can steal identities by creating false documents, such as driver's licenses, Social Security cards, birth certificates, or student IDs. There are even Websites dedicated to helping people create false identities. Here are some things to do when trying to learn about another person:

1. Verify the person's address
2. Search the public records
3. Run a background check on yourself
4. Explore the multitude of Websites that offer background checks, ask people for opinions, and choose the one that best suits your needs

Step 2: Do Your Homework

Make sure the person signs a release form. He or she needs to understand that you will be examining the public records concerning this individual. Learn how the databases to be searched are organized. It is often a good idea to obtain this information before meeting with the person to be investigated. This way you will not find yourself lacking in vital information.

Step 3: Get the Vitals

Make sure that you have the full name of the person being checked along with his or her aliases or nicknames. If there has been a change of name due to a marriage or an adoption, then be sure to obtain these names also. Note that a different name may not mean that something is wrong. For example, many people use their middle name rather than their given name, but this can cause a waste of both time and resources. Make sure that you get the person's pertinent details. These include:

- Date of birth
- Place of birth
- Hometown
- Name of the person's elementary and high school
- Name of post–high school education
- Military discharge papers
- Social Security number
- Passport number
- Driver's license
- Telephone number(s)
- Fax number
- All email addresses
- Names of immediate family members
- Current and past addresses for the last 10 years

Step 4: Making Copies

Make copies of as many documents as you can obtain from the person. Remember to return the originals and provide a written guarantee that upon completion of the investigation, all copied documents will be returned and/ or destroyed.

Step 5: Confirm the Vitals

Make sure that all information is accurate. There are two types of inaccuracies: simple clerical errors (i.e., the person transposed a number) and errors made on purpose. The latter is clearly a red flag, so go to credit bureaus, the post office, college records, etc. All data should match the data that the person being investigated provides. The fact that the person being investigated has provided you with correct or incorrect information reveals a great deal about him- or herself.

Step 6: Begin Your Search

The best and easiest place to begin a background check is by obtaining public records. Public records provide us with vital information, such as places and dates of birth, marriages and divorces, and if said person is alive or dead. This last point may appear to be superfluous, however, it is not unheard of for unscrupulous people to assume the identity of an already deceased person. Upon completion of a public records search, be sure that the person is who he or she says. Cross-check the information given on the application with what appears in the public records, and then do a search of the person's financial history. A financial history search is necessary because a person who has financial problems may become a challenge to the casino or other institutions where he or she seeks employment. Seek information concerning:
- Credit ratings
- Past bankruptcies
- Real estate ownership
- Debts, such as large car payments
- Tax liens
- History of evictions for nonpayment of rent
- Court documents pertaining to financial settlements or problems

Although a person's driving record may not seem to be essential, these records actually tell the investigator a great deal. For example, if the investigated person has a history of speeding or driving under the influence, then new problems may be revealed.

Finally, we live in a world of social media; a great deal of information can be obtained by simply following the person on Facebook, LinkedIn, or Twitter. These social media conduits provide us with a great deal of personal information and reveal much about the person's character.

Step 7: The Criminal Investigation

Unfortunately, it is not uncommon for people with criminal records to apply for security positions or other sensitive positions. Check if the person has a criminal record and/or a record as a sex offender. Be cognizant of the fact that many people who work in the tourism industry have access to a great deal of cash and guests' rooms. One should be mindful of the possible necessity to check more than one set of records. For example, check national, state, county, and city databases. Remember to go back into the history and do not stop at the person's last place of residence. Here is a list of some of the places where you can check on a person's criminal record:

- Municipal criminal
- County criminal
- Statewide criminal courts (most states)
- Statewide criminal check for felonies, misdemeanors, and sex offenses
- State Department of Corrections (47 of 50 states)
- National arrest and court warrants
- National Department of Corrections
- OFAC Patriot Act search
- FBI Most Wanted
- FBI Most Wanted Terrorists
- Interpol Most Wanted
- Sex-offender records

(Hoover, 2012, Criminal Records Searches section, para. 5)

Interview Techniques

Interviews can tell us a lot about a person. Interviews require that the person knows how to interview, and he or she should be able to interpret tone and body language.

One of the most difficult parts of the hiring process is the personal interview. In his book *100 Things You Need to Know: Best People Practices for Managers and HR* (2004), Eichinger noted that: "There are as many interview structures as there are interviews, but research comes down strongly on the side of structured interviewing techniques. A structured interview technique means that the interviewer has done research to figure out what specific competencies are required for a job, and then has a series of questions that will probe the extent to which the candidate has or has not demonstrated these competencies in previous assignments. When multiple interviewers use the same structured interview format with the same candidate, a more robust and precise image of the candidate's skills follows" (2004, p. 226).

From the perspective of security, the interview is an essential addition to the background check. Interviews are highly complex processes, and they should not be seen as merely a conversation. It is best to have a professional interviewer conduct the session and, if possible, tape the session for later reference. Listed below are some interview guidelines to be considered when conducting an interview.

- Make sure to interview the prospective employee in a place that is quiet and in which you can give your full attention.
- Make sure to have all telephone calls held. If you are interviewing a person of the opposite sex, then be sure to have two people in the room. One of these people should be the same sex as the applicant.
- Ask your attorney if you can tape interviews. If you do indeed tape the interview, then you need to inform the applicant that he or she is being taped.
- Always begin an interview with some "small talk/chit-chat." This warm-up period will put the interviewee at ease and give you time to judge body language.
- When interviewing a prospective employee, use a combination of closed and open-ended questions. Closed questions can be answered with a simple yes or no answer, while open-ended questions require explanations. Many interviewers prefer to alternate the type of question they ask. Closed questions should be answered in a strong and firm manner; open-ended questions should demonstrate the person's pensive side.

There is much you can learn about the person by his or her comportment. Here are some tips to avoid common interview mistakes:

- Make sure you begin and end your interview on time.
- Pay attention to the person being interviewed. Do not accept phone calls during the interview.
- Dress the part. How you dress matters. If you are to be the person's boss, then make sure that you play the role correctly.
- Is the person looking at his or her cell phone instead of paying attention?

- Be positive rather than negative. If you were not considering hiring the person, then why interview him or her? If you are considering hiring the person, then your tone and style should set a business pattern for the potential employee.
- Never be rude to an interviewee. You do not have to hire the person, but even if you do not like him or her, politeness is always correct and businesslike.
- Allow the interviewee to ask questions. Questions are really answers with an interrogation mark. We learn as much about a potential employee by the questions that he or she asks than by the answers he or she provides.

OTHER PLACES WHERE PEOPLE GATHER

Casinos are not the only place where large numbers of people gather. The following section deals with three other places of gathering: convention centers, trade shows, and festivals. In the next chapter, additional locales such as parades and sporting events will be considered.

Convention Centers

Many casinos have both hotels and convention centers. For this reason, the attention shifts from the casino floor to the convention center.

Conventions are big business. Some of the largest convention centers, like those found in Las Vegas, Nevada, or Orlando, Florida, can accommodate conventions numbering in the tens of thousands of participants. Other cities may have smaller convention centers, but their economies are still impacted by the convention and meeting business. In all cases, attendees and/or participants may pay registration fees to attend a convention and/ or meeting, while at the same time purchasing lodging, food, entertainment, gas and transportation services, and local souvenirs.

Not only do conventions and meetings serve as a place of gathering, but also they provide a way to showcase a community. Therefore, communities seek out and compete for convention business.

HISTORY OF MEETINGS AND CONVENTIONS

Trade shows and fairs may be some of the earliest forms of conventions and meetings. In fact, trade shows represent one of the earliest forms of capitalism. Ever since people started to communicate and gather information, there has always been a tendency for them to trade with one another. From the earliest of times, human beings had the need to gather together, exchange ideas, and find new ways to present products, services, or ideas. For example, in Biblical days, people understood that selling goods meant more than simply having a good product. They also had to present their goods in an attractive and accessible manner. Early exhibitors understood that location might have meant the difference between success and failure. So, they competed for the best locations at local fairs. Over the millennia, fairs and trade shows have evolved. Today, trade shows are still very much in existence, and they are extremely important to both large industries and to local economies. The trade show also gave birth to the convention and meeting business. Conventions are similar to trade shows in that people share both data and "products." However, the trade show provides samples of an actual physical product, while the convention is more abstract. Conventions provide opportunities to sell ideas or to market collective "wisdom." They may be any event where people gather to learn, exchange ideas and products, and/or create networking opportunities for future personal or business enhancement. Many conventions combine the trade show with the actual convention, or vice versa. This allows people the chance to talk about certain concepts and see how they are translated into actual products that serve current and future needs.

The impact of trade shows, meetings, and conventions often extends beyond the actual delegates or exhibitors. Delegates and exhibitors not only attend these gatherings, but they often turn a "business trip" into a semivacation. Now, it is not uncommon for convention delegates, or those exhibiting at trade shows, to bring family members along with the idea of mixing business with pleasure.

From the perspective of the travel and tourism industries, trade shows and conventions provide major economic boosts to the host community. As mentioned above, those working at a convention or trade show, or attending them, need a great many services, such as hotels, electricians, restaurants, transportation, etc. Additionally, exhibitors may need freight services, in-house coordinators, and service personnel to set up and break down exhibits. Trade shows and conventions do not exist in a perfect world. These large gatherings attract numerous people who seek less than honest ways to make a living. For example, trade shows provide ample opportunities for pilferage and robbery, and conventions contain all of the sociological forces mentioned in Chapter 1. In today's world, conventions need a great deal of security, not only to stop any pilferage, but to also protect both those exhibiting at the convention and those attending it.

Security and conventions are interrelated. Without the convention, there is no need for convention security, and without proper security, a community's convention business may soon wither. Trade show and convention security is more complex than initially thought. From the convention center's perspective, its security forces are responsible for what occurs within the convention center. From the meeting planner's perspective, however, what occurs outside of the convention center or exhibit floor also impacts the show's security.

Thus, there is a cybernetic loop in which security officials need conventions to stay employed, and conventions (or trade shows) need secure areas and communities. In order for a community to attract conventions, the locale needs to understand something about itself. Then, it is essential for both convention and meeting planners to work with private and public security professionals. All groups involved must be aware of the following issues:

- Is the locale appropriate for a convention? Before trying to attract a convention, it is essential that security personnel understand what makes this particular locale special. Security personnel need to be aware of certain questions, such as: Does the community have specific demographics that would add to or detract from a particular convention? Is the community's geography one that would not be appropriate for some age groups or people with special physical needs?

- How safe is the neighborhood in which the convention center is located? It can take as little as one well-publicized incident to destroy a convention city's reputation. Work carefully with your local police department to ensure security is provided in a timely and courteous manner. In a similar fashion, do everything that is possible to enhance the landscaping and environmental beauty of the convention center's neighborhood. Remember, the neighborhood that surrounds your convention center is the one that makes the greatest impression on your visitors.

- Which local businesses, services, and citizens are willing to turn your community into a convention-oriented community? Convention-oriented communities make money when delegates leave the convention center and go into the community. If the community has poor customer service, or simply is not tourism friendly, then conventioneers will speak poorly of the community rather than of the convention itself.

Delegates that enjoy a community are more likely to return as leisure visitors, or recommend the location to their family and friends.

- Understanding what other competitive communities are offering. In a like manner, the security professional needs to understand his or her community's competition. For example, if the community claims its location is centrally located, then determine in what area. The reality is that all communities are centrally located to something else. What makes this location special? How good are your transportation arteries and how cooperative is local law enforcement in aiding needy travelers? Remember, many cities advertise that their residents are special, who offer old-fashioned hospitality. Most meeting planners interpret these statements to mean that the community has nothing unique to offer.
- What size convention can a particular community handle? Often, communities do not think through the logistics of a convention. If you are going to seek to attract a convention, then be sure to know what types of hotels you offer, how close restaurants are to the convention center, and what services a convention center has. At first glance, these issues may not seem to impact the convention center security staff, but they do. Convention delegates and trade-show exhibitors do not live in the convention center; what happens outside of the convention center impacts what happens on the inside.
- What promises is your convention center making, and can these promises be fulfilled? Remind those seeking convention business for your community to make sure that what they promise is real and doable. Meeting planners know all too well how to separate honest offers from those that are cons. The reality is that you may never know what will win (or lose) you a convention's business. The security professional is very much a part of the convention center's marketing team. Customer service is as essential for someone in security as it is for someone in the marketing department.
- What is the security level of the restaurants and attractions in your community? Many security people make the mistake in believing that they are not responsible for what occurs outside of the convention center. Technically, they are correct, but most visitors do not distinguish the boundary between the convention center and the community. Although it is impossible to favor one establishment over another, it is a good idea to try to steer people toward those establishments that will produce the least amount of problems. Facial expressions and body language may be able to convey what cannot be said with the spoken word.

CRIMES AT CONVENTION CENTERS OR TRADE SHOWS

There is a paucity of information regarding crimes at convention and trade-show centers. A review of the literature indicates that convention center crimes tend to be limited to (1) articles and media reports of crimes near a convention center or (2) some form of crime of opportunity at the convention center, such as pilferage, pickpocketing, or the removal of personal items that are left unattended (e.g., handbags, briefcases, laptop computers, etc.). Actual crimes committed at a convention center appear to be low for a number of reasons. Among these are:

1. Most convention centers have well-trained and adequate security forces.
2. Convention centers are highly regulated; there are specific guidelines that both exhibitors and attendees must follow. For example, most conventions and trade shows require some form of identification before allowing the attendee to enter. Also, they require bags, coats, and other paraphernalia to be checked before entering.
3. Convention centers tend to use a combination of high tech and low tech, thus preventing major crimes before they may occur.
4. The negative publicity costs to a convention center of a major crime would be very high. Therefore, convention centers tend to stand at a state of ready alert.

Convention/trade-show centers, however, may need to prepare themselves for an ever-changing set of challenges. Many large convention centers have both security and safety departments, while smaller centers tend to combine these two departments. For reasons of easy reading, this chapter combines the security and safety side by treating them as if they were one department.

Because convention/trade-show centers draw large crowds, it would be impossible to conduct a background check on each person attending. In an age of terrorism, new challenges await these centers, including:

• Issues of cybercrime. Most convention/trade-show centers are now computer dependent. There are daily attacks against Western nations and their economic industrial base from a number of rogue countries. Although at the time of this writing there are no reported cases of major cyber attacks against a large convention center, this does not mean that such an attack may not occur. Convention/trade-show centers must be prepared to deal with everything from the loss of electricity, to computerized sprinkler systems being set off. In all cases, a cyber disruption will have major economic and reputational consequences due to the amount of property on view and the fact that conventions and trade shows are of short-term (usually under eight days) duration.

- Issues of identity theft. Identify theft is a widespread problem, and it is certainly not restricted to convention centers or trade shows. Nevertheless, conventions and trade shows tend to be somewhat loose in their control over personal data. They provide ample opportunities for the stealing of credit card information or loss of personal documents that lead to identity theft.
- Issues of remote bombs being set off by cell phones. Most convention/trade-show centers have fairly well-controlled access. Though, coatrooms and storage rooms are another matter. These rooms may be in bombing access to the convention or trade show floor. Even if they are not, a bomb in such a sensitive location would produce casualties and a great deal of negative publicity.
- Issues of attacks against the edifice's air and water system. Because convention centers tend to be large edifices, they are totally dependent on ventilation and water systems. Many of these locations, especially at the midsize level, have their ventilation systems in locations with fairly easy access. Ventilation systems provide potentially silent attacks in which the victims may not realize that they are being slowly poisoned or harmed.
- Issues of airborne illnesses and planned infections. Closely related to the issue of proper ventilation protection is that of airborne illnesses, which may be impossible to detect. A person can be sent into a convention center with a contagious disease and create an act of terror simply by "planned sneezing." Most convention centers have no way of knowing who has a contagious illness, and who may be the perpetrator of such planned contagion.
- Issues of fire and fire prevention. Convention/trade-show centers are highly regulated with regard to fire codes and protection. These large buildings are regularly inspected and each "show" is treated as a separate entity. From the public's standpoint, this is most likely a minor worry. However, not all fire inspectors are the same, with some doing a better job than others. It would be a mistake to assume that a fire cannot occur at a convention center. Also, the actual fire may cause panic if proper evacuation procedures are not in place. Thus, the interrelationship between fire safety and crowd control is essential.
- Issues of food poisoning. Convention/trade-show centers usually have some form of restaurant or food concessionaire that is highly monitored. Many booths, however, often offer food samples and souvenirs.

Although convention/trade-show center security staff inspect most foods given to the public, many nonregulated products could slip through the cracks.

The list above is a mere sample of the challenges facing the modern trade show and convention center. Many trade shows provide security and safety manuals for their exhibitors. Often, these manuals are tailored to the needs of a particular trade show. Below is a composite of some of the types of security guidelines used at trade shows.

SOME TRADE SHOW/CONVENTION SECURITY PROCEDURES

- Trade shows often have badge-monitoring security guards at the entrance. In many cases, no unauthorized person is permitted to enter the premises before the exhibits open.
- Trade show security usually requires all personnel working at the show, setting it up or taking it down, to use an official ID badge. All persons in the exhibit halls must wear a badge. Badges must be issued from the trade show, and business cards are not an acceptable substitute.
- After the trade show closes for the night, security guards ensure that no one is allowed onto the trade-show floor.
- Exhibitors are reminded that theft and pilferage are most likely to occur when the booth is unattended. This means that the exhibitor must have a method in place to allow a one-person booth to be relieved for personal necessities.
- If there is a large amount of expensive articles on display, such as a jewelry exhibit, then it may benefit the exhibitor to hire a guard for his or her booth. It is a mistake to assume that the trade show can offer total protection.
- Rather than leaving valuables on the display floor, it is advisable to locate secure cages where the exhibitor can store valuables overnight.
- Exhibitors should never leave valuables on display overnight. They should remove, store, or cover the items that are being displayed.
- It is essential that exhibitors have a full inventory of what they are displaying. The inventory should include which items were brought to the show and which were removed after the trade show is complete.
- Exhibitors should never trust anyone with security of their merchandise. Security starts with the exhibitor.

Trade shows are meant for soliciting. This is the primary reason that someone buys space at a trade show. Soliciting, however, has limits. Most trade shows demand that their exhibitors limit their solicitation to their own booth. The use of sexual innuendos, going into the aisles to solicit, or soliciting in front of another person's booth are not acceptable behaviors. Most management companies do not permit unauthorized people to come onto the exhibit area and solicit. Solicitations are then kept only to those persons or companies that have purchased space. In a like manner, it is usually a standard operating policy that exhibitors have something to do with the trade show's theme. Trade shows work on a cluster principle, which means that groups of similar products produce a synergy that helps all to do better. This same principle holds true in other businesses, such as casinos and bookstores.

Building Codes and Restrictions

Most trade shows have very specific booth building codes. These requirements allow a sense of uniformity and permit security and safety personnel to have access to the exhibit hall if necessary. Also, most trade shows also have very specific fire codes. There are special restrictions that deal with the use of combustible fuels, cables, and electronic equipment.

HAZARDOUS MATERIALS

Both indoor and outdoor trade shows have very specific rules and regulations regarding hazardous materials. Common prohibitions include items whose packages contain the words "danger," "warning," "poison," "do not inhale," etc. If an exhibitor is not sure whether a product is allowed, then they need to ask. Local fire departments are very cautious about allowing hazardous materials into a closed environment with potentially large numbers of people present.

ANIMALS (PETS) AT TRADE AND CONVENTION CENTERS

With the exception of a pet or a rodeo show, most trade shows only allow animals that are people specific, such as seeing-eye dogs. Other animals may present numerous health and safety hazards. If they are not trained properly, then they may inadvertently be harmed.

Because we live in a litigious society, most trade shows today have developed their own rules with the help of legal counsel, and they require some form of liability limitation. It is always a wise idea for an exhibitor to review the rules and regulations with his or her legal counsel prior to signing any agreement.

CONVENTION/TRADE-SHOW CENTER SECURITY AND SAFETY PLANS

Convention centers, like trade shows, often tailor their security procedures to the specific needs of the community and the center. In the larger convention centers, located in Las Vegas or Orlando, careful attention is paid to distinguishing between safety and security needs. In the smaller centers, these two departments are often united into one overall department.

A good example of convention center security is provided by the Website of the Los Angeles Convention Center (LACC).[1] The Website indicates that the LACC accepts responsibility for the "the physical and procedural security of the public areas and non-licensed spaces." The LACC also provides meeting times and coordination with the event security director. LACC has a set of emergency procedures, evacuation routes, and potential hazards. The LACC clearly sees security as a joint responsibility with the event. Thus, its Website states: "The event security contractor is responsible for the security of their licensed area(s), including such items as security operations, unlocking of all licensed area doors during occupancy, ADA compliance and support, hazard control, emergency processes, abating and reporting on thefts or loss, and referring those with criminal complaints to local police." There is then a triangle of responsibility here, as seen in Figure 5.1.

Once again, due to the fact that we live in a litigious society, the Website outlines insurance requirements. These include:

a. General Liability insurance in the amount of $1,000,000.
b. Workers' Compensation insurance on file with the Event Services Division of the LACC.

Figure 5.1 Part of event security is to have an event security plan, a crowd-control plan, a line-control plan, and a building security plan.

[1] http://www.lacclink.com/lacclink/security.aspx.

c. LACC and the City of Los Angeles shall be named as an additional insured on both policies.

d. Please forward insurance endorsement forms to your insurance company or agent for completion. The forms should be returned to LACC Event Services Division.

EVENT SECURITY PLAN

Event security plans can be very simple or extremely complicated. To a great extent, the plan depends on the type of event, who will be attending the event, the event's location, and the event's timing. A good overall event-planning site can be found on the Department of Justice Website.[2]

No matter how large or small the event may be, there are certain characteristics that are pertinent to all events. These principles hold true for all events from a small wedding to a major national convention. Among these are:

- Pre-event planning and a risk management plan
- Knowledge of whom is in charge of the event and what the lines of command are
- List of what are the threats and risks to this event
- Understanding of who has what information that is necessary for the event's success
- Types of communication that can be used by the event's organizers and those in charge of its security
- Ways to deal with internal and external traffic issues
- System to determine who should and should not be at the event
- Plan that will determine who is in charge of security and safety
- Clear evacuation routes should they be needed

Outdoor Events

Tourism business and commerce not only occurs inside of casinos and convention/trade-show centers, but a great deal of commerce often occurs at outdoors events and festivals. As a result, this chapter now examines some of the security issues that touch these two areas of tourism and event industries.

In many parts of the world, the summer and fall months are filled with festivals and outdoor events. They can be wonderful opportunities to showcase a community and to produce added revenue. Festivals, however,

---

[2] http://www.cops.usdoj.gov/Publications/e07071299_web.pdf.

require a tremendous amount of work to ensure safety and security. No festival committee should ever permit a festival to take place without the cooperation of the local law enforcement agencies. All too often, law enforcement is "told" about a festival rather than "consulted." This negative result can be anything from a disorderly conduct complaint to a serious tragedy. The moment a festival or event committee sets the date for its event, it is essential that the committee contact and involve law enforcement. Specific regulations and guidelines need to be worked out with local authorities. Because there is such a wide variety of festivals and events, the following is a set of basic universal guidelines dealing with festivals and events.

- In pre-event planning sessions, remember that successful events start with good event planning. Many event planners and organizers are excellent at thinking about the type of event that they wish to hold and where it is to be held. Unfortunately, these same people, at times, tend to overlook other key considerations. Event planners should develop a timeline for the event at least one year prior to when it will be held. It is essential for them to include all of the major stakeholders in the initial meetings. Stakeholders include city organizations monitoring the event, law enforcement, traffic control, local businesses, marketers, and, of course, the local convention and visitor's bureau/ tourism office.

- Determine what type of festival it is and where it will be held. Both the style of the festival and the event's venue have a major impact on security. For example, who has the final word as to event cancelation or postponement due to unstable weather conditions? How close is parking? Are there snakes in the area? Is this a festival in which alcohol is served or is it a "dry" festival? What geographic problems are in close proximity to the event's location? Are there demographic problems such as gangs or other people who might interrupt or become an event security hazard?

- At the event planning stage, do a full threat and risk assessment, which is an area of festival and event planning often overlooked, especially in an age of street violence and terrorism. Review the chapter on risk assessment, then determine what the major risks are. For example, what are the event's demographics? If the event primarily attracts senior citizens, then there is one set of risks. Families produce other risks, while young people or teenagers produce a completely different type of risk. In a like manner, the terrain on which the event is held, the season in which it will be held, and whether it will be an indoor or outdoor event, all impact the type of risks for which you must be prepared. Make sure that the event planners know who will be working at the festival. If money is to be exchanged, then how will the money be secured and what background checks will be used?

- Review all critical factors well in advance of the event. Among these are: What is the sponsoring organization's purpose and experience in running an event? Does this event promote a specific cultural, political, or social agenda? What is the event's history? What has gone wrong in the past? How happy or unhappy is the local community with the event? If the event is to take place on a residential street, then the problems may be quite different than if the same event were to be held in an open field. How can weather impact the event? Think beyond rain. For example, if this is an outdoor summer event, will people suffer from sunstroke? How will they get water and how many restrooms will the event provide?

- Distinguish between different types of risk because not all risk is the same. Physical risks correspond to things that can happen to the person or the place. These are tangible risks and their consequences can be measured. Reputational risk refers to the cost to a community's reputation when something goes wrong. Most people protest that the media are not fair; they tend to emphasize points taken out of context. This is true in many cases, but places that depend on tourism need to have a plan to deal with the media. Another form of risk is the emotional cost to personnel and locales when something goes wrong. Emotional risk means that an event has to have backup personnel in place so that first responders are in good shape to do their job without worry. Finally, there is the fiscal risk present with any event. If people do not show up, or if there is a weather disaster, then event planners need to consider the possibility of recovering from a severe financial loss.

- Determine what are acceptable risk levels for your event. Develop methods to diminish risk by spreading it across the event rather than concentrating it in one location. You can also diminish risk by sharing responsibility with allied agencies, participating in joint training exercises, and continuously monitoring for unexpected or unplanned changes during the event. You need to seek ways to reduce risk, but for some occasions, it may be wise to cancel an event due to unforeseen risks. In such cases, not doing anything may result in a major risk.

- Never hold an event without a good organizational (incident command) structure. Failures often occur due to poor communication between parts of the event. It is essential that prior to holding an event, all stakeholders use the same vocabulary and understand each other. So, it is important to have a system to communicate and practice coordination. Good incident command structures lessen risk; should an incident occur, they are essential in protecting life and property.

- Develop an alcohol consumption plan. The selling (giving away) of alcoholic drinks is always a problem. The best policy, while often impossible to implement, is to not serve alcohol. If alcoholic drinks are served, then plan for these notable security challenges, such as (1) inebriation policies, (2) underage drinking, and (3) the passing of alcoholic drinks from one person to another. These policies should lead to the following questions: What policies do the festival providers have regarding drivers who leave the festival with slight (or major) intoxication, thereby causing an accident? Address the issue of alcoholic consumption prior to the festival with the help of law enforcement.

- Festival security planners must know who will have what access to the event and its booths. Just as in the case of trade shows, the festival security planner must know who can enter the festival area, when it must be cleared out, and who has booth and money access. One of the most difficult parts of running a festival is to determine who has access to what and how those with proper access are to be identified. Festival managers need to worry about money on hand and where it is to be stored, as well as troublesome items such as alcohol, arts and crafts, merchandise, and equipment. If the festival is to be outdoors and takes place over several days, then a safe storage place must be found to protect goods from potential crime and/or the weather. Remember, the festival's guests may be involved in pilferage, and the same problem can occur with people working at the booths.

- Festival security personnel must determine what types of security and safety best meet the event's needs. Security and safety are essential for any successful festival. Security starts with police, fire fighters, and emergency first-aid squads, along with public health officials. Given that police have limited budgets and manpower, consider supplementing professional first responders with private security. In such cases, make sure that both groups coordinate and work together. Conduct a joint evacuation or tabletop exercise in order to verify that everyone knows his or her role.

- Consider all issues of crowd control. Although each festival or event has different crowd-control issues, there are some things common to all festivals and events when considering crowd control. To elaborate, if the event is outdoors and people are not seated, then one of the best forms of crowd control is having security personnel on horseback. However, horses are extremely expensive, and they often involve sanitation issues. A less expensive substitute for horses is to find ways in which some of your security team is above the crowd, like with the use of towers, crow's nests, or even rooftops.

- Crowds tend to take on lives all their own. To ensure an orderly crowd, keep the crowd moving at a slow and steady pace. Crowds tend to turn into riots when they move too quickly, are at a standstill, and there is no simple and clear evacuation system in place. Remember, most people react better to the spoken word than to the written word.

- Events and their security plans are part of the local hospitality industry. Chief Greg Mullen of the Charleston, South Carolina, police department emphasizes the importance of taking event security seriously and integrating it well with the overall tourism plan. Mullen stresses to his police officers that events function as a form of tourism, and they suffer from the same sociological issues, as do other forms of tourism. Thus, when events suffer from a negative occurrence, this situation may have negative publicity consequences and harm the entire local industry. As in all forms of risk management, it is more cost effective to deal with the risk than it is to deal with the damage once it has occurred.

- Measure an event's security success by how well the security staff has mitigated risk, how safe the public felt at the event, the number of crimes that were prevented, and the desire of the public to return because the event "felt" safe and secure. Critical areas of event risk include health and safety issues (especially if food items are being sold); crowd management; alcohol sales and consumption; traffic management, including coming to the festival, parking, and leaving the festival; and personal security should fights break out, a robbery occur, or even a mass killing.

- Evaluate, evaluate, evaluate! A major error in event and festival risk management is failure to evaluate the event or festival after it is completed. Be sure to conduct a thorough after-action review. Include in this review both positive and negative outcomes, what went right, what did not happen due to luck, and what mistakes were made. List areas for improvement. Never be defensive in your review; instead, analyze your plans and document both positive and negative tactics in a written report. This report should be written within 30 days of the event so that memory loss and idealization do not occur.

REFERENCES

Editorial: Casino-crime link is well established. (2013). *Concord Monitor*. Retrieved from http://www.concordmonitor.com/home/5253146-95/editorial-casino-crime-link-is-well-established.

Eichinger, R. W. (2004). *100 things you need to know: Best practices for managers and HR*. Minneapolis, MN.: Lominger Ltd.

Grabianowski, E. (2007). How casinos work. *How Stuff Works*. Retrieved from http://entertainment.howstuffworks.com/casino.htm.

Hoover, J. (2012). How to conduct a background check? *How to Investigate*. Retrieved from http://www.howtoinvestigate.com/articles/basic_background_check.htm#.UmB2phaNBvZ.

Kent, S. (2013). Singapore proof a casino won't spike Toronto crime. *Toronto Sun*. Retrieved from http://www.torontosun.com/2013/01/21/singapore-proof-a-casino-wont-spike-toronto-crime.

Stitt, B. G., Giacopassi, D., & Nichols, M. (2000). The effect of casino gambling on crime in new casino jurisdiction. *Journal of Crime and Justice*, *23*(1), 1–23.

Tapley, L. (2009). Do casinos cause crime? *The Crime Report*. Retrieved from http://www.thecrimereport.org/archive/do-casinos-cause-crime.

CHAPTER 6

Aquatic Tourism: Security at Beaches, Rivers, Lakes, and on the High Seas

INTRODUCTION

Figure 6.1 Welcome to the Panama Canal

Ever since the dawn of time, the rivers, lakes, and seas have fascinated people. As far back as the book of Jonah, human beings have understood that the world's oceans and seas were both a source of food and transportation, and at the same time a source of mystery and danger. These bodies of water created natural barriers and at the same time, river and seaports were a nation's doors to the world. Large-scale bodies of water also play a major role in multiple forms of tourism, including beaches, cruises, fishing, and water sports. Often, but not always, aquatic tourism falls into the category of "Sun, Sand and Sea" tourism.

The phenomenon of water parks may also be considered a part of aquatic tourism. Until recently aquatic tourism principally had to deal with issues of safety such as preventing people from drowning, sea animal attacks such as those of sharks or jellyfish, diving safety, and overexposure to the sun. With the advent of many college students turning local beaches into spring break parties, a number of indirect security issues have developed. Many of these issues do not occur on the water, but cannot be separated from aquatic tourism. Among these are such issues as:

- Larceny and theft
- Sexual assault
- Rowdy and/or socially unacceptable behavior
- Nudity
- Room invasions

In the last decade aquatic tourism has also had to deal with the issue of piracy and/or potential terrorist threats. Because the subject is so broad, this chapter focuses on two major forms of aquatic tourism: beach tourism and cruise tourism.

BEACH/SEA/RIVER TOURISM

Almost everyone seems to love a day at the beach. Beach tourism, often called "sun and sand" tourism, should perhaps better be called shore tourism as it covers a much wider range than simply visiting the sandy shores that are situated next to a lake or an ocean. Included in this wider range of aquatic options are:

- Beach tourism includes both oceans and seas, and rivers, lakes and even swim clubs.
- Water sports both in the water (e.g., water skiing, deep-sea fishing, river tubing) and alongside of the water, such as fly fishing.
- Sunbathing.
- Land activities such as beach volleyball.
- Underwater activities such as scuba diving and snorkeling.

Each one of these activities shares something of an aquatic experience, each tends to produce a carefree atmosphere and in each case a lack of common sense may prove to be highly dangerous or even deadly. Because aquatic tourism can be both fun and dangerous, many places post clear symbolic signage that can be understood no matter what language the visitor or participant may speak. Signage is usually presented in three ways. These are: (1) permitted activities, (2) forbidden activities, and (3) informational signage. Permitted activities often show a picture or representation of an activity presented in green. For example, the sign for "swimming permitted" will be the representation of a swimmer surrounded by a green circle and with the words "swimming permitted" written below the sign. Often the word representation is provided in both the local language and in an international language such as English. Signs indicating a forbidden activity will be in red and once again surrounded by a red, rather than green circle. The activities represented will have a line through it, indication that this activity is dangerous and/or forbidden. Once again written words will be placed beneath the sign in both the local language and in an international language. Informational signage tends to be square rather than in a circle. It may come in a variety of colors and will have a word or phrase below the sign. Information signs may indicate when a lifeguard is on duty, where one may bar-b-cue, or water depth.

In most cases, aquatic tourism has spent more time on issues of safety than it has on questions of security. Although the potential along a crowded beach for a terrorist attack exists, these types of attacks have so far rarely occurred. At present the major issues in aquatic tourism are:

- Physical and sexual assault
- Theft
- Car break-ins
- Petty larceny

And safety issues that include:

- Drowning
- Food spoilage
- Sunburns and sun poisoning

Safety Precautions

Many beaches and other public swimming areas have at least some form of signage warning the public about changing sea conditions and if a lifeguard is or is not on duty. However, lifeguard protection along beaches is often sparse or nonexistent and hotels tend to place more emphasis on not being sued than on individual safety. Thus, the most common sign at a hotel swimming pool is "No lifeguard on duty, swim at your own risk."

Around the world there are a number of international signs that indicate ocean beach safety, although there is some variation and different beaches may use different colors. It is traditional to indicate the state of a beach's safety with colored flags.

Bathers may find other signs asking them to take their cell phones to the beach and dial the local emergency number such as 911 in case of emergency. This "do-it-yourself" safety, however, causes other problems. These include: the cell phone now must be watched while the person is in the water, and in case of a water emergency, the victim may have already drowned by the time that help arrives.

Protection against the Sun

Beaches and water sports have other safety problems, among them the need to have proper protection against the harmful rays of the sun. Although the sun is not a security issue, it certainly is a safety issue. Many a vacation has been ruined by overexposure to the sun. Fifty years ago, people believed that the sun was beneficial and that a deep tan was a sign of good health. Medical experts no longer hold this belief. The sun and sunburns cannot only cause a great amount of discomfort and distress, but may also be a cause for cancer.

Children need special protection against the sun, and many people forget that there is not necessarily a relationship between the sun's strength and the atmospheric temperature. For example, high mountains in tropic regions may benefit from cool weather, but the sun is still a tropic sun! The sun is not only strong on land, it is also strong on the water. People who are fishing or engaging in other water sports need to take just as many precautions as those who are sunbathing on the beach. Before engaging in any form of aquatic activity, beach and water sports enthusiasts should consult a physician. Signs should be posted reminding people that just as the sea can be dangerous, so too can the sun, and that cloudy weather is no protection against illness and skin damage.

Boating Safety

A second area, about which whole books have been written, deals with boating safety, whether on the open seas or on a lake. In either case, the potential for a boating accident and for a drowning exists. When considering boating security and safety, take into account the following:
- Boating is a popular U.S. sport.
- Boat sizes range from a small canoe or even a tire tube to large yachts that can traverse the seas.
- Boating is often tied to sports fishing.

Once again, the term "fishing" can encompass anything from deep-sea sports fishing to fishing with a rod on a river's edge. In all cases, however, certain precautions will need to be taken:
- Proper clothing and lotions to provide adequate protection from the sun.

- Use of proper safety equipment such as life preservers.
- Understanding that water can be dangerous.

In the case of the open sea, the realization that the sea is both capricious and dangerous and conditions can change at a moment's notice. Fish and other forms of sea life do not exist for human beings' enjoyment. It is imperative to remember that the sea life is at home in the sea, and that human beings are merely guests of the sea. In the case of large bodies of water, the U.S. Coast Guard provides a great deal of information on its Website. It is wise to check with the Coast Guard or other police agencies prior to venturing into the sea.

CRIMINAL ISSUES AND ISSUES OF TERRORISM AT AQUATIC LOCATIONS

As noted above, the world of aquatic tourism is not without its problems. Problems can range from crimes of opportunity to sexual and physical assaults. Many of the key principles discussed in earlier chapters became prevalent in aquatic tourism. For example, there may be a tendency to leave valuables in shoes or under beach towels. Articles left on the beach without any protection are invitations for theft. This problem is especially acute where beaches and swimming pools do not provide safe locations for valuables to be stored. Criminals know that many visitors will carry at least some cash for incidentals such as drinks or light meals. Visitors often wish to remember their vacation on film with cameras and/or do not want to be disconnected from the world and so bring smartphones to places such as the beach where they are left unprotected while the owner enjoys the water. Once left on the beach, they become targets for theft. Aquatic areas, almost by definition, are areas in which people often wear minimal clothing. There is greater potential for sexual assaults, especially in isolated areas or at night. Sexual assaults may come from both the local population that believes that the visitor may not press charges and from other visitors. In some cases, these assaults are very much intentional; in other cases these assaults may arise from the mistaken belief that in a "party atmosphere" such as spring break all inhibitions cease to function. In both cases, an assault is an assault, and excuses do not compensate for the action.

An additional threat at any aquatic area is to children. These threats fall into two broad categories: (1) assuring that children are safe and (2) the prevention of illegal acts such as kidnapping. Children are a special problem because they can disappear at a moment's notice and in a world of violence are always the potential targets of kidnappers.

The use of closed-circuit TV (CCTV) cameras may be of some help in limiting beach and swimming pool incidents, but it is a mistake to become totally dependent on cameras as a security measure. CCTV cameras do not substitute for lifeguards and security personnel.

CRUISE TOURISM

Human beings are both fascinated by and fear the sea. As such, boats and ships have allowed humanity to reach the far corners of the world and served as platforms for exploration, commerce, and trade. Cruises may be as old as civilization itself. The Bible makes reference to "cruises" on several occasions. For example, the story of Noah, read in the original Hebrew, very much appears to be about a cruise to "nowhere." If we read the text not as a "history" but as insights into the sociology of cruises, then these passengers' Hebrew names represent types of cruiseline passengers and teach us a great deal about the sociology of cruising. We can translate the Hebrew name Noah as "to rest or to relax." Thus, the Hebrew name provides us with a clue as to the definition of cruises. Cruises are more than voyages from a place to another place; their goal is not the "there" but the "getting there." In the world of cruises the voyage is the journey and the cruise just as in the case of Noah and his ark acts as an all-inclusive floating hotel rather than as a means of transportation.

Noah's three sons, who join him on "their cruise to nowhere," also represent some of the more difficult parts of the sociology of cruise security. We can translate his three sons' names, Shem, Japheth, and Ham, as someone who believes he or she is a big deal, pretty or playboy, and one who is convinced that the world revolves around him or her. The Biblical text hints at the fact that those who take cruises may be challenges to security personnel and that self-victimization or lack of common sense may be a constant problem for cruise security officers and professionals. Often cruise security personnel must work hard to protect passengers from doing things that may turn out to be harmful to them.

A second Biblical tale tells a more fearsome account of man's love–hate relationship with the sea. In the Book of Jonah the reader learns that Jonah saw the sea as a means of escape, and yet Jonah soon came to realize that the sea is a friend and a foe, a place of tranquility, and, at the same time, subject to the forces of nature. Once again, if we choose to read the text not as history but as a paradigm of sea travel, many of the security problems found at sea are noted in this Biblical vignette.

The Jonah story provides the student of tourism security with a host of ethical and practical problems. In fact this text can be used as a training manual for anyone working on a cruise ship. For example, the text forces the modern security specialist to ask questions such as, What was the responsibility of the crew toward Jonah? Is it a crew's responsibility to protect its passengers or does the crew have a greater responsibility to protect the ship? Does the crew have the right to allow a passenger to engage in harmful behavior? If not, then in the case of the Jonah story, was their crew complicit in what must have been believed to be an act of suicide? Reading the text on a still deeper plain and from the perspective of an age of terrorism, modern security specialists need to ask:

- Should Jonah have been allowed on the ship? Should his sudden departure have aroused suspicion?
- How do we determine if a passenger is a security threat?

FROM THE BIBLICAL TEXT TO THE MODERN WORLD

From the time of Jonah until the latter half of the twentieth century, sea travel was either an extremely uncomfortable means of transportation or an attempt at ultimate luxury mixed with the romance of the seas. The *Titanic* serves as a symbol of that period. It would provide the ultimate touches of luxury packaged as safe travel. The ship was considered to be unsinkable. We may view the *Titanic*'s sinking and loss of life as the end of an era of cruise innocence.

The modern cruise industry sought to transform this situation and in so doing, at least to some extent, conquer the sea. It is only after World War II that we note a new era of sea travel. The modern cruise industry, based on trips to nowhere, is more about the sea experience than about the ports-of-call. Indeed, we may argue that these ports-of-call are mere "excuses" for the cruise experience. Cruise travel is travel for the sake of travel in which modern hotels float across seas and visit ports for no other reason other than that of rest and relaxation.

A Short History of Cruises

At the end of the nineteenth century and in the beginning of the twentieth century, destination travel was mixed with upper-class pleasure. These semi-cruise ships allowed people to travel, especially across the North Atlantic, in style. While the goal of these ships was transportation between ports, the ship attempted to provide every conceivable luxury to make the trip both safe and pleasant. The White Star line claimed that the *Titanic* disaster of April 14, 1912, would not impact business. A *New York Times* article of April 16, 1912, stated, "Most of the steamship people said that they could see no reason why the sinking of the 'unsinkable' should affect the summer traffic in any way" ("Titanic sinks four hours after hitting iceberg," 1912). There may have been debate regarding the impact of the *Titanic*'s sinking on the North Atlantic passenger route business, but there can be little doubt that the two world wars clearly put an end to leisurely sea travel. With the end of World War II, sea travel now had to face the added competition of air travel and the fact that travel time between Europe and North America could now be measured in hours instead of days. We may argue that with the demise of sea travel as a form of transportation, but rather relaxation, the modern cruise industry was born.

Although ship travel has long been a part of human history, the idea of the pleasure cruise is relatively new. Kelly Ann Whiting (2010) notes that the modern cruise industry, which promoted the idea of traveling for pleasure rather than purpose, can be traced back to the 1980s (Witting, 2010).

In 2010, Nassim Nicholas Taleb published his book on the improbable called the *Black Swan*. The book was an extension of his ideas first found in his 2001 book, *Fooled by Randomness*. Taleb argues that there are times when the unexpected impacts both business and history. The U.S. cruise ship industry may be an example of the Black Swan phenomenon. Starting in 1977 (and in production until 1986) first American television viewers, and then audiences from around the world, became enthralled with a television show called *The Love Boat*. It featured voyages to nowhere, romanticized the idea of the cruise, and seemed to indicate that cruises were places where love blossomed and good times flourished. The show's influence was enormous. For example, Josh Dale (1997) has written in his academic article entitled "Cruising the Love Boat: American Tourism and Postmodernism Sublime": ". . .the Love Boat promoted the cruise ship experience as exciting and glamorous; suddenly, to take a cruise was to enter a mobile, never-ending party" (p. 166). Dale goes on to state: ". . .when Carnival Cruises also began aggressive promotion of the party-ship concept, the stage was set for the revitalization of the cruise ship industry and a revolution in American tourism. Today, cruise ships are a seven billion dollar industry in the United States alone, and the overwhelming majority of their passengers are Americans" (p. 166).

The Sociology of Cruise Passengers as Tourists

The ideal tranquil seas, as depicted in *The Love Boat,* have not always been a reality. Cruise passengers, above all, are tourists. Although they have special needs, their basic actions and needs are those of other tourists. Cruise ships, however, have special needs. These are floating hotels often in international waters. Their crews are often composed of a myriad of nationalities; all must adhere to the ship's policies, but the staff members do not come with the same set of cultural baggage. Passengers and crew from multiple countries and cultures occupy the same limited space and often come to the cruise with different perceptions of what is or is not acceptable behavior. These cultural differences when combined with the intensity of close quarters of a cruise ship and often little alone time on the part of both crew and passengers may lead to special problems. This cacophony of personalities at sea without a means of physical separation translates into both psychological and physical challenges. In such a closed social environment, we can view acts such as pilferage from an entirely different perspective.

To a great extent, a cruise ship is an all-inclusive hotel on the high seas. As such, much of what applies to lodging security also applies to cruise ships. The makeup of many of the cruise industry's passengers, however, may be different. It should be noted that cruise ships often cater to special niche markets such as the over-50 crowd or gay tourists. Each of these groups may have special safety and security needs.

Because the people are away from home, their homes also become more vulnerable. For example, a CNN report stated that:

> This weekend's hot story involves a now former Royal Caribbean employee who has been accused of using customer information to burglarize cruise travelers while they were off on vacation.
>
> CNN.com reports that Bethsaida Sandoval, 38, has been arrested and charged for 24 counts of burglary in Palm Beach County; Sandoval admitted that she and her husband were involved in the crimes, according to the probable cause affidavit, using her position with the cruise line to source victims' home addresses.
>
> **("Royal Caribbean employee arrested," 2010, para. 2–3)**

Issues of Cruise Security and Safety

Despite famous shipwrecks in modern history, cruises were not only "not seen" as dangerous, but also the public perception of the cruise was that it was a glamorous, safe way to travel. This perception of safety was based on a number of assumptions or lack of knowledge, including:

- The media presented that rare ship disaster as the exception rather than the rule. Thus, despite such incidents as the 1956 collision between the *MV Stockholm* and the *Andrea Doria* resulting in its sinking off the coast of Massachusetts, most people tended to view these incidents as exceptions.
- Being on the sea rather than in the air gave the psychological perception of a greater sense of personal control.
- Crimes on cruise ships were rarely reported, thus increasing the perception that crimes ranging from robbery to sexual assault rarely if ever occurred.
- Piracy was considered part of a romantic past.
- Despite the 1985 terrorist acts against the *Achille Louro* resulting in the murder of Leon Klinghoffer, terrorism was not taken as a serious threat to the cruise industry.
- Shipboard illnesses were rarely reported.

In the second decade of the twenty-first century, the public became acutely aware of the fact that cruise security was much more complicated than first believed. For example, the Carnival cruise ship *Splendor* was in the news in 2010, as it dealt with a major shipboard fire. The fire that knocked out the cruise ship's electricity forced passengers to live in both uncomfortable and at times less than sanitary conditions. The fire was also a major marketing nightmare and produced headlines such as "As tugboats haul in unhappy passengers, how safe is a cruise?" (Elliott, 2010). *Splendor's* fire resulted in the following:

- A major loss of revenue for the Carnival cruise ship line.
- Thousands of inconvenienced and unhappy passengers. There was also a considerable cost to Carnival as the company had to refund the passengers' full fares.
- The fact that the United States had to send Coast Guard ships to rescue the passengers has now turned into an open question as to who is obligated to pay for rescue operations.
- Carnival received a great deal of unwanted publicity in the world media.

Splendor's misfortunes serve as an example of the interrelationship between the various components of tourism surety. These components consist of (1) security, (2) safety, (3) reputation, and (4) economic or financial liability. In the above case, the safety/security mishap turned into both a reputational fiasco and a financial loss.

If the *Splendor's* troubles were not enough, cruise passengers have had to face crimes during their shore visits. For example, on the eastern Caribbean island of St. Kitts, some 17 cruise ship passengers on a tour bus were robbed at gunpoint (Askin, 2010). Although the cruise line cannot be blamed for what goes on off the ship, the fact that 17 of its customers were robbed during a planned shore excursion points to the fact that cruises are more than mere love boats in the sun, that cruise security and land security are often intertwined, and that what happens on board can impact a cruise's port-of-call and vice versa.

Tourism Safety, Security, and Surety

There can be little doubt that these cruise mishaps have had an impact on the industry's reputation. In June 2013, CNN reported that: "Nearly 20% of cruise (passengers) reported problems on cruises" (Ebrahimji, 2013). Many of these problems are not necessarily security or safety issues, but the fact still remains that, according to CNN, about 18% of cruise passengers report having had some problem. In a parallel article, CNN reports the following issues:

- *Emergency systems aren't designed for a pleasant trip.*
- *Itineraries can change without notice and cruise lines may change a ship's course midvoyage.*
- *Passenger compensation often is not required.*
- *Cruise ship inspections vary by ship and country.*
- *Passengers may have a legal case.*

(Hunter, 2013)

It should be noted, however, that although there are problems with cruise ships, the great majority of passengers indicate a willingness to return for another cruise. Despite the negative publicity, most cruise passengers travel without incident, and based on the number of repeat cruise takers, they appear to be satisfied with their cruise experience.

As noted in previous chapters, security has been divided into issues of safety and of security. As in other forms of tourism, these two aspects merge into what this book calls tourism surety. Tarlow has written extensively on tourism surety, noting that although many disciplines make a clear distinction between security and safety, tourism scientists and professionals do not. There is no one standard distinction between safety and security. In this book we define safety as the act of protecting people against unintended consequences of an involuntary nature. We define security as the act of protecting a person or object against a person or thing that intentionally seeks to harm. For example, a spontaneous fire is a safety issue, but when the fire is lit on purpose, it becomes arson and is now a security issue. Because tourism safety/security are customer driven in the travel and tourism industry, both a safety and a security mishap can destroy not only a vacation but also a local travel and tourism industry. Another reason for the use of the term "surety" (a term borrowed from the insurance industry) is that surety refers to a lowering of the probability that a negative event will occur. Tourism surety must not only worry about known potential problems such as health risks, but also always be aware of the potential for a "Black Swan incident." Surety specialists would be foolish to promise perfection, but rather they can offer nothing more than improvements in security and must constantly remind the public that to live is to risk.

As in other forms of tourism, cruises are vulnerable to a host of issues and the cruise's risk manager must take a number of realities into account. Among these are:

- The public demands total safety/security although there is no such thing in life as 100% security and safety.
- Any incident on board a cruise ship will become fodder for the media.
- Cruise ships provide an enclosed environment, that means that health issues may spread quickly.
- Risk managers and security personnel must deal with a number of concurrent tourism safety and security issues as passengers, in most cases, are not only on the sea, but also visiting ports of call.
- There are numerous layers of laws enforced during the cruise, which means that as the cruise ship's position changes, so do the regulations and laws to which the ship, its crew, and passengers are subjected.
- Cruise tourism must take into account that the floating hotel is subject to both man-made and nature-made disasters.
- Man-made disasters are both of a criminal and terroristic nature.
- Recovery on sea may take longer and be more difficult than recovery on land. Additionally, on land, many communities have established special police units to aid in the tourism industry, but there are still a great many questions concerning how tourism security should be handled on the sea and at the ports serving both air and sea transportation.

The Component Parts of Tourism Surety

In previous chapters we have divided the field of tourism surety into six component parts or challenges:

1. Customers/travelers do not always use common sense
2. Issue of anomie
3. Decrease of inhibitions
4. Increase of stress
5. Increase of both risk-taking and fear
6. Increased sense of the importance of time

Although these phenomena occur in all areas of tourism, aquatic tourism has its own special spin on these six phenomena. Thus, when it comes to cruise surety, these challenges still exist but now become even more difficult. Table 6.1 lists some of the similarities and challenges between land and cruise surety components.

Other differences or further complications between land and cruise tourism are:

- *Traveler Protection.* Tourism surety assumes that security professionals and police will need to know how to protect visitors from locals who might seek to do them harm, from other visitors who may be in transit for the purpose of committing crime, and less than honest staff members. Tourism surety also seeks to protect the visitor from tourism professionals who may be willing to commit fraud or sell them a product that is defective. In the world of cruising this task is especially challenging and must be broken down into several parts. Due to the fact that the cruise is a traveling hotel, it is a hybrid between land and sea travel. This means that there are multiple law enforcement agencies and laws involved during the cruise. There is also the need to protect cruise passengers from staff members and from other passengers. Also there is the problem that cruises must adhere to schedules and if a passenger does not return to the ship or is the victim of a criminal incident while on land, a great deal of confusion may ensue. Included in this confusion is how are criminal complaints made, does the ship remain in port, and do unsavory characters take advantage of the fact that shore time is limited and that police may not be able to do anything to protect a victim in the short time allotted to shore time?

- *Protection of Staff.* A cruise industry that does not care about its staff (workers) cannot long survive. The second aspect of a tourism surety program is to find ways to ensure that honest staff members can work in an environment that is crime free and not hostile. To work on a cruise is a high-pressured industry and it is all too easy for staff members to be abused or for tempers to flare leading to a hostile work situation. Staff members must often bunk with someone from a different culture. Sharing a room is never easy, but when there are potential cultural or values differences, slight disagreements can turn into security issues. Staff

Table 6.1 Land versus Water Tourism

Phenomena	Commonality with land tourism	Difference with land tourism
Lower levels of common sense	As in the case of land tourism, people often tend to react rather than think and make mistakes that they would not do were they not on vacation.	The sea presents additional dangers such as rough waves, issues of illness, and the risk of falling overboard.
Anomic behavior	High levels of anomic behavior may manifest themselves.	Each port-of-call may have a different language, laws, and customs, meaning that what is true in one place may not be correct in another place.
Lower levels of inhibitions	Inhibition levels are often determined by the people with whom one is traveling. Younger people or people alone and in situations of anonymity may be more prone to lowering of inhibitions.	Sea travelers often have a false sense of security. This, mixed with high levels of alcoholism, late-night parties, and cultural differences, may result in sexual assaults or other antisocial activities. There is the sense that what happens on the water is really not reality.
Increase of stress levels	Land travel often produces stress, especially when air travel is involved.	Once on-board ship, most levels of stress decrease. The same cannot be said for ports-of-call.
Increase in risk and fear levels	Ironically, there appears to be a psychological bifurcation between the human fear mechanism when faced with the unknown and a denial mechanism when traveling.	Many people have a bifurcated attitude toward risk and fear. On one hand they fear the sea, but on the other hand they are willing to take personal risks with people whom they may not know well.
Issues of time and time management	Time is of the essence and a time problem can produce a great deal of both stress and anger.	Cruises are self-contained time machines. When something goes wrong there is a sense not only of loss of time, but of being out of contact and control.

members may also have to deal with unruly passengers who have left their common sense and inhibitions at home (see Table 6.1).

- *Ship Protection*. It is the responsibility of the cruise security team to protect the ship from undue damage. Ship protection can range from simply dealing with a person who becomes hostile due to too much to drink to an act of terrorism and/or piracy. Often, cruise passengers simply forget to care for furniture, appliances, or equipment. Ship surety then also takes into account the needs of the cleaning staff and engineers and seeks to ensure that the environment is both attractive and as secure/safe as possible.

- *Ecological Management*. Closely related to and yet distinct from site security is the protection of the area's ecology. In the world of cruising ecological management is especially important as the world worries about the "health" of its oceans and the ever-decreasing sea life populations. Cruise ecology, however, should not only be restricted to the physical; it also involves cultural ecology. It behooves specialists in tourism surety to protect the cultural ecology of an area that is visited. Often, ports-of-call complain of "temporary invasions" in which thousands of passengers disembark for a few hours, turn their cities into traffic challenges, and then suddenly depart. Strong cultures tend to produce safe places. On the other hand, when cultures tend to die, crime levels may tend to rise. Protecting the cultural ecology along with the physical ecology of a locale is a major preventative step that tourism surety professionals can do to lower crime rates and to ensure a safer and more secure environment.

- *Port Protection*. Although tourism security specialists tend to concentrate on the need to protect cruise passengers while they are at a port-of-call, the other side of the coin must also be noted. Not all visitors are nice or follow local customs and laws. Visitors may choose to purchase illegal products, engage in illegal sex, or do physical damage to the locale. These issues become highly complex as legal entanglements may develop between various overlapping agencies.

- *Economic Protection*. The cruise industry is a major generator of income for both the ship's homeport and for places where the cruise ship passengers visit. As such, it is open to attack from various sources. For example, terrorists may see a tourism site as an ideal opportunity to create economic havoc. Criminals do not wish to destroy a tourism locale, but rather view that locale as an ideal "fishing" ground from which to harvest an abundance of riches. As such, law enforcement agents and cruise security professionals have a special role in protecting the economic viability of each locale. How security professionals act and the methods that they use can reinforce the marketing department's message or undercut it.

- *Reputation Protection.* We only need to read the newspaper to note crimes and acts of terrorism against cruise liners receive a great deal of media attention. The classical method of simply denying that there is a problem is no longer valid and in a world of 24/7 news it is counterproductive. When there is a lapse in cruise security, the effect is long term. Some of the consequences to a ship's reputation include the ship's moving from upper- to lower-class clientele, the need to drop prices, the general deterioration of the cruise product offered, and the need for a major marketing effort to counteract the negative reputation.

General and Cruise Ship Concerns

Cruise ship passengers share a great deal of sociological commonality with other forms of leisure travelers. In *Tourism in Turbulent Times*, Tarlow (2005a, 2005b) has written of the sociology of tourists. The following is an adaptation of these principles to the world of cruise travelers.

- Travelers often tend to leave their commonsense at home. Most vacationers tend to assume that the place to which they are traveling is safe. This is certainly true of cruise passengers, many of whom believe that they are in a closed and protected environment. As such, there is a tendency to leave one's worries at home, to assume that someone else is looking out for the person traveling and that nothing will happen. Tarlow notes that the word "vacation" gives us an insight into this phenomenon. We derive the word "vacation" from the French word "vacances," meaning "vacant." A vacation then is a time of mind-vacancy, a period when we relax and tend not to think.
- It is often easy to identify cruise travelers at a port-of-call. These travelers often fail to blend in with the local culture. They may use neither local dress nor speak the local language. Unlike other forms of tourists, cruise travelers' time frames are a great deal shorter than other forms of tourism and therefore have less time to adjust to the place. Land tourism is based on a place (or group of places) that acts as the destination; in the world of cruise tourism, the cruise is the destination.
- Travelers are often in a state of anomie. To travel is to be confused. There are many reasons for this anomic state. Often cruise travelers simply ache from cramped quarters or may have had too much to drink. French sociologist David Emile Dukheim was the first to identify

and name this sociological state of disorientation. Durkheim (1893) called this disoriented state "anomie." Anomic cruise travelers are not only liable to make silly travel mistakes, to let down their guard, or simply to be careless, but those who would prey on them are well aware of this state.

- Visitors often drop inhibitions when they travel. People tend to do things on the road that they might not try at home. This lowering of inhibitions may result in experimentation, be it with drugs or sex, or simply being ruder than usual. For many, the cruise is a place where inhibitions can be safely lowered.

- To travel is to be stressed. Cruises promise stress-free vacations, but often the search for fun results in stress. Stress-related issues in cruise security mean that people tend to enter into higher levels of anomic states, tend to think in less rational ways, and are often anger-prone.

- Closely related to stress is the issue of time. Cruise passengers, like other forms of tourists, seem to be able to forgive almost anything other than loss of time. One merely has to observe how people line up for shipboard events and become frustrated if an event begins late. In such situations it is not uncommon to see the anger, disappointment, frustration, and stress on passengers' faces to understand how powerful time is in travel.

Cruise Ship Security and Safety Issues

Both tourism security specialists and law enforcement agencies fear that cruise ships can become sitting targets. Due to their size and bodily structure, cruise ships are slow-moving, carry a large number of human beings with personal wealth, and emphasize fun over security. Furthermore, they are often located far from police or military units that can come to their immediate rescue. These fears were first realized in the Mediterranean Sea when Palestinian terrorists attacked the unarmed Italian cruise ship *Achille Lauro* on October 7, 1985. After capturing the ship these terrorists murdered a disabled 69-year-old American man named Leon Klinghoffer and threw him overboard. Kinghoffer's vulnerability was that he was an American Jew who was at the wrong place at the wrong time.

After the *Achillie Lauro* incident there was a long period of quiet. In the latter part of the twenty-first century's first decade, cruise ships have had to deal with a rebirth of piracy. This phenomenon has been especially marked in the waters of the Indian Ocean off the coast of Africa. Acts of piracy and the fact that Palestinian terrorists in the 1980s attacked a cruise ship meant that cruise ships are vulnerable to at least five types of surety problems:

1. Criminal activity committed by passengers against other passengers or staff
2. Criminal activity committed by staff against passengers or other staff
3. Issues of health safety
4. Possibility of a port security breach
5. Possibility of a terrorist attack on the high seas

As of the writing of this book there are no cases of a cruise ship being attacked in the Caribbean, but pirates have attacked smaller ships and there have been a number of incidents against ships docked at Caribbean ports.

To simplify the issues of cruise safety and security, this chapter touches on several subsections as if they each were an independent entity. The reader, however, is cautioned, as an academic simplification done for reasons of readability does not necessarily translate into real-world realities where multiple situations may occur simultaneously.

Due to both safety and security issues, the cruise industry has adopted the following Cruise Passenger Bill of Rights. This Bill of Rights states:

> *The Members of the Cruise Lines International Association are dedicated to the comfort and care of all passengers on oceangoing cruises throughout the world. To fulfill this commitment, our Members have agreed to adopt the following set of passenger rights:*
>
> 1. *The right to disembark a docked ship if essential provisions such as food, water, restroom facilities, and access to medical care cannot adequately be provided onboard, subject only to the Master's concern for passenger safety and security and customs and immigration requirements of the port.*
> 2. *The right to a full refund for a trip that is canceled due to mechanical failures, or a partial refund for voyages that are terminated early due to those failures.*
> 3. *The right to have available on board ships operating beyond rivers or coastal waters full-time, professional emergency medical attention, as needed until shore-side medical care becomes available.*
> 4. *The right to timely information updates as to any adjustments in the itinerary of the ship in the event of a mechanical failure or emergency, as well as timely updates of the status of efforts to address mechanical failures.*
> 5. *The right to a ship crew that is properly trained in emergency and evacuation procedures.*
> 6. *The right to an emergency power source in the case of a main generator failure.*
> 7. *The right to transportation to the ship's scheduled port of disembarkation or the passenger's home city in the event a cruise is terminated early due to mechanical failures.*

8. *The right to lodging if disembarkation and an overnight stay in an unscheduled port are required when a cruise is terminated early due to mechanical failures.*
9. *The right to have included on each cruise line's Website a toll-free phone line that can be used for questions or information concerning any aspect of ship-board operations.*
10. *The right to have this Cruise Line Passenger Bill of Rights published on each line's Website.*

(Parrotta & Peikin, 2013, Passenger Bill of Rights section)

Cruise Ship Security Issues

The following principles translate into very specific tourism surety challenges:

*   Cruise vacationers tend to be either more reserved than the general population or more "fun-seeking" than the general population. That means that cruise crews must discern between those who seek to be pampered and those who are more adventure-seeking at sea than they would be on land.
*   Cruise-goers tend to bring large amounts of luggage that makes luggage control difficult.
*   Lowering of inhibitions may be manifested by demands and rudeness to staff.
*   Reality loss, especially on shore leave, may become dangerous.
*   Many communities have mixed feelings toward cruises and often do not have adequate police forces.
*   Cruise-goers often transfer any form of discomfort into anger.
*   As on airplanes, anger can easily be displaced onto staffs.

Other reasons to be concerned about cruise ship safety:

*   Most of the factors that apply to places of lodging apply to cruises.
*   Cruise ships are often in international waters, outside of the protection of any specific government and open to attack.
*   Cruise ships provide all four potential reasons for terrorism as noted in the section on terrorism.
*   Cruise ships may be considered by some religious fanatics to be symbolic of a decadent Western culture.
*   Cruise ships are open and historically have been easy to penetrate.
*   Few people are surprised to see great variations in dress and language on a cruise ship.
*   It is not uncommon to hide one's identity on a cruise ship.
*   Inhibitions often disappear on a cruise ship.

OTHER SECURITY ISSUES SPECIFIC TO CRUISE SHIPS

Cruise ships are moving hotels and as their passengers are both on and off the ship, the potential for security challenges is never ending. For this reason cruise security cannot be placed in a single box. Here are a few of the reasons that explain the need for cruise security to be fluid.

- Protection must be multi-tiered. Ships' passengers may be vulnerable in three places:
  1. on the open seas,
  2. at/near a port, or
  3. off-ship/on-shore.
- Passengers' profiles may attract terrorists.
  - Passengers may be wealthy.
  - Passengers may be multinational.
  - Passengers may not speak English.
  - Passengers may not report suspicious behavior.
  - Crews may be multinational and respond in different ways.
- Ship routes may bring ships close to points from which attacks are easy.
- Terrorists may be passengers or may choose to attack from another ship or plane.
- Because once an attack has occurred crisis management is difficult at best, passive protection methods are necessary.
- Evacuations may be difficult and will turn almost instantaneously into major news stories.
- Terrorism may come in the form of illnesses or contaminated food.
- Even the perception that an illness or a food poisoning incident may have been caused by terrorism may damage the industry.

Issues of Health and Cruises

To a great extent, cruise vacations are about eating. An example of the vulnerability of cruises is what happened to the cruise ship *Splendor* in November 2010. During its voyage *Splendor* lost electricity and therefore its refrigeration, resulting in the loss of much of the ship's food supply. Headlines such as "Cruise Passengers Endure Stench, Cold Food" indicate just how strong the challenge of food safety and viability are (Spagat & Watson, 2010).

Food plays not only a vital physical role in keeping us healthy, but also a vital economic and emotional role in how people often judge a vacation.

This social phenomenon is important for a land vacation but even more important for a cruise vacation, where passengers expect all-you-can-eat gourmet dining experiences. This means that the dining experience is not merely one of safety but is part of the total psychological package that the cruise line is selling to its customers. Not only must cruise lines develop the highest food safety levels possible, but also they must accomplish this safety within the confines of small quarters and in a manner that promotes the cruise experience.

Cruise Health Issues

Starting around 2006 the media reported that the cruise industry suffered from what some people at the time believed to be an issue of food terrorism. In reality no such thing happened; rather, it was a case of employees not washing their hands properly. Table 6.2 lists some of the major outbreaks in 2007 and 2008 as an example of the impact on a cruise liner due to lack of sanitation.

Like other forms of tourism, cruise ships are subject to routine sanitation inspections, and while officials report that cruise ships have demonstrated above-average sanitation procedures, even the slightest outbreak of any cruise ship irregularities attracts media attention.

OTHER HEALTH ISSUES

Viruses, such as the Norwalk virus, gain headline attention, but there are also numerous other health issues that must be considered on cruises. Assuming the crew is healthy, cruises still form a closed environment, cabin sizes are small, and ports of call may range from places where sanitation is excellent to those who have under-par sanitation standards. While it is not fair to blame a

Table 6.2 Sea Illnesses

Date of outbreak	Cruise boat struck	Number of people infected/stuck
December 2006	*Freedom of the Seas*	400 people
January 2007	*Queen Elizabeth*	300 people
May 2007	*Norwegian Star*	130 people
December 2007	*Queen Victoria*	133 people
January 2008	*Holiday*	143 people

Source: Sardone (2014)

cruise liner for an individual's overeating or sexual escapades, cruises are places where passengers often lower their moral and ethical standards, resulting in overeating, overdrinking, and sexual encounters that may result in a host of social problems. An additional problem may be "death at sea." That is, that due to a preexisting medical condition, a passenger suddenly dies. The body must be cared for and both medical and legal arrangements are needed to bring the body home.

The most recent scares of a terrorist attack indicate the importance of port security. Cruise ship and airplane travelers have major differences, for example, no one vacations on an airplane. Below are some of the social manifestations of each of these forms of travel followed by a section on port security.

Crimes on Ships

Crimes on ships are distinct from crimes against cruise ships. On the whole the cruise industry has done a good job of downplaying media attention regarding shipboard crimes. Yet a cruise ship is nothing more than a small village floating on the open seas. Joyce Gleeson-Adamidis (2010) addresses the crime situation on cruise ships by stating: "Does crime exist onboard cruise ships? Yes. Is it a common occurrence? No. Does anyone care what happens to you onboard ship? Absolutely. A mechanism of protection is in place affecting each passenger for their entire time onboard" (para. 1). Gleeson-Adamidis also notes that:

- *Cruise ships carry thousands of people and as such incidents are bound to occur.*
- *Cruise ships have extensive and constant surveillance, consisting of video cameras, security personnel, crewmembers, and a willing army of eyewitnesses to any and all events.*
- *Cruise ships are subject to regulatory laws for all ports. When problematic situations occur, local authorities are contacted and their laws adhered to.*
- *She further notes that in the case of American passengers (who make up the great majority of cruise passengers) it is standard procedure to contact the FBI when American passengers are involved.*

2010, Crime at Sea section

In opposition to what Gleeson-Adamidis states, there are a number of media reports to the contrary. For example, Boston television station WCVB-TV reported May 26, 2010, that "Investigation: Crimes on Cruise

Ships Often Not Reported." The television exposé noted "When something happens on land, you have the police involved," said Carolyn Latti, a maritime attorney in Boston who has represented hundreds of victims of crimes on-board cruise ships. "When you're on a cruise ship, when you leave the port, you basically leave your rights."

Currently, cruise ship companies are not required to report crimes to any American law enforcement. The Federal Bureau of Investigation (FBI) told Boston television news program Team 5 that there is no way to know how many vacationers become victims. Many people think that because they are U.S. citizens, the same rights apply to them once they get on the boat. However, this is simply not the case. Supporting this sentiment is an incident in which Carnival, the world's largest cruise line, reluctantly admitted in court in 1999 that its crew members had assaulted both passengers and fellow crew members 108 times from 1993 to 1998—almost twice a month. A CNN exposé even reported the following:

> *"Travelers have this idea they are in a special cocoon where nothing bad can happen," says Charles Lipcon, a leading maritime lawyer in Miami, Florida, who is representing the alleged victim from the Coral Princess and has handled more than a hundred cruise assault cases in the last decade. "That's just not true."*
>
> *Addressing cruise ship violence has become an important issue for lawmakers as the $22 billion cruise industry proliferates. About 12 million North Americans will set sail on a cruise this year, according to the Cruise Lines International Association, a trade organization representing the industry.*
>
> *Cruise crimes have made headlines in recent years, like the Connecticut newlywed who vanished from his Royal Caribbean honeymoon cruise in 2005. Last Tuesday, the U.S. Coast Guard began searching for a passenger who went missing on a Carnival cruise ship.*
>
> *Though cruise companies don't display crime statistics to the public, they are required to report serious incidents involving Americans to the FBI and U.S. Coast Guard. Salvador Hernandez, deputy assistant director at the FBI in 2007, told lawmakers that "the FBI opened 184 cases on crimes that occurred aboard cruise ships between 2002 and early 2007."*
>
> **(Chen, 2009, para. 4–7)**

It is hard to ascertain exactly what reality is. Are there crimes that occur aboard cruise ships? The answer to this question is yes, but is the rate of crime worse than on land? The answer would appear to be no, because these crimes become news and were they an everyday occurrence then the probability of these incidents becoming news would be limited. Below is a listing of some of the other forms of crime that do exist. However, it must be cautioned that there is no clear statistical data on how many, how often, or where these assaults happen.

Some forms of passenger crimes are:

- Robbery
- Stealing
- Sexual assault
- Drunken and lewd behavior

Not mentioned in the literature but also a problem is the issue of staff-on-staff violence and passenger pilferage and potential violence toward staff members.

Issues of Terrorism and Piracy

The renewal of piracy, especially off the eastern coast of Africa, means that cruise lines must now take into their risk management plans not only protecting passengers from safety issues caused by alcoholism and potential sexual assaults but also from an outside attack against the ship. Tourism security and risk managers are well aware of the multiple problems that they face on a ship. While cruise passengers exhibit all of the sociological characteristics of land-based tourists, additional complications may arise at sea. Among these are issues of international law: the fact that the crew may be composed of staff from a variety of nations, the close quarters of a cruise ship, the fact that the sea may provide additional safety challenges, and now the issue of piracy. While at the time of this writing pirates have yet to hijack a cruise ship successfully, security officials are well aware of this possibility and the ensuing media nightmare that would follow.

For example, on Saturday, November 5, 2005, CNN reported:

> *A luxury cruise line will re-evaluate whether to offer future cruises off the coast of Somalia after pirates attempted to attack one of its ships early Saturday. The pirates were in two small boats and were carrying machine guns and a rocket-propelled grenade when they attempted the attack on Seabourn Cruise Lines' "Spirit" about 5:35 a.m. local time Saturday, Deborah Natansohn, president of the cruise line, told CNNRadio.*
>
> **(Cherry & Moyer, 2005, para. 1–2)**

Africa was not the only place that caused risk managers dealing with cruise ships a great deal of worry. The Website "CruiseBruise" reported that in 2009 the following areas were open to potential piracy issues. Among these were:

Africa and Red Sea

- Gulf of Aden/Southern Red Sea
- Somali waters—eastern and northeastern coasts are high-risk areas for hijackings. Ships not making scheduled calls to ports in these areas should stay away from the coast.

- West Africa
- Abidjan
- Conakry
- Dakar
- Douala
- Freetown
- Lagos
- Tema
- Warri

South and Central America and the Caribbean
- Brazil—Rio Grande
- Venezuela
- Haiti—Port au Prince
- Dominican Republic—Rio Haina
- Jamaica—Kingston
- Peru—Callao

("Pirate Attacks on the High Seas," 2010)

Already some signs of piracy against tourists have been reported in the Caribbean. For example, according to an article that first appeared in the *Los Angeles Times*, "Attacks on yachters across the Caribbean have marred the luxurious cruising life with increasing frequency as the number of vessels sailing the lush islands grows year to year, and with it the lure of the sailors' valuables to thieves and drug traffickers in the region" (Williams, 2008, para. 5). The article then goes on to state another problem in tourism security, lack of ability to prosecute criminals, and states: "'Even if arrests are made in crimes against yachters, the victims are seldom able to return to identify or testify against their attackers,' said Chris Doyle, author of popular cruising guides for the Caribbean" (Williams, 2008, para. 18).

It is not clear if there is an interaction between politically motivated terrorist acts and economically motivated pirates. To add to a difficult situation, even when an attack is thwarted on some level the cruise industry has lost a round in the media war.

Port Security
It is impossible to separate port security from cruise security. While there may be a terrorist attack against a cruise ship on the open seas, there is a much

higher probability that such an attack will occur from a port. The reasons for this probability are numerous and include:

- Ships at port are in much shallower waters.
- An attack on a cruise ship in port might not only destroy the vessel but could do considerable damage to the buildings and neighborhoods surrounding the port.
- A terrorism attack on a cruise ship docked at port might well convince other nations to ban cruise ships for fear of a similar situation occurring on their soil.

Just as at hotels and attractions, ports are centers where visitors often need protection. The busy traveler often is running to/from gates, may have minimal control over his/her luggage, and often has no idea where his or her documents may be. Ports, especially seaports, may be centers of prostitution and the underworld, and security must always be aware that damaging the site not only knocks out the landed infrastructure (terminals or docks) but may also cause cessation of transporting of goods and passengers. In the case of the cruise industry an attack at a port might not only cause death, but also would be a major blow to the industry's economic vitality.

The connection then between the protection of a cruise ship and its port-of-call are highly interlinked. Cruise ship companies must cooperate with port security in multiple nations around the world. This multinational approach is another challenge for cruise officials. Different nations not only have different standards, but there are also different political philosophies that must be taken into consideration. In order to have cruise security there must then also be in-port security. The following are just a few of the things that port/cruise security managers must take into consideration:

- Port officials must assume that their ports, be they for shipping or air, will be targets of terrorism. This does not mean that every port will be attacked, but it does mean that any port can be attacked or can become a conduit for an attack. Ports are doorways to the transportation system. Thus, a terrorist may use one port in order to gain access into the sanitized area of another port.
- The media today is highly conscious of port security. An attack at any airport or seaport (or if an attack is launched from that port) may result in a great deal of negative publicity and economic damage for a long period of time.
- Ports are not only places through which visitors egress but also ingress. Thus, if a nation's airport is not deemed safe, the reputation loss may be felt throughout the entire local tourism industry.

Here are some suggestions to help ports adapt to a world in which destruction exists for its own sake:

- Recognize that there is a fundamental paradigm shift in the travel industry. Old assumptions will no longer hold. From a business perspective these old assumptions are very dangerous. Those parts of the travel and tourism industry that emphasize security will have a good chance of surviving. The venues that provide good security mixed with good customer service will flourish. Those parts of the travel and tourism industry that hold on to the old way of thinking will fade away.

- Cruise and port security officials need to invite specialists to help train people and to set a paradigm shift in motion. The worst thing you can do is bring in someone who is not a specialist in both security and travel and tourism. Remember this is not a passing emergency, but a new way in which people think. Port security officers must not only think security but also how that security impacts the economy of an area and the marketing potential of their actions.

- Port security and cruise security specialists must be careful never to create a false sense of security. Gas masks will do nothing in case of a biological or chemical attack, while sealed rooms may be very useful. Do not panic people, but deal with safety and security issues in the most professional manner possible. People begin to panic not when you take precautions in a professional manner, but when you fail to take precautions.

- Develop security coalitions with all components of the community. Ports are not stand-alone communities; they are part of a living community. Make sure that your port security/police department is trained and understands tourism, and that the local tourism industry understands how it needs to cooperate with port security officers. In too many cases port security personnel and tourism personnel do not even know each other's names.

HOW PASSENGERS DEAL WITH CRUISE EMERGENCIES

In today's world, most cruise ship passengers carry some form of recording device. Cruise lines and staff are aware of the fact that during onboard emergencies, these devices are often immediately activated to record multiple aspects of the emergency and how the crew handles the emergency. Often passengers post photos of the incident within hours of the event and news outlets may then broadcast these images around the world. Often passengers will state that the crew did not seem to know what to do. The reality, in most cases, however, is quite different. John Franceschi, the owner and president of Marine Safety Solutions, notes that crewmembers are well trained and that when we know the emergency response structure on a cruise ship then we can understand the crew's actions.

Franceschi notes that all ships have a document dictating the emergency response duties of the crewmembers. This document is called the *Emergency Station Bill*. All crewmembers receive an emergency duty corresponding to the station bill, in addition to their regular shipboard jobs. Common emergency duties on cruise ships include firefighting and damage control, passenger evacuation, operation of the lifeboats, and many other duties specific to protecting the lives of passengers and crew during an emergency.

Crewmembers receive regular training in their specific emergency duties. No matter how well a crewmember is trained, initial confusion is part and parcel of an emergency. Reasons for this initial confusion may be:

• Lack of initial information. The crew may at the outset not know much more than the passengers about the specific emergency.
• Lack of credible information. The exact emergency must be diagnosed.
• Dealing with potential panic on the part of passengers.

What sets the crew apart from the passengers, however, is that once the crewmembers understand what the emergency is about, they are able to move to a professional stance. Crewmembers know from training and practice drills where their proscribed emergency station is located and what to do to perform their emergency duties. Passengers often confuse what may appear to be confusion among the crew with the fact that what they see is crewmembers moving to their various stations from all parts of the ship.

Often these emergency procedures may frustrate passengers. The basic sociological principles stated earlier in this chapter kick in and passengers enter into anomic states. During the initial phase of an emergency, crewmembers may not have the time or information to answer passengers' questions satisfactorily. For example, if one crewmember's duty is to control the damage during an emergency, their training does not cover passenger evacuation and lifeboat operations, and therefore may be unable to direct passengers to their assigned lifeboat location. The average crew response time in a general emergency on a cruise ship is 5 to 8 minutes. By that time, the majority of the crew would be at their emergency stations and would be able to direct passengers as necessary. During that time, regular announcements are made from the bridge informing passengers of the nature of the emergency.

Very few incidents on cruise ships require passengers to assemble at their lifeboat stations. Far fewer situations require that the passengers actually enter the lifeboats. Cruising is one of the safest forms of vacation travel and emergency situations sensationalized by the media do not give a true reflection of industry safety standards.[1]

REFERENCES

Askin, D. (2010, November 15). Update: 17 Celebrity Cruises Passengers Robbed at Gunpoint in St. Kitts. *cruisecritic.co.uk*. Retrieved from http://www.cruisecritic.co.uk/news/news.cfm?ID=4232&sr=us,%20Nov%2015,%202010.

Chen, S. (2009, June 22). Sexual assaults on the high seas come under scrutiny. *CNN Travel*. Retrieved from http://edition.cnn.com/2009/TRAVEL/06/22/cruise.sexual.assault/.

Cherry, M. & Moyer, A. (2005, November 5). Cruise liner outruns armed pirate boats. *CNN World*. Retrieved from http://www.cnn.com/2005/WORLD/africa/11/05/somalia.pirates/.

Dale, J. (1997). Cruising the Love Boat: American Tourism and the Postmodern Sublime. *The Japanese Journal of American Studies*, *8*, 165–190. Retrieved from http://www.academia.edu/430628/Cruising_the_Love_Boat_American_Tourism_and_the_Postmodern_Sublime.

Ebrahimji, A. (2013, June 29). Nearly 20% report problems on cruises. *CNN Travel*. Retrieved from http://www.cnn.com/2013/06/28/travel/cruise-customer-satisfaction-survey/index.html.

Elliott, C. (2010, November 14). As tugboats haul in unhappy passengers, how safe is a cruise? *Courier-Post*. Retrieved from http://www.courierpostonline.com/article/20101114/LIFE/11140311/As-tugboats-haul-in-unhappy-passengers-how-safe-is-a-cruise.?nclick_check=1.

Gleeson-Adamidis, J. (2010, November 7). Crime at sea. *Cruise Critic*. Retrieved from http://www.cruisecritic.com/articles.cfm?ID=240.

Hunter, M. (2013, February 15). Five things we've learned about cruising. *CNN Travel*. Retrieved from http://www.cnn.com/2013/02/14/travel/cruises-five-things/index.html?iref=allsearch.

Parrotta, L., & Peikin, D. (2013, May 12). Cruise industry adopts passenger bill of rights. *Cruise Lines International Association*. Retrieved from http://www.cruising.org/news/press_releases/2013/05/cruise-industry-adopts-passenger-bill-rights.

Pirate attacks on the high seas. (2010). *CruiseBruise*. Retrieved from http://www.cruisebruise.com/Pirate_Attacks/Pirate_Attacks_Main_Menu.html.

Royal Caribbean employee arrested for burglarizing cruise travelers. (2010, June 13). *eTN Global Travel Industry News*. Retrieved from http://www.eturbonews.com/16676/royal-caribbean-employee-arrested-burglarizing-cruise-travelers.

Sardone, S. B. (2014, January). Sea sick: The Norwalk Virus strikes. *About.com*. Retrieved from http://honeymoons.about.com/od/cruising/a/Seasick.htm.

Spagat, E., & Watson, J. (2010, November 12). Cruise passengers endured stench, cold food. *Associated Press*. Retrieved from http://www.today.com/id/40150294/ns/today-today_travel/t/cruise-passengers-endured-stench-cold-food/#.UrCw-Xnn00Z.

Tarlow, P. E. (2005a). Terrorism and tourism. In J. Wilks, D. Pendergast, & P. Leggat (Eds.), *Tourism in Turbulent Times* (pp. 79–92). Oxford, UK: Elsevier Inc.

---

[1] Marine Safety Solutions provides safety assessment and training to the cruise industry. If you would like to know more, visit www.marinesafetysolutions.com.

Tarlow, P. E. (2005b). A social theory of terrorism and tourism. In Y. Mansfeld, & A. Pizam (Eds.), *Tourism Security and Safety* (pp. 33–47). Oxford, UK: Elsevier Inc.

Titanic sinks four hours after hitting iceberg; 866 rescued by Carpathia, probably 1250 perish; Ismay safe, Mrs. Astor maybe, noted names missing. (1912, April 16). *The New York Times.* Retrieved from http://timesmachine.nytimes.com/browser/1912/04/16/P1.

Williams, C. J. (2008, June 1). Caribbean's lush isles are a pirates' paradise. *Los Angeles Times.* Retrieved from http://articles.latimes.com/2008/jun/01/world/fg-pirates1.

Witting, K. (2010). How has the cruise industry evolved. *cruiseshipguides.com.* Retrieved from http://www.cruiseshipsguide.com/Article-CruiseIndustryEvolves.html.

CHAPTER 7

Transportation: Travel by Air, Car, and Train

INTRODUCTION

On July 6, 2013, Asiana Airlines Flight 214 from Seoul, South Korea, destined for San Francisco with 307 people on-board, crashed, injuring 182 people and killing 2. The incident dominated the U.S. news. Newscasters and media journalists analyzed every minute of the crash and the events leading up it. For at least 2 days, it appeared as if nothing else occurred in the world. In reality, a great deal was occurring, from a bloody civil war in Syria, to major economic crises in Europe, to gang murders in Chicago. Other news simply ceased to exist while the attention of the U.S. media became fixated on the crash of Asiana Flight 214, with the media paying a great deal of attention on issues of human error.

This chapter does not enter into the engineering details of plane crashes; however, it does examine the public's perception of what it perceives to be a danger in the skies and how these perceptions are translated into the world of tourism surety. "Surety" is the key word here for numerous reasons. The Western world is as dependent on air traffic for travel and commerce as the ancient world was dependent on water transportation. In other decades control of the seas and rivers meant not only control of economies, but it also transformed into military prowess. In today's world, sea travel is still necessary for commerce and often for military success, but ever since the Berlin airlift of 1948, the public has understood the importance of aviation as a military and political tool. By the 1960s, businesses became international and began working across borders and in many different countries. This internationalization meant that many businesspeople became dependent on efficient and safe air travel in order to conduct business around the world. The aviation industry also promoted air travel as a luxurious experience, and thus people could now fly with ease and comfort to their vacation spots or combine air and car travel in what was called a "fly-drive vacation." In all of these areas, the public assumed that despite the fact that a person was thousands of miles above the earth, air travel was safe and efficient. Air safety became of paramount importance, especially as the world of aviation entered into the age of the jumbo jets.

THE DISTINCTION BETWEEN SECURITY AND SAFETY

If we distinguish security from safety, in the earlier decades security was a different issue in aviation. The hijackings of multiple planes to Cuba in the 1960s were often taken at first in a somewhat light-hearted manner. In most cases, airplanes were hijacked for a short while and the passengers and plane were soon returned. In October 2012, Patrick Weidinger, a specialist in aviation security and hijackings, called the period between 1958 and 1970 the "golden age of hijackings." In 1969, there were 82 planes hijacked from the United States to Cuba. During this period, it was not clear what was to be done with hijackers or how to prevent hijacking. Although these hijackings were relatively benign, they alerted the public to the fact that not only did air travelers have to worry about the flight's safety but also about the flight's security. To add to this confusion, no one was quite sure if these were political acts, criminal acts, copycat actions, or pranks. Not only did hijackings destroy people's travel schedules, but also no one knew where the rash of hijackings would lead. This so-called Golden Age came to its conclusion in 1973 when (1) Cuba and the United States agreed that hijackers would be returned to the United States for criminal prosecution, and (2) the United States introduced the metal detector.

Table 7.1 indicates that the U.S. hijackings may have begun with political motives, but soon became vehicles for robbery and extortion. The preferred weapon of choice was a gun, but the claim that a bomb was on-board became an important new weapon. What began as an inconvenience soon turned into a very different and more deadly experience. By the 1980s, hijacking (or "skyjacking" as it came to be known) was no longer a mere inconvenience, but had become a deadly political weapon. A few incidents show the extent of how deadly hijacking had become.

NOTABLE HIJACKINGS

The Entebbe Hijacking, June 27, 1976

On June 27, 1976, Palestinian and German terrorists hijacked an Air France plane flying from Tel Aviv to Paris via Athens with 250 passengers on-board. They diverted the plane to Entebbe, Uganda, where it came under the protection of the Ugandan President Idi Amin. He supported the hijackers with both extra troops and arms. The hijackers separated passengers who were either Jewish or Israeli and on July 1, 1976, released the non-Jewish passengers who were then flown to Paris. The crew was given the choice of leaving, but chose to stay with the plane and remaining passengers, all of whom

Table 7.1 A List of Some of the Most Famous U.S. Hijackings

Hijacking	Date and destination desired	Name of hijacker	Weapon used
US Airlines Convair #440	May 1, 1961/Cuba	Antulio Ramirez Ortiz	Knife and gun
Pan Am #281	Nov. 24, 1968/Cuba	Three men, one called Castro	Gun
Eastern Airlines #1320	March 17, 1970/ Boston	John Divivo	Gun
TWA #727	November 1971/ Africa (intended) Cuba (actual)	Charles Hill, Ralph Lawrence, and Albert Finney	Guns
Northwest Orient #305	Nov. 24, 1971	Dale Cooper	Bomb in suitcase
Braniff # 39	Jan. 12, 1972/ Unsuccessful attempt to get to South America	Billy Gene Hurst, Jr	Gun
TWA #2	January 28, 1972/LA to NYC	Garrett Trapnell	Threatened to crash plane
American Airlines # 119	June 23, 1972/St. Louis to Tulsa	Martin J. McNally	Copies Dale Cooper's 1971 attempt
Delta # 841	July 31, 1972/Algeria	Three men, one woman	Guns
Southern Airways #49	November 10, 1972/ around U.S., ends up in Cuba	Melvin Cale, Louis Moore and Henry D. Jackson, Jr	Threaten to crash plane into building or city

were then transferred to an airport terminal building. On July 4, 1976, Israeli commandos attacked the Entebbe Airport and rescued most of the passengers. The death toll included 3 passengers, 20 Ugandan soldiers, all 7 hijackers, and 1 Israeli soldier. The Israeli commandos also destroyed 11 Russian MIG fighters. The remaining 97 passengers were flown to Tel Aviv.

TWA Flight 847, June 14, 1985

Members of Hezbollah and Islamic Jihad hijacked TWA Flight 847 enroute from Rome to Athens and took the plane to Amman, Jordan. After murdering a U.S. naval diver, the plane was taken on an odyssey to other Arab capitals including Algiers and Beirut. Many of the passengers were not released until the end of June. The capture of the TWA flight proved that, as a political and propaganda tool, hijacking was a very powerful instrument. It attracted a great deal of media and was a successful instrument in convincing the Israeli government to release some 700 prisoners. It would also lessen airline passengers' sense of security. Not only might they be inconvenienced, but also they might be held captive for weeks, and, in a style reminiscent of the Nazi era, people might be killed due to their nationality or religious affiliation.

Indian Airlines Flight IC-814, December 24, 1999

Five Pakistani hijackers took control of Indian Airlines Flight IC-814 traveling to Delhi from Kathmandu with 180 passengers on-board. The terrorists killed a number of passengers and took the plane first to Pakistan and then to Dubai where 27 hostages and the body of Rupen Katyal were released. The plane then left for Kandahar, Afghanistan. The other passengers were released in India, freeing three terrorists. Once again, it became clear that hijacking was a successful terrorism tool.

September 11, 2001

The hijackings that occurred on September 11, 2001, may be the world's most famous cases of plane hijacking. These multiple acts at the same time changed the course of aviation security and demonstrated clearly to the world that a civilian aircraft could be used as a weapon of mass destruction. Prior to the attacks on September 11, most hijackings were of a limited scope, and although there were actions such as the Entebbe raids, most people did not necessarily integrate these acts of terror into their private lives. The 9/11 attacks not only demonstrated how vulnerable a major world power was to a well-coordinated hijacking used for military purposes against civilian targets, but created a major economic shock wave that impacted a great deal of the United States and world economies. The attacks demonstrated that tourism was now at the forefront of nonconventional warfare, that civilian homefront populations were highly vulnerable to attack, and that in a world of interconnected economies, such an attack could damage national economies around the world. The attacks not only resulted in the deaths of thousands of innocent victims, but also further demonstrated how much both U.S. and international businesses had become dependent on the air transportation system over the last few decades.

ISSUES OF COMMONALITY IN HIJACKINGS

There are certain goals that most hijackers have in mind when planning a hijacking, which include:

- *Media attention.* Most hijackers do not seek financial gain, but rather seek publicity or political success for a particular cause. The old adage that "all publicity is good publicity" is true for hijackings. The hijacking of a plane receives wide media coverage. This coverage means that the group's cause and name now become public. From the hijackers' perspective, the longer the incident lasts, the more publicity their cause receives.

- The airline industry is a major part of not only the transportation industry but also the tourism industry. In fact, anything that hurts the tourism industry also hurts a state or nation's overall economy. When terrorists hijack a plane, they not only receive media coverage, but they also cause both immediate and long-term economic loss. A terrorist hijacking may also result in loss of life. Even failed attacks produce a great amount of inconvenience for the traveling public. The case of Richard Reid, the infamous "shoe bomber," serves as a perfect example. On December 22, 2001, Reid attempted to bomb American Airlines Flight 63 from Paris to Miami. The public was still reeling from the 9/11 attacks that had occurred earlier that year, and Reid was apprehended by a flight attendant and other passengers. Although Reid was arrested, he succeeded in further damaging the airline industry by causing a new policy to be implemented. Passengers in nations such as the United States were now required to remove their shoes for inspection before boarding a flight. This measure was meant to be an additional protection measure, but many airline passengers questioned if shoe removal was nothing more than a bureaucratic overreaction. It is not clear if shoe removal made air travel safer.

Some scholars have attempted to measure airline security on a cost–benefit basis. In an essay titled "Assessing the Risks, Costs and Benefits of United States Aviation Security Measures" by Stewart and Mueller, the authors note that although the hardening of cockpit doors has proved to be cost-effective, the use of air marshals has not. Their analysis reduces hijacking to a statistical number. Such a number may have great value from an actuarial perspective, but tourism is not only about numbers. It is a business with a long after-life and often lives as much on perceptions as it does on facts. Thus, the traveling public, especially the leisure traveling public, often panics and this sense of panic may, if enough media attention is given to the incident, last for many years (Mueller & Stewart, 2008).

Hijacking then takes on at least three different aspects. First, on a national level, it may become part of the political or economic narrative within that country. Many nations have developed both preventative and legal policies to deal with internal hijackings. Second, on the international level, hijackings can become a more complicated issue. For example, the hijacker may take the plane to a country that has no diplomatic relations with the nation of origin or is at a state of war with the latter nation. The United Nations has enacted a number of conventions and protocols to deal with hijacking and considers it an unlawful act. These acts, however, do not mean that any particular nation may choose to respect the protocols of an enemy nation, or protect its citizens. Thus, there is the potential for innocent civilians to be held as hostages or pawns. Third, the hijacking may do great harm to a nation's tourism industry, to its reputation, and to its overall economic well-being.

COUNTER-HIJACKING MEASURES

For all of the above reasons, tourism industries, airlines, and national governments have joined forces to prevent airline hijackings. Although at first most people did not realize the seriousness of hijackings. (There are a few exceptions to this statement, such as the Israeli airline, EL AL. In fact, EL AL has built a reputation on being a secure airline and has often been able to charge higher fares due to the fact that the airline is perceived to be safe.) After 9/11 most people understood that hijacking was an act of asymmetrical warfare. Once that perception entered into the public, governmental, and business consciousness, new rules were developed and it soon became clear that simply asking for a person's driver's license and if the passenger packed his or her own bags was not enough.

Current counter-hijacking measures are based around a series of concentric circles. These include:
- Encouraging passengers to become aware of their surroundings and fellow passengers.
- Hardening the airport's defenses and creating "sanitized" zones.
- Greater examination of luggage.
- Making the plane itself more secure.

Each one of these steps has a series of substeps. Often visitors turn to popular Web sources for information concerning what to do. The following is an example of one of these popular Web-based sources and the information that it gives to its readers. In the e-line news service "wikiHow," six steps are given for passengers to protect themselves against a terrorist attack. These include:

1. Before boarding the plane, be alert to what is going on around you. There should be no unattended luggage. Passengers want to be sure that they have full control of their own luggage and that no piece of luggage is ever left unattended. In a like manner, the now famous phrase "see something, say something" is an important part of personal security. If you feel something is wrong, then listen to your gut.
2. Being aware of what other terrorists have done in the past, such as the shoe bomber and the underwear bomber. The authors point out that alert passengers are safe passengers.
3. Choose proper clothing. Airplanes are not meant to be fashion shows; they are meant as forms of transportation. Wearing light, comfortable, and nonflammable clothing is an important part of a personal evacuation should that ever be needed. Women should not wear heels, and people should use vision aids that are least likely to fail during an emergency.
4. Listen to and read about the plane's safety steps. Too many people simply do not listen to the flight attendant's briefings and then review visually the passengers who are in close proximity. Ask yourself in case of an emergency: who is the strongest person in close proximity, where are children located, and how close am I to an emergency exit?
5. Have a plan in mind should there be an attack. The old pattern of simply doing nothing and thereby appeasing the attacker may no longer be the best plan. However, you do not want to stand out in a crowd or raise the attacker's suspicion or anxiety level. Decide if you want to attack first or be submissive and establish a rapport with your abductors.
6. Should you decide to fight: be prepared that the person may have a knife. Do not try to take the attacker on alone, but rather think how you can get other passengers to aid in the attack. Your highest chance of success will come if you can catch the hijackers off guard (http://www.wikihow.com/End-a-Plane-Hijacking).

HARDENING THE TERMINAL

Experts in security use the word "hardening" to mean making a target less vulnerable or making it less susceptible to an attack. It should always be remembered that there is no such thing as 100% security. All life, reputations, and locations are always vulnerable and there is nothing made by human beings that cannot be destroyed. Nevertheless, experts can lessen a locale's vulnerability, and this lessening is called "hardening."

In the United States, airport and security professionals after the 9/11 attacks realized that they could not merely depend on passengers, but that airport terminals would have to become harder to target. To make the airports less likely targets, numerous measures have been taken around the world. Many airports were built, however, in a different era, and the airport's architecture does not lend itself easily to airport security, checkpoints, and metal detectors. Often airports need to be redesigned so as to accommodate a world that demands greater security. Airports have developed numerous ways to increase security. These include:

1. Vehicles are not permitted in close proximity of the terminal.

2. Vehicles are examined before being allowed to enter the terminal's premises. The preparking scan, however, is not easy to accomplish, as passengers normally carry baggage with them, and the opening of car trunks or the random scanning of vehicles hardens the target, but does not ensure security. Newer airports are taking into account the principles of CPTED (crime prevention through environmental design) and the CPTED offshoot TPTED (terrorism protection through environmental design). For example, many airports have found ways to remove blind spots from their security observers so that security personnel have a clear line of sight not only from the naked eye, but also via observational points and cameras.

3. The use of body scanners and metal detectors. Perhaps the most common way to protect a large part of the airport and its airplanes is through the use of mechanical devices such as body scanners and metal detectors. Certainly these machines have proved themselves effective in having found numerous weapons and other prohibited objects. Nevertheless, it should be noted that they are only as effective as the people watching the machine. Although a great many weapons have been caught, there are still too many that get past these machines. Furthermore, often airport security machine personnel demonstrate lack of motivation (or overmotivation), a poor understanding of the travel experience, and signs of both physical and mental fatigue.

4. Airport peripheral areas. Security personnel have questioned some of the security measures that governments have instituted. Although the areas beyond the security checkpoints are relatively safe, the precheckpoint areas are another matter. The same can be said for many airports where people must go to pick up luggage. Not only are many of these areas minimally guarded, but because so many security personnel have been moved into other areas of the airport, there is often no one guarding luggage as it comes off the conveyor belt. This lack of human supervision produces not only luggage that is taken by mistake, but means that luggage is open to being stolen or having a foreign object placed within it.

5. Other areas of concern. Some of the other areas of concern are airport parking lots and garages, many of which are connected to the terminal and intertransportation (that connects to other forms of transportation, such as rails and bus service with the heart of the airport).

GREATER EXAMINATION OF LUGGAGE

Another method of making an airplane (and the same also applies to cruises) more secure is through the examination of cargo. In the world of air travel, cargo tends to fall into three categories:

1. Shipped cargo (e.g., packages and mail)

2. Personal cargo (e.g., checked luggage)

3. On-board cargo (e.g., carry-on luggage, handbags, medical equipment)

Each of these forms of cargo requires special treatment. From the tourism security perspective, the security professional must be able to enforce rules while acting in a civil and professional manner. Because tourism is such a media-covered industry, any mishandling of a passenger will almost immediately become a news item. On the other hand, the public demands full protection and does not tolerate security mistakes.

In the United States, as in most nations, civil aviation authorities and law enforcement agencies such as the police have been given the authority to inspect all baggage and also the traveler's person. This means that if security believes that a passenger's luggage or person may be a threat to the aircraft, other passengers, or the airport, the security professional has a right to investigate as he or she believes is necessary, or to deny boarding for that passenger. Most countries also have the following policies:

1. If the passenger refuses to cooperate, then that passenger is subject to the laws of the nation from which the aircraft is to depart. Carriers have the right to deny a passenger boarding rights should he or she not cooperate with security personnel.

2. Each nation has lists of who may perform baggage and personal examinations. The aircraft's captain always has the right to conduct further investigations even after the passenger has boarded the aircraft.

There is little doubt that the Transportation Security Administration (TSA) still has problems with its current system(s). In December 2008, it was announced that full-body scanners would be used at U.S. airports. The full-body scanners were not only disliked by the public, but took a great deal of time to pass through and, despite the government's assurances to the contrary, many people questioned their impact on personal health due to the fear of radiation. Furthermore, there were questions as to the protection of personal privacy.

The scanners were disliked enough that on May 31, 2013, Fox News reported that:

> The full-body scanners that caused an uproar for taking semi-scandalous snap-shots of fliers at security checkpoints have been removed from America's airports. The move comes after a congressional mandate and several complaints lodged by privacy-rights activists who likened the scanners to a virtual strip search. Instead, airports will now use scanners that only show generic images of bodies, according to a letter released Thursday from TSA officials to members of the House Homeland Security Committee. "As of May 16, 2013, all AIT units deployed by TSA are equipped with (the body-masking) capability. Additionally, TSA's procurement of next gen-eration AIT requires" the same body-obscuring capability, TSA Administrator John Pistole wrote in the letter, according to The Hill.
>
> **("TSA gets rid of full-body scanners at US airports," 2013, para. 1–4)**

Furthermore, many other types of scanning machines often find false-positives such as peanut butter jars, baseballs, or sports equipment. Some experts believe that the rate of false-positives falls between 18% and 35% of all baggage examined. Other experts note that screeners became less care-ful as the number of false-positives increases. Freelance writer Beth Pinsker quotes Isaac Yeffet, formerly of EL AL airlines (considered to be the world's safest airline), as stating, "Let's say I'm a screener, and I open the luggage to do a search and find chocolate or peanut butter—I'm happy because I found what the machine flagged" (Pinsker, 2003, para. 10). Yeffet goes on to state: "I can assure you, from my experience and knowledge. . .that most of the explosives will be in a false bottom" (para. 10). Yeffet notes that EL AL trains its personnel not to be machine operators, but rather to be "security profes-sionals" who can think on their own. Pinsker goes on to ask the question: "What constitutes success? The answer of course is a machine that identifies every bomb while keeping false positives to a tolerable level. That's a for-mula sure to please passengers. . ." (para. 23).

In the United States, the TSA publishes a regularly updated list of what is allowed and not allowed on planes. For passengers confused as to what may or may not be allowed, the TSA provides an online Web service that allows passengers to ask questions. Some of the items that have long been on the TSA's not-allowed list include:

• Sharp objects
• Sporting goods that may cause harm
• Guns and firearms
• Tools that can become weapons
• Martial arts and self-defense items that may become weapons

- Explosive and flammable materials, disabling chemicals, and other dangerous items
- Other items as determined by TSA agents

Perhaps the best way to handle the "what to bring" question is to realize that flying is a privilege and not a right, and that when we are on an airplane we are dealing not only with our own personal safety but also that of our fellow passengers and that of the crew.

MAKING THE PLANE ITSELF MORE SECURE

There have been various methods to ensure the hardening of the aircraft itself, especially once it is in the sky. Although no one will provide (nor should it be provided) a full list of on-board security policies, some have become well known. Among these are:

1. The use of air marshals on selective flights.
2. The locking of the cockpit door.
3. Additional training for all flight attendants. Being aware of what is happening on the plane may be a major deterrent.
4. Because most cargo is not passenger cargo (it is estimated that the number is well below 50%), it is important that cargo also be inspected. To ensure the plane's security, air cargo is subject to random searches and X-raying; other suggestions (some of which have been implemented) include the reinforcing of cargo holds and passenger plane airframes. A number of transportation companies have developed "blast-proof baggage containers" and it is rumored that EL AL now has multiple devices on board to deflect an incoming missile.

It is almost impossible to write about airline safety and ignore the EL AL model. There are those people who approve and there are those who disapprove of some of EL AL's practices, but most people have come to see this model as the standard for the industry. Although there is a great deal we do not know about EL AL security, there is also a great deal that has been made public. Included in these known facts are:

1. Airport security personnel are well-educated professionals who speak at least two languages.
2. Airport and national security agencies work together and share intelligence.
3. Israeli security agents are tested throughout the world and throughout the year. If a security person fails an infield test, he or she immediately loses his or her job.

4. When it comes to the security of its planes and passengers, EL AL ignores issues of political correctness. In EL AL, world profiling is not a bad word and is done along psychological lines.
5. Psychological profiling is also accomplished by interviewing all passengers prior to boarding the plane. EL AL does not have technicians. Instead, it has security specialists who are trained to read signals given off from every part of the body.
6. EL AL was the first to not only lock cockpit doors, but also to reinforce them.
7. EL AL planes use a system called "flight guard." This system, developed in Israel, protects planes from incoming missiles and/or flares sent off to confuse the airplane's protection system.
8. EL AL uses air marshals and well-trained flight personnel who work in concert to make sure that every EL AL flight is safe.

ISSUES OF FIRE AT AIRPORTS

Because many parts of an airport are one-way streets (entrances without exits), fire safety and design are especially important, especially in a period of time in which the majority of emphasis is on counter-terrorism. It should be remembered that a terrorist has a great many tools in his or her arsenal and the use of fire as a weapon to destroy both property and lives should not be discounted. For example, security specialists tend to see airport check-in, security, and immigration customs lines as challenges. These lines may produce bottlenecks where orderly lines quickly melt into chaos. Airports must have a fire evacuation strategy that permits the exiting of potentially large numbers of people in areas that are not designed for two-way pedestrian passages. What is true of the public areas of an airport is also true of the airport's "off-limit zones." Cargo areas are prime locales for a fire and this fire may then quickly spread to any number of locales. Should the fire in any way mix with fuel services, then a tragedy can easily turn into a catastrophe. Airport security specialists then need to identify all areas where a fire may break out and have a plan in place to contain the fire and evacuate large numbers of people in a minimum amount of time. Because airports welcome people from around the world, airport signage must be such that a person can understand it even if the person does not read the local language.

OTHER SUGGESTIONS IN HARDENING AIR TRAVEL

There are numerous methods that have been tried around the world. The author does not endorse any of the ideas found below; they are merely creative ideas. It is necessary, however, to make sure terrorists understand that we are constantly changing our security models and that we are not merely reacting to what "was," but working hard to ensure that it "will not be." Here are a few suggestions:

1. Require all flight personnel and especially pilots to have a background check, and use the top psychological models to make sure that pilots are not suicidal.
2. Consider allowing police officers to fly at a deep discount if they carry a weapon and handcuffs.
3. Determine what passengers really can and cannot carry. The belief that a plastic baggie worth less than a penny can protect a plane from exploding toothpaste is simply silly.
4. Take protective measures at both check-in counters and bag claim.
5. Have an air marshal on every flight and have this person in a different seat each time.
6. Provide pilots and other air crew with pepper spray or other similar substances.
7. Use some form of iris screening to identify passengers.
8. Develop new techniques so that if the pilot is incapable of landing the plane, others can land it with or without knowledge of special equipment.
9. Run a counter-terrorism video on the airplane prior to take-off, telling people that in case of a terrorist attack, not to panic and that the pilot may take certain precautions.
10. Make sure that the cockpit is totally isolated from the rest of the plane; use double doors or nonbreakable doors.
11. Require all crewmembers to be trained in counter-terrorism techniques.

ISSUES OF HEALTH

Although terrorism often grabs the headlines, perhaps an even more important issue is that of health. Health issues in the air take on three separate dimensions:

1. Passenger health, the ability not to get sick while flying.
2. Cross-continental and transnational health issues. This topic includes the transporting of illnesses from one place to another, and the exposing of populations to risks that normally do not exist in the host society.
3. Use of illness as a "weapon" of mass destruction. In this case, a person who is intentionally ill is sent to another airport or nation for the expressed purpose of carrying an illness from one location to another.

There are a number of health risks that can impact any airline passenger, especially when the passenger is on a long trip (4 hours or more) and seated with minimal legroom. Deep vein thrombosis, for example, may be one of the traveler's greatest risks. Most airline Websites offer some guidance on how to avoid this problem through the use of exercises in place, the encouragement of taking a walk every few hours, and care in drinking a minimum of alcohol. For example, the United Airlines Website offers the following suggestions:

- *Wear comfortable clothing and shoes.*
- *Get a good night's sleep before your trip and rest as much as possible during the flight.*
- *While away, get as many hours of sleep every day as you normally would at home. Taking short naps of 30–40 minutes will refresh you as you adjust to the new time zone.*
- *Drink plenty of water and/or juice before and during the flight to stay hydrated.*
- *Eat light meals during your flight. Also avoid caffeinated beverages and alcohol.*
- *Don't remain in one position too long; perform the simple stretches as seen below and walk when possible.*

("Tips for healthy travel," 2013)

Flying entails other risks. For example, an article written by various doctors found on the Federal Aviation Administration Website notes that:

1. *Aircraft are pressurized to be somewhere from 6,000 to 8,000 feet above sea level. This higher altitude especially for people from sea-level communities means that there is less oxygen and that gases in body cavities expand more rapidly. The doctors also note that: "Furthermore, an increase in cabin altitude will cause gases in our body cavities (abdomen, middle ear behind the ear drum, sinuses) to expand as much as 25%. This can cause problems in the abdomen (bloating or stomach cramps), ears (a crackling sensation or ear block), and respiratory tract/sinuses. . .."*
2. *Issues of jet lag, especially when one is crossing several or more time zones.*
3. *Infectious diseases. Just as in any other confined space there is a chance that an infectious disease may pass from one person to another.*

(Bagshaw et al., 2002)

Because air travel is the most common form of travel, there are bound to be in-flight emergencies ranging from the birth of a child to a heart attack. The Centers for Disease Control and Prevention published a book on health for travelers. Chapter 6 of this book states:

Worldwide, more than one billion people travel by commercial aircraft every year, and this number is expected to double in the next 20 years. Increasingly, large aircraft combined with an aging flying population makes the incidence of onboard medical emergencies likely to increase. Approximately 1 in 10,000 to 40,000 passengers has a medical incident during air transport. Of these, approximately 1 in 150,000 requires use of in-flight medical equipment or drugs. The most commonly encountered in-flight medical events, in order of frequency, are the following:

1. *Vasovagal syncope*
2. *Gastrointestinal events*
3. *Respiratory events*
4. *Cardiac events*
5. *Neurologic events*

Deaths aboard commercial aircraft have been estimated at 0.3 per 1 million passengers; approximately two-thirds of these are caused by cardiac problems.

(Marienau, Illig, Kozarsky, & Gallagher, 2013)

In addition to standard first-aid kits, depending on the size of the aircraft and applicable regulations, enhanced emergency medical kits may include, but are not limited to:

- Automatic external defibrillators
- Intubation equipment (pediatric and adult)
- CPR masks (pediatric and adult)
- Intravenous access equipment and solutions
- Intravenous dextrose
- Antihistamines (oral and injectable)
- First-line cardiac resuscitation drugs (atropine, epinephrine, lidocaine)
- Nitroglycerin
- Bronchodilators
- Analgesics

DISEASES CARRIED FROM ONE NATION OR CONTINENT TO ANOTHER

In 2011, the movie *Contagion* was released as a major motion picture. The movie is part of an ongoing genre of movies dealing with pandemics. Scientists and pandemic experts noted the accuracy of *Contagion*. The movie deals with a fast-moving pandemic. As in real life the medical community must not only scramble to find a cure, but it is unclear who may be transmitting the disease and what the role of air transportation may be in the spreading of the pandemic. The movie underlines the fact that it is not only the disease that is creating social havoc on a macro level but also the human proclivity to panic in the face of a silent killer. The panic causes the unraveling of much of society and this unraveling becomes a crisis in and of itself.

Although the movie is pure fiction, it serves to remind the tourism security professional that travelers, especially international travelers, may transmit diseases from one part of the world to another, either knowingly or unknowingly. This potential hazard is especially true if the host country has wiped out the disease and its population is not immune to it. Because airlines are not only an enclosed space but also carry people from multiple nationalities the potential to transmit disease is extremely high. Furthermore, most airlines use a hub-and-wheel method for flights and this means that people from various parts of the world may be feed into one hub. Thus, the passengers on a plane may have originated in various locations. The potential for illness may begin in the host locale, pass onto one or more terminals, be carried on an airplane, and finally infect people in the receiving locale. In June 2012, CNN provided a list of the 10 top airports for spreading diseases in the United States (Table 7.2).

Table 7.2 Air Travel Risk

Rank for spreading disease	Name of airport	Location
1	John F. Kennedy (JFK)	New York
2	Los Angeles (LAX)	California
3	Honolulu (HNL)	Hawaii
4	San Francisco International Airport (SFO)	San Francisco, California
5	Liberty Airport (EWR)	Newark, New Jersey
6	O'Hare International Airport (ORD)	Chicago, Illinois
7	Dulles International Airport	Serves DC, in Virginia
8	Hartsfield-Jackson (ATL)	Atlanta, Georgia
9	Miami International Airport (MIA)	Miami, Florida
10	Dallas/Fort Worth International Airport, (DFW)	DFW (Grapevine) Texas

To add to the problem is the case of a media scare concerning a new pandemic. At least during the initial period it may not be clear where transmission is found or what the incubation period may be. Some of the airborne illnesses that have worried both medical personnel and travelers alike are:

- Tuberculosis
- Severe acute respiratory syndrome (SARS)
- Common colds
- Influenzas
- Meningococcal diseases
- Malaria
- Dengue
- Measles
- Food-borne illnesses

A good example of a false panic is SARS. The so-called SARS pandemic became a media event and did a great deal of damage to both Hong Kong and Toronto, Canada. In the case of Toronto, there were many more traffic fatalities than there were deaths caused by SARS and no one outside of a hospital environment was stricken with the illness. Another example is the 2006 outbreaks of avian (bird) flu (H5N1) in various nations around the world. These outbreaks caught the tourism industry's attention. Despite the great amount of publicity given to avian flu, it is important to note that as of this writing there have been less than 700 people so far who have contracted the disease.

The SARS panic caused far fewer deaths than did traffic accidents in the impacted places, but the panic that SARS caused created economic havoc. Although the media was a major component in scaring the public, reality proved to be different than what was stated on television. The tourism security officer then needs to be aware of not only the facts but also the perception of the facts as presented in the media. As a tourism security specialist you need to know that:

- *Tourism is highly vulnerable to a panic situation.* The days after 9/11 ought to have retaught the tourism industry that for most people travel is a leisure purchase based on want rather than need. If travelers become afraid they may simply cancel their trips. In such cases, there may be massive layoffs of tourism workers.
- *You must be prepared to take care of sick employees and their families.* The people staffing the tourism industry are also human. That means that their families and they are also susceptible to illnesses. Should large numbers of staff (or their families) become sick, hotels and restaurants may have

to close simply due to manpower shortages. Tourism industry people need to develop plans on how they will maintain their industry while suffering from manpower shortages.

- *Security personnel must be prepared to take care of visitors who fall ill and may not know how to contact local medical authorities or even speak the language of the local doctors.* Another problem to be considered is how the tourism industry will aid people who fall sick while on vacation. Medical notices will need to be distributed in multiple languages; people will need ways to communicate to loved ones and to describe symptoms to medical personnel in their own language.

- *Security personnel must be prepared to fight against a pandemic not only from the medical perspective, but also from the marketing/information perspective.* Because the public may well panic it is important that the tourism industry be prepared to offer concrete and credible information. This information should be given to the public almost immediately. Every tourism office should have an information plan ready should a pandemic occur in its area. Develop creative Websites so that people can gain information any time of the day and without regard to where they may be located.

- *Security personnel must be prepared to counter negative publicity with an action program.* For example, in areas that have been impacted by a disease, make sure to advise travelers to stay current with their vaccinations and create medical information sheets. It is essential that the public know where to go for information, as well as what is true versus what is false. For travelers who may not be up-to-date with current shots, offer lists of doctors and clinics willing to accept traveler's insurance.

- *An up-to-date first-aid kit and proper preventative procedures at hotels and other places of lodging.* For example, make sure that employees use antibacterial hand wipes and encourage hotels to provide these for travelers.

- *Security personnel must be prepared to work with travel insurance companies.* In case of a pandemic, travelers may not receive value for money and may desire to either cancel a trip or cut it short. The best way to maintain good will is by working with such organizations as the United States Travel Industry Association (in Canada, it is called Travel and Health Industry Association of Canada). Develop travel health programs with these organizations so that visitors feel financially protected.

- *Be prepared to work with the media.* A pandemic is like any other tourism crisis and should be treated as such. Prepare for it before it strikes. If it should occur, set your action plan in place and make sure that you work with the media. Finally, have a recovery plan set so that once the crisis has abated you can begin a financial recovery program.

The bottom line is that air travel may not produce illnesses, but the transfer of large numbers of people from one place to the next may be a source of worry not only for medical authorities, but also for tourism security professionals.

TERRORISM-BASED ILLNESSES

If an unintentional disease or pandemic can send the tourism industry into a panic, then an intentionally planned attack could have catastrophic results. Tourism security specialists realize that their industry could be used as part of some form of biological warfare.

Tourism is based on the premise that we live in an interconnected world. For the most part, this interconnectivity has brought a great deal of benefits to millions of people. Nevertheless, there is nothing gained in this world without a price. One of the prices we all pay for bringing the world together is that we are not only open to new cultural experiences, but also new biological threats. As *Newsweek* noted in its April 29, 2009, issue in reference to the swine influenza:

> The central driver is the increasingly interconnected world we live in. Even the most remote areas of the planet can now be reached in less than 48 hours. Diseases now plaguing those in refugee camps, heavily populated and growing slums or the most remote tropical rainforests can, without warning, show up in far-flung towns and cities. A devastating hemorrhagic-disease epidemic in Africa or South America could rapidly become the hemorrhagic epidemic of Boston or Bordeaux. Even good clinicians rarely have the knowledge to diagnose and treat exotic tropical diseases. Until a month ago, our attention was focused on Asia—the source of the last two influenza pandemics, in 1957 and 1968—as the likely source for the next one. And yet it appeared in Mexico while we weren't looking.
>
> ("Opinion: Swine flu is a wake up call," 2009, para. 3)

The tourism industry is particularly vulnerable to biological warfare, especially in the form of contagious illnesses such as smallpox. Because tourism is a peacetime and often leisure industry, it can become the perfect undercover delivery system. Here are just a few reasons for this:

1. Traveling today, especially in a world with limited visa restrictions, is relatively easy.
2. Airports are hubs with thousands of people going to any number of places. These are easy centers in which to expose people to contagious diseases and they will then act as carriers to any number of other places.

3. Often travelers make more than one stop. These additional stops mean a greater potential for infection. It can also become exceedingly difficult to develop the common thread that unites all of the infected victims.

4. Tourism receives a great deal of publicity. Once the epidemic (pandemic/disease) is identified by the media, there is a high probability of some form of panic.

5. Tourism is a major economic generator in and of itself and numerous other industries are also dependent on the travel industry. If the public fears travel, the economy will be severely injured if not destroyed.

What makes many of these potential diseases scary is that they are easy to produce/make, and the delivery system may be almost impossible to detect. Furthermore, were terrorists to use a powder of anthrax or get someone ill with smallpox organisms, these diseases would be almost impossible to detect until it was too late. To make matters still worse, the physicians attending the sick might lose valuable time until they were able to determine the cause of the illness. Additionally, health workers might panic, leaving the sick unattended and the public in a state of alarm.

Finally, tourism security specialists and professionals will need to be concerned about not only the movement of people, but also the threat to food and the movement of contaminated food from one location to another. These are special threats to people who may eat contaminated food, then board an airplane and not realize that they are sick until they are at the next locale or in the air. For example, the World Health Organization notes that:

> During 1996, tourists who travelled to yellow fever endemic areas without having had yellow fever vaccination imported fatal yellow fever infections into the United States and Switzerland. During the same year approximately 10,000 reported cases of malaria were imported into the European Community, with one fourth of them reported from the United Kingdom. When cholera re-entered Peru in 1991, after a long absence, it found an opportunity to spread through the existing sanitation and water systems, causing over 3000 deaths. Seafood exports were embargoed from Peru and tourism decreased, costing an estimated loss of at least US$770 million to the Peruvian economy in one year.
>
> **("Global infectious disease surveillance," 2013, para. 2)**

The world is an interconnected planet. The good news is that tourism allows people to get to know each other and understand each other from around the world. The bad news is that often we bring other baggage when we travel than merely our suitcases!

TRAIN TRAVEL AS TOURISM

Although air travel, especially in tourism, is the most preferred form of public transportation, other forms of transportation have long played a part in tourism. In an earlier chapter, we discussed the cruise industry and its impact on tourism. In this chapter, we turn to two other forms of land tourism travel: travel by train and travel by bus and motor coach.

Perhaps no form of travel has captured the public's imagination as much as the train called the *Orient Express*. Portrayed in film and in literature, this train has come to be the epicenter of both intrigue and romance within nineteenth-century Europe. The actual train began service from Paris to Constantinople (now Istanbul) in October 1883. The media dubbed the train the "Orient Express," and the name stuck. The "luxury" train became a favorite of European royalty and was also known as the "spies express." A number of movies portrayed the train as a center of spies and even murder, and this portrayal added to the train's acquired glamor (Zax, 2007). The *Orient Express* was not the only train to be considered romantic in the nineteenth- and twentieth-century world of train travel. U.S. trains have also become part of what we might call the "romance of the Old West."

Train travel began in the United States in the early part of the nineteenth century. With the expansion toward the western states, train travel had the advantage of comfort and speed over horse travel, especially over long distances. Trains in the United States had three main purposes: transportation of goods, transportation of people, and in the latter part of the century, more luxurious trains provided tourism experiences to parts of the United States that were relatively unknown to a large part of the nation's eastern population. Train travel, however, was not without problems. Not only was there the problem of derailments and other mechanical breakdowns, but there were also issues of attacks by "hostile" natives and by robbers. Many of these "security issues" became part of the U.S. movie industry and added to a sense of adventure. In 2010, *National Geographic* published its list of the top 10 train trips in North America. The list included:

- *Peak Experience: Colorado's Durango and Silverton Narrow Gauge Railroad*
- *Revolutionary Railway: New York to Vermont* Ethan Allen Express
- *Northwest Passage: Oregon to British Colombia Canada,* Amtrak Cascades
- *A Ride in the Woods: West Virginia's Cass Scenic Railroad*
- *Westward Ho: Chicago to California* California Zephyr
- *Mountain Climber: British Colombia to Alberta,* Rocky Mountaineer

- *On the Rim of Copper Canyon: Mexico's Chihuahua Pacific Railway*
- *Hail to the Chief: Los Angeles to Chicago,* Southwest Chief
- *Wilderness Alaska the Easy Way: Years 1988–2013*
- *Grand Old Time: Arizona's Grand Canyon Railway.*

(Duckett, 2010)

In the latter part of the twentieth century, train travel, which had fallen into a downward spiral, began to take on new life in tourism. The reasons for this renaissance were economic and involved issues of security. These included:

- Trains were considered to be more ecologically friendly. They can carry more people for less use of energy.
- Trains were considered by some to be safer. There was less publicity given to a train disaster than to an air disaster.
- The introduction of the bullet train in Japan and Europe made train travel a lot faster than it had been in the past.
- The "EuroPass" gave thousands of young North Americans a train travel experience that they had not had at home.
- Senior citizens and young people had the extra time to travel by train and see the countryside as they traveled.

Despite the fact that train travel is somewhat immune to accidents, violence, and even terrorism, the reality is that it is not immune. Found below is a listing of some of the worst train accidents in the last 25 years:

- *July 12, 2013: Six people are killed and nearly 200 injured just south of Paris when four cars slide off the tracks as a passenger train speeds through the small French town of Brétigny-sur-Orge.*
- *April 22, 2012: A woman dies of injuries a day after two trains collide head-on in Amsterdam. At least 16 people are seriously injured.*
- *April 13, 2012: Three people are killed and 13 injured in a train crash near Frankfurt when two trains collide and derail.*
- *March 3, 2012: Two trains collide head-on in southern Poland, killing at least 8 people and injuring around 50.*
- *January 30, 2011: A head-on collision between a cargo train and a passenger train kills at least 10 people and injures 23 near the eastern German village of Hordorf.*
- *December 9, 2010: One person is killed and two others are injured after a train derailed in southern Greece between the southern cities of Argos and Tripoli.*
- *August 6, 2010: A train derails in southern Italy, killing one passenger and leaving about 30 injured on the outskirts of Naples, its destination.*
- *July 23, 2010: Switzerland's popular Glacier Express tourist train derails in the Alps, killing one person and injuring 42 on its spectacular journey between Zermatt and St Moritz.*

- *February 15, 2010: A train wreck in Buizingen, Belgium, kills 18 people and injures 55.*
- *July 1, 2009: Thirty-two people are killed and 26 injured when a train carrying liquefied gas derails and explodes while traveling through a downtown neighborhood in the Tuscan seaside town of Viareggio.*
- *October 6, 2008: A local passenger train runs into the back of a long-distance train near Budapest, Hungary, killing 4 people and injuring 26 people.*
- *January 27, 2008: A passenger train derails in central Turkey, killing at least 9 people and injuring dozens of others, possibly due to ice on the tracks.*
- *September 2006: The Transrapid magnetic levitation train, which floats on a magnetic cushion, hits a maintenance vehicle on a test track in the Emsland area of Germany, killing 23 people.*
- *July 3, 2006: A local passenger train crashes in the southern city of Valencia, killing 41 people. Excessive speed is blamed.*
- *January 2006: Up to 46 people are killed and 198 injured when a packed train derails and plunges into a ravine outside Podgorica, the capital of Montenegro.*
- *January 2005: Seventeen people are killed when a passenger train and a freight train crash north of Bologna, Italy.*
- *June 2003: A Spanish passenger train travelling to Cartagena from Madrid crashes into the path of an oncoming goods train at Chinchilla, killing 19.*
- *May 2003: Thirty-four people are killed in Hungary when the Budapest-Nagykanizsa train hits a coach full of mainly elderly German holidaymakers at a level crossing near Siofok.*
- *November 2000: A fire in an Austrian tunnel engulfs a funicular train packed with skiers, killing 155 people.*
- *October 1999: Two trains collide near London's Paddington station, killing 31 people. One of the trains had gone through a red signal.*
- *June 1998: A high-speed train derails near the village of Eschede in Lower Saxony, Germany, killing 101 and injuring 88. It was caused by a single fatigue crack in one wheel that caused the train to derail at a switch and collide with a road bridge.*
- *December 1988: Thirty-five people die in a crash involving three trains at Clapham Junction in London. Slack safety measures are blamed.*

("European train crashes," 2013)

One of the most recent tragic incidents involving train travel occurred in Spain in July 2013. The crash is important not only in that it was one of Spain's worst disasters since 1944, but also because it symbolizes that all forms of transportation carry risk. The accident took place near Santiago de Compostela, a major tourism center, especially for religious tourism. Although it will take some time to know all of the facts, as of this writing, we know that at least 79 people died when the train derailed. The train's conductor has pled guilty to having spoken on a cell phone while taking a major curve at a speed well above what the law permitted. It is clear from the evidence given that human error caused the crash. The victims came from numerous nations around the world, and to quote one news source: "The crash has cast a pall over the town, a Catholic pilgrimage site. Santiago officials had been preparing for the religious feast of St. James of Compostela, Spain's patron saint, the day after the crash, but canceled it and turned a local sporting arena into a morgue" ("Driver in Spain train crash," 2013, para. 23).

Tragedy has struck the Spanish rail system in other ways. For example, on March 11, 2004, bombs went off almost simultaneously in various commuter trains entering the city of Madrid. These explosions killed 191 people and wounded over 1,800 other innocent victims. The bombings may have not only murdered and injured a great many people, but may have caused the prime minister at the time to lose the election. Spain's new government then pulled out of its involvement in the Iraq war.

From both the train accidents and terrorism attacks, a number of facts begin to emerge:

- Although train travel is considered less dangerous than air travel, the reality is that in both forms of transportation, there is always risk.
- Although most governments place their resources into airline protection, the possibility of a terrorism attack against a train, especially against a commuter train, is ever present.
- Currently trains are a weak link in the world of tourism security.
- Nations would be wise to consider the consequences of attacks against not only people but also against cargo. Often trains carry dangerous chemicals or other substances through populated areas.

Train transportation then is an area about which not only tourism security officials need to concern themselves, but general security officials also.

BUS TOURISM

It would be incomplete to consider tourism transportation security and not also mention the motor coach part of the market. In reality, there are several areas that we might call "bus tourism." These include:

1. Local buses used by both members of the local population and at times visitors to the community.
2. Intercity buses used by both members of the local population and visitors.
3. Buses that are rented for either a party or an affinity group, such as a school or business association.
4. Tour buses. These may be local buses that work with larger companies such as a cruise line or they may have set routes by which they take visitors to specific attractions in a specific locale. The English Double

Decker city tour buses are a good example of this type of bus. Often both European and American cities have day-long and half-day tour buses that provide an overview of the locale.

5. Motor coaches, which may be considered a more luxurious form of tourism and are used specifically for the visitor industry. We may define a motor coach as somewhat akin to a cruise on land.

Motor coaches, however, are both similar and different from other forms of tourism transportation for the following reasons:

1. They tend to have either affinity groups or groups that become affinity groups. That is, they do not accept passenger traffic along the way.
2. Unlike cruises, they provide lodging and food in other accommodations such as hotels or motels.
3. There tends to be a relationship between the driver and the passengers.
4. Baggage may be taken off the bus at every overnight stop.
5. Like the tour bus, their goal is the visitation of specific sites, but unlike the tour bus, the drivers tend to develop a relationship with the passengers over time, and the travel duration is much more than a day.

Motor coaches must distinguish between issues of safety and security. In both cases, there is safety and security on the bus and off it. Table 7.3 illustrates some of the many complex issues facing motor coach companies in regard to issues of safety and security.

Although a motor coach is vulnerable to all of the above, few incidents occur. Most incidents tend to be with tour buses that are sometimes confused with motor coaches. Part of the reason for motor coach safety and security is that the National Tour Association (NTA) spends a great deal of time encouraging both mechanical and human safety and security. In

Table 7.3 On- and Off-Bus Security and Safety Challenges

Issues of bus security, such as:	Issues of bus security:
Condition of the tires	Protection from:
Engine maintenance	Robbery
Conditions of roads used	Acts of terrorism
Driver fatigue/illness	Active shooter
Passenger illness	Fights between passengers
Fire on bus	
Safety issues off the bus:	Issues of off-bus security:
Food safety at local restaurants	On-road robbery
Hotel air filtration and cleanliness	Robbery and room break-in at hotel
Accidents caused by another driver	Terrorism attacks
Fires outside of bus	Security of the bus while parked

the appendix of this chapter, for example, you will find the Crisis Management Plan Structure. The Advocates for Highway and Auto Safety would
disagree. This organization argues that there have been between 1990
and 2012 at least 317 deaths and some 3,111 injuries. However, it is essential
to note that the organization then states that:

> The list (of the dead and injured) is compiled by Advocates for Highway and Auto
> Safety from reports documented in the media and investigations conducted by the
> National Transportation Safety Board (NTSB) and is not a census of all bus crashes
> or fatalities. For the purposes of this list, the term motorcoach refers to an over-the-
> road bus that carries more than 15 passengers including the driver.
>
> **("Motorcoach crashes and fires since 1990," 2014)**

It should be noted that tourism bus safety in many places does not meet
international standards. The rape of tourists in front of other passengers
while the bus was traveling to Rio de Janeiro notes a lack of security. In
countries such as Peru and Mexico, road and travel conditions are more than
lacking. Below are two of the many bus tragedies that made the news around
the world.

Attack in Mexico

On February 25, 2012, some 22 passengers were robbed and assaulted on a
Mexican tour bus traveling near the tourist city of Puerto Vallarta. Luckily
there was no loss of life, although there was loss of property. The attackers
"intercepted" the bus as it passed through the town of El Nogalito. The incident followed on the heels of another incident in Mexico where an American mother and her daughters were among seven passengers who lost their
lives in Pachuca (state of Veracruz). It should be emphasized that these were
not motor coaches per se, but tour buses. Nevertheless, this incident teaches
us several important security points:

- The robbers had inside information as to where the buses would be.
- There was no special dispensation given to visitors.
- In the case of the Puerto Vallarta incident, the robbers specifically tar-
  geted people on a tour bus.

Bus Disaster in Italy

A more typical situation is what occurred in July 29, 2013, in Italy. Some 39
people died when their bus plunged off a ravine in southern Italy. It should
be noted that this was not a tour bus. The tragic news, however,

demonstrated that both locals and tourists are forced to use often-substandard roads, bridges, and other public arteries.

The bus world is highly complex and it is essential for tourism security personnel to be aware of the different forms of bus travel and the different challenges that each one of these subcategories faces.

APPENDIX: NTA'S CRISIS MANAGEMENT PLAN STRUCTURE[1]

The following outline will help tour operators develop and personalize a step-by-step management plan to put into action at a time of crisis. Tour operators should share their crisis plan with suppliers they will use on tour to ensure there is coordination in the time of a crisis.

Coordination Team: Internal Leader/External Leader

- Develop holding statement immediately.
- Contact team leaders (who makes up the Coordination Team).
- Meet with Coordination Team.
- Determine current situation (identify what is known, what must be verified).
- Make key assignments to team leaders.
- Determine if "on-site" team needs to go.
- Prepare statements with legal/finance review (but legal does *not* have the final call on statement—company leader/Coordination Team leader does).
- Alert all systems/staff (reservations, IT, etc.).
- Assign a scribe to record all events chronologically—right hand to internal team leader (consider a report/time sheet for key individuals to complete as things happen and regularly submit to the scribe).
- Internal communications—employee nurturing—critical to remember the care and feeding of the staff.
- Develop succession plans for when key players are not available and/or shift controls on rotation (i.e., if internal team leader is not available, who takes that role, and then who fills his/her role, etc.).
- Always keep looking forward—ANTICIPATE (let the teams deal with the details and minutia so the whole process keeps moving forward).
- Ongoing evaluation of process for adjustments as needed and for future use.
- Wrap-up session as crisis ends (or key stages come to an end).

[1] The Crisis Management Plan Structure in this Appendix is reprinted with permission of the National Tour Association (NTA). Copyright 2013. All rights reserved.

General Inquiries (Brings an Anticipation of What General Inquiries Will Be)

- Immediately tell employees and customer service personnel how to respond—develop a holding statement ("Yes there is a situation. We are aware of it and investigating it, and we'll find out the details and get back to you.").
- Dependent on the situation, share appropriate messages of condolence. Don't forget to reference staff, drivers, etc.
- After the Coordination Team meeting—develop official statements for customer inquiries.
- Prepare written statements for email inquiries.
- Coordinate with agency team because agents will be calling reservation center line first.
- Coordinate with the guest relations and media teams for messages.
- Run manifest of guests on tour for reference during inquiries.
- Develop rotation system so everyone can be better prepared and rested for their shifts.
- Consider special touch-tone message or 800 line with prepared statements to public (depends on situation).

Media Team (Includes Suppliers/DMOs/Aassociations, etc.)

- Contact external PR assistance.
- Establish media site (off-site of main management area, like a local hotel)—be sure there is meet-and-greet staff and phone reception for all media inquiries.
- Establish spokesperson(s) (may be more than one depending on situation, never more than two—may be one at home and one on-site).
- Remind/inform all employees to refer all media calls to media team and make no comments outside of statements provided. Give them talking points to pass on to the media team, so that it is handled properly and positively).
- Review initial "holding statement" (or create specific to media as needed) and revise as possible with updates.
- Recognize the power and immediacy of social media.
- Have email/phone number for key media people for quick access, including national media, depending on crisis.
- Identify who if anyone will speak to media on-site—especially before on-site team arrives (local supplier, tour director/staff, officials).

- Be sure that anyone in proximity who could be approached by media is briefed with statements (e.g., shared tenants).
- Ongoing:
  - Monitor news and social media (online, TV, radio, etc.).
  - Coordinate closely with all communications teams to ensure messages are consistent.
  - Gather as much information as possible for other trams.
  - Notify/update partners, suppliers, NTA, etc.
  - Have hard copy, updated lists of contact information and keep current.

On-Site Team (Involves Elements of All Other Teams, Handled at the Scene)

- Locate "go bag" (prepared in advance and ready for travel to site; contains satellite phone, if necessary; cameras; crisis manual; employee contact lists for 24/7 coverage; cash access; corporate credit cards).
- Provide direction to on-site interim staff for actions prior to On-site Team arrival.
- Complete logistics of getting to the site (flight arrangements, lodging, etc.).
- Coordinate with suppliers at the scene (coach company, DMO).
- Instigate roles with the on-site team and consultant team, if appropriate.
- Establish location of all involved.
- Establish On-site Command Center and distribute contact information to HQ, suppliers, etc.
- Coordinate with Media Team for on-site spokesperson/media needs.
- Provide counseling/comfort for those involved.

Operations/Logistics Team (Fact Checkers, Logistics, Resources)

- Coordinate with On-site Team to develop interim on-site team by identifying who is in the immediate area (tour directors, drivers, supplier representatives).
- Identify other resources in the area (other suppliers/contacts the company has access to in local area).
- Prepare the tour director (on-site staff) with "holding statement" and initial talking points particularly for media—refer media as possible to Media Team at HQ.
- Run manifest for who was involved.

- Begin verifying facts—determine fatalities, injuries, causes of accident/situation, etc.
- Conduct ongoing analysis of the situation.
- Key: Internal/external communication plan must be solid and consistent.
- Prepare information for contacting families/next of kin as needed—turn over to customer service center.
- Coordinate logistics for anyone else who needs to get to the site, such as family members, suppliers, other staff, etc.

Legal/Contract/Finance

- Review supplier contracts.
- Review insurance forms.
- Review passenger manifest.
- Check insurance coverage—what is financial exposure.
- Notify insurance broker and legal counsel.
- Coordinate with Operations Team on potential liabilities/exposure:
  - Driver record.
  - Equipment record.
  - Supplier record.
  - Company record.
- Hire accident investigator as needed.
- Fund tour directors—wire money—have plan for weekends, holidays, etc. (may need to rely on local contacts/suppliers).
- What did the participants lose?—What will the company need to replace (passports, keys, clothing, valuables, etc.).
- Get police report, if applicable.
- Begin looking at future impacts from incident (insurance increases, contract clauses, etc.).

Miscellaneous Points

- First, determine who "owns" the crisis—is it your company's, carriers', etc.?
- Anticipate appearance of cell-phone video of the incident. Social media is everywhere and coverage will be instantaneous of everything.
- Suppliers must have 24/7 emergency contact to reach company.
- Let suppliers and partners know what you expect of them in a crisis situation—suppliers need to have emergency kits with critical emergency information for reaching company.

- In Europe, government is more involved with control of accidents than in the United States. What may happen in this specific location?
- Assist people who can't get their belongings—company must provide prescriptions, glasses, clothing, other needs.
- Short-term costs pay off in the long run.
- Be sure you document your due diligence (any resources used to determine safety and security of destination).
- Most overlooked or neglected component is staff: What if the trauma devastates the employees' work? Needs to be a major focus of your business continuity plan.
- Contact cascades—who contacts whom—especially in a catastrophic event at all levels have contingencies.

Internal Communications Issues

- Initial notification.
- Internal updates: What? When? How?
- Interteam communication.
- Communication beyond HQ.
- Critical especially with shift rotations—is there a paper trail or central location for people to get briefed?
- Assign company contact(s) for suppliers to deal directly with at HQ and provide backup contacts.
- Consider relevant time differences.
- Emergency card with contact numbers and essential logistics number provided to all staff and a checklist on other side of top dos and don'ts so they have an immediate reference of what to do first.

REFERENCES

Bagshaw, M., DeVoll, J. R., Jennings, R.T., McCrary, B. F., Northrup, S. E., Rayman, R. B., et al. (2002). *Medical guidelines for airline passengers*. Alexandria, Virginia, USA: Aerospace Medical Association. Retrieved from, http://www.asma.org/asma/media/asma/travel-publications/paxguidelines.pdfBa.

Driver in Spain train crash provisionally charged with negligent homicide (2013). *Fox News*. Retrieved from http://www.foxnews.com/world/2013/07/29/driver-in-spain-train-crash-charged-with-negligent-homicide/#ixzz2aYvaXNtT.

Duckett, R. H. (2010). *North American train trips*. *National Geographic*. Retrieved from http://travel.nationalgeographic.com/travel/top-10/north-american-train-trips/#page=2.

European train crashes—a recent history (2013). *The guardian*. Retrieved from http://www.theguardian.com/world/2013/jul/25/european-train-crashes-recent-history.

Global infectious disease surveillance (2013). *World Health Organization*. Retrieved from http://www.who.int/mediacentre/factsheets/fs200/en/.

How to end a plane hijacking (n.d.). *wikiHow*. Retrieved from http://www.wikihow.com/End-a-Plane-Hijacking.

Marienau, K. J., Illig, P. A., Kozarsky, P. E., & Gallagher, N. M. (2013). Conveyance & transportation issues. *Centers for Disease Control and Prevention*. Retrieved from http://wwwnc.cdc.gov/travel/yellowbook/2014/chapter-6-conveyance-and-transportation-issues/air-travel.

Motorcoach crashes & fires since 1990 (2014). *Advocates for highway & auto safety*. Retrieved from www.saferoads.org.

Mueller, J., & Stewart, M. G. (2008). *Assessing the risks, costs and benefits of United States aviation security measures*. Retrieved from http://www.saferoads.org/files/file/Motorcoach%20Crash%20List-%20February%202012.pdf; http://polisci.osu.edu/faculty/jmueller/stewarr2.pdf.

Opinion: Swine flu is a wake up call (2009). *Newsweek*. Retrieved from http://www.newsweek.com/opinion-swine-flu-wake-call-77043.

Pinsker, B. (2003). *Confessions of a baggage scanner*. Wired, 11(9). Retrieved from http://www.wired.com/wired/archive/11.09/bagscan.html.

Tips for healthy travel (2013). United. Retrieved from http://www.united.com/web/en-Us/content/travel/inflight/health.aspx.

TSA gets rid of full-body scanners at US airports (2013). *Fox News*. Retrieved from http://www.foxnews.com/politics/2013/05/31/tsa-gets-rid-full-body-image-scanners-at-us-airports/.

Zax, D. (2007). A brief history of the Orient Express. *Smithsonian.com*. Retrieved from http://www.smithsonianmag.com/history-archaeology/brief_orient.html?c=y&page=2.

CHAPTER 8

Tourism Security Legal Issues

TOURISM SURETY, STANDARDS OF CARE, AND THE LAW

In Chapter 1, we discussed the issue of tourism surety versus tourism safety and security. We noted that tourism surety involves not only questions of visitor safety and security, but also involves the economic viability and reputation of the tourism host locale. In today's litigious society, almost any tourism entity is open to lawsuits, and they can be extremely costly. Just as good customer service is all about treating guests with more than respect, good customer surety is about treating them with a sense of responsibility and care. It is then essential that the tourism security manager/professional take the time to consult national and international organizations to know what is expected of him or her.

Being safe and secure can mean different things to each of tourism's different players. For example, to the tourism provider being safe and secure means not only preventing physical disasters, but also knowing how to take the proper steps so that a physical disaster does not also become a financial disaster. From the consumer's perspective being safe and secure means the ability to visit a place, enjoy the experience, and return safely. From the perspective of the site itself, safety and security means having visitors come and doing relatively little damage to the site, be that damage ecological, such as in the Gálapagos Islands, or physical, such as Plymouth Rock in Massachusetts.

Because we live in a highly litigious society, tourism security is more than mere weapons and muscle power. To be safe is to know how to defend oneself on all fronts from the legal to the media, from the physical to the mental. From this perspective it is essential for any tourism entity to have a proper security staff and to consult with that staff often. A good tourism security team should have the following:

1. A risk manager
2. A medical and/or public health specialist
3. A legal person or staff (depending on the size of the business)
4. A specialist in both physical and human security
5. A marketer and/or public relations specialist

ISSUES OF RESPONSIBILITY, LEGALITY, AND STANDARDS OF CARE

One of the most frequently heard complaints in the world of travel and tourism is that when things go wrong, few people accept responsibility. Instead, tourism and travel professionals "abuse" visitors with a jet stream of excuses, or customers merely see a shrug of the shoulders or are simply ignored. In today's world, travel and tourism are challenging, and when travel and hospitality professionals simply look the other way or ignore a problem, the situation becomes both stressful and often intolerable. Taking responsibility is more than merely listening and smiling, it is providing good service. Taking responsibility is the ability to attempt to fix the problem or to find reasonable alternatives to travel and hospitality problems. All too often tourism professionals tend to forget that the only person who is satisfied with an excuse is the person who makes it.

There is another aspect of tourism responsibility, which is the industry's responsibility to provide a sustainable industry that does more good for local communities than it does damage. This means thinking about tourism's social and economic impact, how it changes the culture of a locale, and what the industry needs to do in order to ensure that a beautiful or culturally special location is not overwhelmed by growth.

MAKING DECISIONS

One of the most frustrating things about tourism is when an employee cannot make a decision and passes responsibility onto another person who cannot make a decision either! There are, however, exceptions to this rule. For example, several U.S. hotel chains, such as the Ritz Carlton, provide all employees with a small budget so that they can solve issues on the spot. Not only does such a program lower tourism frustration, but it also serves as an excellent method to transform a negative situation into a positive one. From the hotel's perspective, empowerment provides additional benefits. Janggon Kim has written:

> Indeed, employee empowerment is a well-known tool for retaining employees, boosting operation productivity and recovering customer services. Improper use of empowerment can also impact negatively on such things as employees' poor decision making and management's fear of giving up control. Employee empowerment, however, has more positive impacts on the front desk operations and this paper will suggest how to overcome those negative aspects by showing the best practices used in hotel operations.
>
> *(Kim, 2011, pp. 3–4)*

STANDARDS OF CARE

If students of tourism security were to go to court and view the forms of litigation that lawyers pursue against members of the tourism industry, they might very well conclude that it is ignorance of or refusal to obey what is commonly called "standards of care" together with issues of "foreseeability" that dominate tourism issues in court. Another term for standards of care is "standards of practice." In both cases, the phrase refers to a set of professional or industry guidelines. Standard of care is what both the public expects from that industry and what the industry expects from itself. Often an industry has specific written standards and some may be written into local or national law or become industry-wide international regulations. For example, it is a common standard of care that a public place of lodging will have both a lock on the guest's door and a smoke alarm in the guest's room.

Because tourism is a multifaceted and composite industry, each subgroup within the tourism industry may have its own basic standards of care. For example, there are different standards of major events, medical tourism, spectator sports tourism, and the travel component of tourism (airlines, trains, buses, cruises, etc.). It is beyond the scope of this book to list every standard of care. It is essential for tourism professionals, and especially those who work in the field of risk management, to meet with their legal staff on a regular basis and learn what the standards of care are in every possible aspect of their industry. Because new standards of care arise, reflecting societal changes and new threats, tourism professionals should never assume that these standards of care are fixed in time. Instead, these standards are ever dynamic and changeable.

A lawyer did not write this chapter. All legal decisions should be between the client and his/her lawyer.

All too often tourism and travel businesses do not know what the proper standard of care is for any particular subject. For example, where does a tour operator's responsibility lie, what is a hotel responsible for, or how liable is a travel agency? It is essential to consult the company's legal experts to be sure that your business is (1) aware of the current standards of care and (2) operating within these proper standards.

Standards of care and laws governing tourism are not uniform across the world. Thus, if a tourism business is multinational it is essential that its staff know its nation's laws and standards of care and also those of other nations in which the business may be operating. For example, travel providers and travel agents, tour operators and travel insurance companies all need to know for what and to whom they are responsible both within their home country and within the countries in which they are doing business. That means taking the time to know not only what the legal things to do are, but also what is both moral and ethical. Remember that tourism is a business that can live within the letter of the law, but it can only be successful if it goes beyond it. Going beyond the letter of the law means knowing what a particular business is willing to provide and what it cannot provide, and then providing all that it can within those limitations.

One way to accomplish this legal form of security is to be able to demonstrate that the tourism security professional has proper checklists regarding the standard of care that he or she provides his clients. Checklists come in many formats. The reason for these lists is not only because they provide an outline of the basic security procedures needed for the security professional's business, but if questioned, the security professional is able to demonstrate the science of his or her procedures rather than merely arguing that safety and security procedures are haphazard.

The safety and security professional should also consult nontourism and travel professionals whose expertise may impact his or her business. For example, the professional may not be expected to be an expert in every aspect of fire or food safety but is expected to consult those who are experts. In the case of fire or food safety at a smaller hotel or attraction, it is their responsibility to work with the local fire or health department. The hotel must be able to prove that it knows the most up-to-date codes and that it follows these codes. For example, a security officer may wish to run a tabletop exercise with a fire department to determine what may occur and what needs to be changed in order to be fully prepared. It is wise for tourism professionals to request that first responders, such as fire fighters, and first-aid experts inspect a locale from their perspectives and review with them hazards to visitors and employees' safety and security, health, and air quality.

LEGAL VULNERABILITY

In the tourism industry, legal vulnerability may be a two-way street. For example, Americans traveling abroad may still sue a foreign hotel for an act that has occurred abroad if that hotel has resources in the United States. What is true of the United States may also be true in other situations. Thus, depending on his or her clientele, a security professional may need to become almost an expert on a variety of laws and regulations, not only for his or her nation but also for those nations from which guests come. To aid the security professional in this quagmire and web of legalism, consider checking with such international tourism organizations as the World Tourism Organization, and national professional organizations. Take the time to ask insightful questions and to learn what is expected of you, then go beyond these standards and become a model for best practices.

TOURISM LAW

It has been noted throughout this book that tourism and travel form one of the world's largest and fastest-growing industries. In fact, if we do not count the international arms industry, then tourism may be the world's largest industry. Because it is a composite industry, however, its exact economic strength is impossible to estimate. The reason for this lack of precision is that tourism is not a tangible product, but rather an amalgamation of products. For example, is the building of a new international airport part of the tourism industry, the building industry, or both? The answer depends on how we define tourism, and which components are added into the economic impact assessment. One standard that is often used is from the World Travel and Tourism Council. According to the World Travel and Tourism Council's economic impact research, tourism contributed US $2.2 trillion and produced 101 million jobs and 5.4% of world exports in 2013 (World Travel and Tourism Council, 2014). Of course, these figures are open to debate, but no matter whose figures we use, few would argue against the notion that tourism is big business. As such, around the world today, new laws and regulations are being developed to protect the tourism industry, its clientele, and its employees.

Tourism law, however, is not easy to define. Travel often consists of crossing physical, social, and cultural borders. What may be correct or proper in one society is not necessarily "acceptable" behavior in another society. Not only can one place's norms be different from those of another locale, but also international visitors are not required to prove knowledge of local norms before entering another country. Travel and tourism professionals can never forget that their profession is not only one that evokes high levels of emotions, but is often open to all sorts of liability cases that range from the frivolous to the extremely serious. Furthermore, what is legal in one country, or section of a particular country, may not be legal in another place. Often, visitors may not only sue in the location in which an incident occurred, but also once they have returned home.

In the Western world, an example of this inconsistency is in the area of marijuana usage; for example, there are parts of Holland where it is legal to smoke or use small quantities of pot. However, what is true of Amsterdam may not be true of other Dutch cities. This inconsistency of law is a perfect example of tourism anomy, as discussed in Chapter 1. Another example of norm variance may be in proper dress or eating habits. For example, a woman's proper dress or the consumption of alcoholic beverages and pork products is totally different in the Western nations than in many Middle Eastern nations.

These differences mean that even defining tourism law can be a challenge. We might argue that tourism law is a composite of international law, local laws pertaining to the tourism industry, best practices and standards of care, and questions of foreseeability. Many of these principles are based on elements from the far and recent past and combine with current international, national, and local regulations. In an article titled "Travel and Tourism Law," published on the Website of the American Bar Association, Alexander Anolik (2010) defines travel law as "the nexus of federal, state, common law, and international laws that regulate the day-to-day workings of the travel industry" (2010, para. 3). Anolik then goes on to state that: "Travel law incorporates elements of contract law, employment issues, tourism and hospitality procedures, anti-trust rules, regulatory and agency compliance, and knowledge of certain international treaties into a comprehensive guide for the travel industry" (para. 3). When it comes to codifying standards of care into law, Anolik notes that such proposals as an airline passenger "bill of rights" would be an example of a potential standard expected by the public that becomes law.

A Word of Caution

The author wishes to remind his readers that he is not a legal expert, and as such, it is strongly advised that readers check with their local, personal, or business legal advisor prior to making any decision. The author wishes to emphasize that the material contained in this chapter is merely intended to provoke creative thinking and questioning and to help the reader in holding intelligent conversations with his or her legal advisor. No decisions should ever be made solely on the basis of the material in this chapter or book but rather only after carefully having consulted with expert and licensed legal advisors.

Having noted that tourism law is fluid, below is a listing of items that the tourism professional may want to consider. Again it should be emphasized that a legal professional should always be consulted prior to making any specific decision.

- The first rule of thumb is that tourism professionals in any aspect of their work need to work defensively. That is, they should always be open to the possibility of a lawsuit. To travel is to deal with risk and whenever there is risk, then potential litigation exists. Tourists, passengers, and attraction-goers have sued for everything from an accident on their property to weather. Unfortunately, even when a tourism entity wins, it still loses. The entity has not only suffered a monetary cost, but may have also suffered a publicity cost, especially in a world dominated by social media. The basic rule of thumb is that if there is a risk, then be prepared to be sued by someone and be prepared to defend yourself not only in court but also in the court of public opinion.

- Learn to live with stochastic models by distinguishing between possible and probable. Many people in tourism tend to confuse these two terms. Almost anything is possible. For example, it is possible but not likely that aliens from outer space will attack Earth. What is possible, however, is not necessarily probable. The key is to develop priority lists in which you rank the probable. The more probable the problem, the more attention should be paid to it. A good rule of thumb is that tourism marketers tend to stress the possible, while lawyers and security specialists look at the probable.

- When it comes to lawsuits know that the rule of foreseeability rules! Make sure that you and your staff go over this principle with your lawyer or legal advisor. In layman's terms, we can explain foreseeability in the following way. Ask yourself if a prudent person would have noted a clear and present physical or other type of danger (e.g., a contagious illness) that might result in some form of harm to your guest staff or anyone else on your premises. Foreseeability never works in the realm of the possible, but rather, just as in the case of tourism risk management, seeks out the probable. Thus, it is highly probable that a slippery floor may result in a visitor's falling and bodily injury, but it is a lot less probable that a well-constructed and maintained building will collapse.

- Know your business's history and any special circumstances that may have occurred at your business or tourism site. It is possible for courts to examine past incidents on your premises. If your locale has a history of accidents or specific crimes, then it is going to be a lot more difficult claiming that you could not reasonably predict a reoccurrence. Ask yourself how past events, geography, and demographics have impacted the safety and security of your guests. Were you aware of them? What counter-measures did you take to correct potential damage to life, limb, property, or mental state? In your part of the world, do you run the risk of natural occurrences such as tsunamis, earthquakes, or hurricanes? If so, are you prepared and have you taken these natural occurrences into account when it comes to your security and safety plan?

- The best way to avoid legal issues is with a good risk management plan. Make sure that it covers all aspects of your business from the physical plant to technology. Ask yourself not only what can go wrong, but also how you would solve the problem if something were to go wrong. For example, if there are water sports involved, is there a high probability that someone may be injured, hurt, or even die? If children or people with special needs are present, then know what other special precautions you have in place. Is all of your life-saving equipment up-to-date and in good working order? Do you train your personnel and staff not only on safety issues but also what to do in case of an emergency? Make sure to review with your legal staff if someone can attack you or your business for issues of poor communication or negligence.

- Overlooking the simple things may cause a great deal of legal problems. Review negligence issues on a regular basis. Often the best plans fail simply because someone fails to check to see if these plans are being carried out. For example, are doors that are supposed to be locked, actually locked? Are all of your light bulbs in working order? Do you check your smoke alarms on a regular basis, and do you hold regular fire drills when your staff least expects it?

- Do not just write down your risk management plan; actually practice it! Too many tourism entities tend to write down their plans, put the plans on the shelf, and then when something happens, use the plans as nothing more than a legal fig leaf. Also all too often top management has a copy of the risk management plan, but has never shared it with those who actually must carry it out. In case of a crisis ask yourself if the upper ranks of an organization will be able to communicate effectively with the staff. If not, what is the value of the risk management plan? Consider all aspects of your tourism business from workplace violence to lack of adequate staffing. Where are your weak points? Remember in the end it is not about avoiding a lawsuit but about keeping people from being injured and saving lives.

- Be mindful that not every tourist and visitor is a good person and criminals and terrorists also travel. Protect yourself and your reputation with carefully placed observation tools. All too often we find visitors who seek out their own harm as a way to make money, steal from insurance companies, or create unsupported litigation as a means of gaining financially. Such actions are just another form of theft. Just as you need to protect your community or business from fraud and theft, so, too, you have to protect your business from dishonest forms of litigation.

TRAVELERS' RIGHTS

As noted above, there is a close relationship between physical travel and one's psychological mood. Travel produces stress. Often when things go wrong small incidents become large incidents. In fact, often what would not bother a person at home becomes a major crisis when that same person is on the road or away from home. More than one person has called vacations a "stressful search for fun." One of the ways that the travel and tourism industry has begun to address this continual state of stress in travel is through the development of industry standards. These standards act as a rulebook for both the supplier and the consumer. The consumer knows what he or she can expect and the supplier has at least a minimal standard of what is expected from his or her business.

TRAVEL AGENTS

Although many people prefer to book their travel via the Internet or phone, there are others who prefer to use the services of a travel specialist. These specialists are able to recommend locations, types of vacations, and which travel product may be correct for his or her client. According to Zigmund Sepanski, travel specialists have six major duties. He notes that the Court decisions over the last 20 years favor the consumer quite heavily. According to Sepanski, the primary duties identified by court decisions and state statutes are:
1. Duty to disclose vendor identity
2. Duty to warn and inform
3. Duty to investigate
4. Duty to confirm
5. Duty not to overpromise or misrepresent
6. Duty to protect client funds
(http://www.authorizedagents.com)

In February 2003, British travel agents published their code of conduct. This code acts as a rulebook for British travel agents and offers precise definitions of industry terms and a code of conduct between members of the association and other members and clients. The code requires member agents to provide customers with the most accurate information possible and to be honest in their advertising.

ISSUES OF TRAVEL LAW AND TRAVEL AGENTS

It is imperative that a travel agent know that even though his or her business is not located in a state that has created a corpus of travel law, the fact that a customer in that state may use the agency's Website may make you liable under a different state's law. Currently U.S. states such as California, Florida, Hawaii, and Washington have some of the tightest travel legislation. It behooves a travel agent to speak to an attorney who specializes in interstate travel law so as to avoid cross-state lawsuits. Travel legal specialists can also advise what registration a travel agency needs in order to avoid problems in another state. Listed below are some of the major issues about which a travel agent needs to be aware on a state-by-state basis. It should be noted that the reader should check to make sure that the data presented here are as current as possible and that laws and regulations have not been changed since the writing of this book. Below are some of the regulations that different states require.

California

- All sellers must register, except those independents registered as a host and who are individuals, not corporations.
- Fee: $100 per location.
- Penalty: $5 per day.
- Felony for some infractions.
- Other fee: Travel Consumer Restitution Corporation (TCRC) $275.
- Trust or bond: yes.
- Seller ID on all advertising.
- TCRC info on all agreements.

Independent agents to be exempt must:
1. Belong to a registered host.
2. Have a written host contract.

3. Sell only host-covered travel.
4. Specific disclosures required.
5. Specific refund requirements.
6. Trust accounts.

Florida

- Florida requires registration, bond, or trust for anyone selling to Floridians.
- Those who are ARC approved for the last 3 years are exempt from bond.
- Fee: $300 annual.
- Penalty: up to $5,000.
- Exemption: ARC 3 years.
- Trust or bond: yes.
- Seller ID on all advertising.

Independent agents to be exempt from fees/bond, not registration must:
1. Belong to a registered host.
2. Have a written host contract.
3. Sell only host-covered travel.
4. No direct client commission.
5. No unused ticket stock.
6. Cannot issue documents.

Hawaii

- All sellers must register.
- Fee: $95.
- Trust account: yes.
- Trust penalty: criminal.
- Disclosure required: yes.
- Funds: in Hawaiian bank.

Illinois

- Sellers of travel must provide the usual disclosure statements, including trust account.
- No formal registration.
- Trust account: yes.

Iowa

- A travel agency doing business in this state shall register with the secretary of state as a travel agency if it or its travel agent conducts the solicitation of an Iowa resident.
- The required bond or evidence of financial responsibility and the registration fee must accompany the registration statement. Independent agent falling under registered host does not have to have bond or security.
- Trust account: yes.
- Disclosure required: yes.

Massachusetts

- Disclosures required, including names, addresses, tour operators.
- Cancelation terms, refund policies, penalties, etc., in writing.

Nevada

- All must register. Independent agent must also register, but does not need bond if the host is registered.
- Fee: $125.
- Penalty: $100 first/$250 second.
- Trust account: yes.
- Bond: $50,000.
- Seller ID on all advertising.

Washington

- Registration is required if you sell into state unless you are an independent agent and your host is registered. Your host needs to list you as an independent agent.
- If you are not a member of a registered host you must register and pay.
- Fee: $145.
- Trust: yes, all funds go to trust or you must have letter of credit.
- $1 million liability.
- Disclosures: yes.
- Seller ID on all advertising.

Travel agents do not only have to deal with issues of law and best practices, but both airlines and cruise lines have established specific travel agency guidelines.

ADDITIONAL ISSUES FOR TRAVEL AGENCIES

The major American insurance company AON notes that: "The basis of a travel agency/client relationship can also be used to justify the amount of liability imposed on a travel company defendant." It is unclear, however, exactly what that relationship is. For example, some courts have held travel agencies to be "agents of the supplier." In this case, the travel agency holds minimal responsibility as they are nothing more than a third-party salesman, selling the product of another company. For example, the agency does not sell airline tickets, but facilitates the sale of a particular airline's ticket to a passenger. The fact that the agency does not receive any income from the sale of the ticket, but rather merely receives a commission is another argument in favor of the agency having a minimal amount of responsibility to the passenger. It may also be assumed by the courts that the less a traveler knows about travel, the greater the responsibility the agent has to provide information to his or her client. The courts often, but not always, assume that the travel agency knows more about the supplier than does the traveler.

A third possibility, and currently the most common, argues that it is inconsequential if a travel agent is a supplier or not of another business, the agency still has certain responsibilities. Often this third point is called *General Standards of Care and Responsibilities*. From this perspective it is assumed that the travel agency knows more about the supplier than does the client and therefore has a duty to inform the client about potential problems. AON notes that: "Even in states where courts have held that travel agents are agents of suppliers, the more recent trend in litigated cases is that agents have an obligation to disclose anything they know which is of material importance to the traveler, so long as the traveler would not already know the same thing." The courts then tend to see travel agent advice as professional advice and therefore the agent assumes at least some of the liability when information that should be given is not provided. Thus, a travel agent cannot be held responsible for a delayed flight but might be held responsible if this flight is always delayed and therefore the probability of making a connecting flight has been greatly reduced. In a like manner the courts assume that a person who travels less often has a greater need for professional advice than a person who travels on a more regular basis ("Insurance solutions for the travel industry," 2013).

Perhaps no area of the travel industry produces more anxiety and anger than the airline industry. The literature and urban legends are filled with horror stories about passengers who have been stranded, kept for long hours on the tarmac, and lost children. Added to these stories are tales and woes of late or canceled flights, lost baggage, and a fear of flying. It is easy to see that many passengers are not happy with the airline industry. To add to this general feeling of anger and frustration, the public has had to learn to deal with no or little food, poor service, multiple fees, and a sense that no one cares or is listening. These many problems have created a demand for an air travelers' bill of rights. As of the writing of this chapter this bill of rights has still not been promulgated in the United States. Nevertheless, there have been a number of steps taken in the United States and in Europe (where a bill of travelers' rights already exists) toward lessening or eliminating the problem.

THE AIRLINE PASSENGER BILL OF RIGHTS

As of the writing of this book there is still no official air passenger bill of rights in the United States. Progress, however, has been made. For example, in April 2011, the U.S. Department of Transportation released a set of consumer protection measures that amounted to an airline passenger bill of rights. Among the "rights" that Secretary Ray LaHood announced were:

- *Lost bags and bag fees.* Airlines will now be required to refund any fee for carrying a bag if the bag is lost. Airlines will also be required to apply the same baggage allowances and fees for all segments of a trip, including segments with interline and code share partners. Airlines are already required to compensate passengers for reasonable expenses for loss, damage, or delay in the carriage of passenger baggage.
- *Full disclosure of additional fees.* Airlines will also have to prominently disclose all potential fees on their Websites, including but not limited to fees for baggage, meals, canceling or changing reservations, or advanced or upgraded seating. In addition, airlines and ticket agents will be required to refer passengers both before and after purchase to up-to-date baggage fee information, and to include all government taxes and fees in every advertised price. Previously, government taxes and fees were not required to be included in the up-front fare quotation.
- *Bumping.* Today's rule doubles the amount of money passengers are eligible to be compensated for in the event they are involuntarily bumped from an oversold flight. Currently, bumped passengers are entitled to cash compensation equal to the value of their tickets, up to $400, if the airline is able to get them to their destination within a short period of time (i.e., within 1 to 2 hours of their originally scheduled arrival time

for domestic flights and 1 to 4 hours of their originally scheduled arrival time for international flights). Bumped passengers are currently entitled to double the price of their tickets, up to $800, if they are delayed for a lengthy period of time (i.e., over 2 hours after their originally scheduled arrival time for domestic flights and over 4 hours after their originally scheduled arrival time for international flights). Under the new rule, bumped passengers subject to short delays will receive compensation equal to double the price of their tickets up to $650, while those subject to longer delays would receive payments of four times the value of their tickets, up to $1,300. Inflation adjustments will be made to those compensation limits every 2 years.

- *Tarmac delays.* The new rule expands the existing ban on lengthy tarmac delays to cover foreign airlines' operations at U.S. airports and establishes a 4-hour hard time limit on tarmac delays for international flights of U.S. and foreign airlines, with exceptions allowed only for safety, security, or air traffic control–related reasons. Carriers must also ensure that passengers stuck on the tarmac are provided adequate food and water after 2 hours, as well as working lavatories and any necessary medical treatment. The extended tarmac delays experienced by passengers on international flights operated by foreign carriers at New York's JFK Airport during the December 2010 blizzard was an important factor in the Department's decision to extend the tarmac delay provisions to foreign air carriers and establish a 4-hour tarmac delay limit for international flights.

The Department of Transportation's rule will make air travel simpler and easier in a number of other ways, including:

- *Requiring airlines to allow reservations to be held at the quoted fare without payment, or canceled without penalty, for at least 24 hours after the reservation is made, if the reservation is made 1 week or more prior to a flight's departure date.*
- *Requiring airlines to promptly notify consumers of delays of over 30 minutes, as well as cancelations and diversions. This notification must take place in the boarding gate area, on a carrier's telephone reservation system, and on its Website.*
- *Banning post-purchase fare increases unless they are due to government-imposed taxes or fees, and only if the passenger is notified of and agrees to the potential increase at the time of sale.*
- *Requiring more airlines to report lengthy tarmac delays at U.S. airports with DOT, including data for international flights and charter flights. Previously, only the 16 largest U.S. passenger carriers were required to file this data, and only for domestic scheduled flights.*

(*"U.S. Department of Transportation Expands Airline Passenger Protections,"* 2011, Tarmac Delays section)

These measures have clearly helped passengers, but as the newspaper *USA Today* reported on July 17, 2013, there is still a long way to go. To its credit, the Department of Transportation has taken numerous positive steps, but travel advocacy groups argue that there is still a great deal more that needs to be accomplished. For example, when flights are delayed or canceled, there is no standardization on what a passenger's rights are. It is the airlines themselves that determine what a passenger's rights may be and not only do these rights vary from passenger to passenger, but they also may vary according to the passenger's status with that particular airline. *USA Today* notes that among the key problems for airline passengers:

- *Each domestic airline publishes its own Contract of Carriage, so there is no industry consistency*
- *Even attorneys have trouble dissecting the vague language imbedded in these contracts*
- *Finding these documents on airlines' Websites has become a challenge unto itself, and hard copies have become a thing of the past*
- *Not all airline employees—and outsourced airline representatives—are familiar with interpreting the contracts*
- *Federal preemption seriously curtails passengers from redressing grievances*

(McGee, 2013)

Europe, on the other hand, has a specific passenger bill of rights for both air travel and train travel. The passenger has specific legal recourse regarding issues such as denied boarding, flight cancelations, extended flight delays, knowing which airline is actually the carrier in cases where there is code sharing, and issues of price transparency. In the United States, these "policies" are currently handled on a piecemeal basis by each airline. The European Union (EU) also provides a travelers' bill of rights when it comes to people who may have a disability and therefore suffer from reduced mobility ("Your passenger rights when travelling by air," n.d.). The Website of the EU also tells the consumer exactly where he or she is to go to lodge a complaint. The Website reads in part:

What should you do if you believe your passenger rights have been infringed? If you consider that your entitlements under air passenger rights legislation have been breached:
- *You should first contact the airline or—for issues related to persons with reduced mobility—the airport.*
- *If you are not satisfied with their response, you can lodge a complaint with a National Enforcement Body (NEB).*

- *In case of issues related to lost, delayed, and/or damaged luggage, you may wish to contact the European Consumer Centre (ECC) in your country: ec.europa.eu/consumers/ecc/index_en.htm*
  You may also wish to contact the national consumer organizations: ec.europa.eu/consumers/empowerment/cons_networks_en.htm#national
  Note: *Complaints should in principle be filed in the country where the incident took place.*
  (From www.wttc.org/research/economic-impact-research/. April 1, 2014)

U.S. CRUISE PASSENGERS BILL OF RIGHTS

On May 22, 2013, the cruise industry announced that U.S. cruise passengers would receive a passenger bill of rights. This development may have come about due to problems in the cruise industry. The Cruise Lines International Association (CLIA) universally adopted this bill of rights and the document acts as a standard against which all cruise line companies are responsible. Within the Cruise Passenger Bill of Rights are the following:

- *The right to disembark a docked ship if essential provisions such as food, water, restroom facilities, and access to medical care cannot adequately be provided on-board, subject only to the Master's concern for passenger safety and security and customs and immigration requirements of the port.*
- *The right to a full refund for a trip that is canceled due to mechanical failures, or a partial refund for voyages that are terminated early due to those failures.*
- *The right to have available on-board ships operating beyond rivers or coastal waters full-time, professional emergency medical attention, as needed, until shore-side medical care becomes available.*
- *The right to timely information updates as to any adjustments in the itinerary of the ship in the event of a mechanical failure or emergency, as well as timely updates of the status of efforts to address mechanical failures.*
- *The right to a ship crew that is properly trained in emergency and evacuation procedures.*
- *The right to an emergency power source in the case of a main generator failure.*
- *The right to transportation to the ship's scheduled port of disembarkation or the passenger's home city in the event a cruise is terminated early due to mechanical failures.*
- *The right to lodging if disembarkation and an overnight stay in an unscheduled port are required when a cruise is terminated early due to mechanical failures.*
- *The right to have included on each cruise line's Website a toll-free phone line that can be used for questions or information concerning any aspect of ship-board operations.*

- *The right to have this Cruise Line Passenger Bill of Rights published on each line's Website.*

(Parrotta & Peikin, 2013, Passenger Bill of Rights section)

TRAIN AND BUS TRAVEL

The European Union provides a set of rights for train travelers:

- Buying a ticket without hassle.
- Traveling in safety.
- Equal service for passengers with reduced mobility.
- Information on accessibility for passengers with reduced mobility.
- Compensation in case of injury or death and liability for luggage.
- Protection from rail companies failing to meet their liability obligations.

Each one of these broad categories provides within it numerous other protections for the train traveler.

In the United States, the situation for both rail and bus travel is a bit more complicated. In the past, different train companies, just as in the case of airlines, may have had different rules regarding compensation. Today most passenger rail traffic is handled by Amtrak, yet there appears to be no standard policy protecting U.S. rail travelers and none is mentioned on the Amtrak Website.

When it comes to passenger rights on buses, the U.S. lags far behind Europe. Although the Federal Motor Carrier Association sets standards for bus drivers, almost no attention is given to the customer side of the equation. Several bus companies have policies to help passengers when there is a problem, but these policies are set by the companies themselves and in reality the passenger is at the whim of the bus company employee.

FIRE CODES

Almost since the start of civilization humanity has had a love–hate relationship with fire. On one hand, fire provides both warmth and a way to cook food and boil water; on the other hand, fire is a deadly force that can rapidly destroy whole cities or great forests. The National Fire Protection Association reports that:

US fire departments responded to an estimated average of 3,700 structure fires per year at hotel or motel properties between 2006 and 2010. These fires caused average annual losses of 12 civilian deaths, 143 civilian injuries, and $127 million in direct property damage each year.

Facts and Figures

- *In an average year, 1 of every 12 hotels or motels reported a structure fire.*
- *Smoking materials started 10% of the fires in hotels and motels; these fires caused 79% of the deaths.*

- *Only 8% of hotel and motel fires were intentionally set, but these accounted for 12% of the associated property damage.*
- *Twelve percent of fires in hotels and motels began in a bedroom; these fires caused 72% of the associated civilian deaths and 31% of civilian injuries.*
- *When sprinklers were present and operated, 91% of sprinklers in hotel or motel fires operated effectively when present.*

(Hotels and Motels, 2013)

All hotels are expected to have smoke alarms and hotels should have (but are not required by law) sprinkler systems in each guest room. Other protections that are recommended for rooms in places of lodging include at least some of the following:

- Fire sprinklers
- Smoke and fire detectors
- Duct smoke detectors
- Automatic alarm systems
- Connection between air handling units and alarm systems
- Manual alarm systems (the pull-boxes you see near stairway doors and elevators)
- Fire department standpipes (in stairways)
- Emergency lights
- Emergency egress system
- Fire resistivity of construction
- Exits and exit signs
- Pressurized stairways
- Smoke control systems
- Portable fire extinguishers
- Staff emergency response plans
- Staff training
- Gas supply shut-off devices
- Fire alarm system required in hotels/motels
- Helicopter landing sites in high-rise buildings

Following notable fires in the 1970s and 1980s, the federal government took efforts to ensure the majority of its employees traveling on official business stay in accommodations offering minimum fire safety features. As a result, Congress passed Public Law 101 391 known as the Hotel and Motel Fire Safety Act of 1990, requiring 90% of all federal travel nights to be at properties that meet the requirements of this act.

The law established as policy that federal employees stay in accommodations meeting certain life-safety standards for fire protection whenever commercial lodging is required. The law required that Federal Emergency

Management Agency (FEMA) maintain a list of those places of accommodation that met the federal requirements. The list came to be known as the National Master List (NML). To meet the requirements of the act, a hotel or motel must have hard-wired, single-station smoke alarms in each guestroom. In addition to the smoke alarm requirement, if the property is four or more stories, each guestroom must have the added protection afforded by an automatic fire sprinkler system. The smoke alarms and fire sprinkler system must meet accepted national standards. Properties that do not meet the act's requirements (or comply, but do not appear on the NML) risk losing federal government travel and conference business. As of 2011, more than 43,000 properties meet the federal hotel and motel fire safety requirements for inclusion on the NML. The NML database is available online to federal employees and the public (Hotel and Motel Fire Safety Act, 2008).

IN EUROPE

The EU bases its standards on the *Council Recommendation of 22 December 1986 on fire safety in existing hotels*. The proposal offers a large number of recommendations regarding fire safety and protects visitors to places of lodging that have at least 20 beds.

The following fire safety measures are suggested:

- *Safe escape routes*: The free passage of persons in the event of fire is secured.
- *Solid building construction*: The hotel will remain stable for at least as long as it takes to evacuate all occupants.
- *Safe materials*: Constraint on the use of highly flammable materials in surface coverings retards the outbreak of fires.
- *Safe technical appliances*.
- *Functional alarm systems*: All occupants must be able to hear the alarm in case of fire.
- *Safety instructions*: Each room displays a plan of the escape routes and emergency procedures.
- *Equipment*: Functional emergency fire-fighting equipment.
- *Training*: Hotel staff is provided with suitable emergency instruction.

The Recommendation and the guidelines it puts forward have been adopted by the national legislatures in all Member States, though not consistently ("Fire safety in buildings," 2011).

Fire prevention and fire-fighting experts agree that the preventative equipment listed above should work in concert, that is, be part of an overall fire prevention/fighting system. The reason for this "system approach" is based on the theory of "redundancy." Redundancy comes from the concept that if one part of a system fails, then there are other parts of the system that compensate for that failure. From the perspective of "redundancy," all security systems should have a backup system that can compensate for any breakdown in the security system. It is important to remember that often a breakdown in the system can come from a very simple and basic element. For example, in the case of fire protection, the leaving of a fireproof door in an open state may allow a fire to spread quickly and to places where the door was supposed to have acted as a fire break. One of the key elements, therefore, in any fire protection method is staff practice. Almost any prevention system can be defeated by human error or ignorance. In the case of security, practice makes perfect (Hotel Fire Safety, n.d.).

It should be noted that neither the United States nor Europe has standard safety, security, or fire regulations for small establishments such as bed and breakfasts. In many cases, being a guest at a bed and breakfast is not different from that of being a guest at someone's home. Nevertheless, a bed and breakfast is expected to charge its guests a lodging tax and is subject to local building and fire codes. In some states, such as Ohio, regulations on the serving of food depend on the number of guests served in a given day. As of the writing of this book, bed and breakfasts are regulated on a state-by-state basis. In an article published January 2013, the *Wall Street Journal* noted:

> Be aware of regulatory requirements—*Before exploring any aspect of whether the business might work, establish whether you're allowed to open it first. New York State and New York City, in particular, have cracked down on "illegal hotels" and established strict rules about what qualifies as a hotel service that impact on bed and breakfasts; guesthouses and online temporary stay services such as AirBnB. On the way, some established guesthouses have gotten caught up in the melee, prompting them to form a lobby group called "Stay NYC" and petition for an exemption for their group of tax-paying, registered businesses from the law. The lesson? Consult an attorney about zoning, tax and licensing requirements...*
> *(Bischof, 2013, para. 6)*

SUMMARY

Because this chapter focuses on a myriad of topics a general summary is offered. The following basic principles and concepts apply to all topics, and they act to summarize this chapter.

Try to envision problems and then prevent them from occurring. The best way to solve a problem and to prevent a crisis is to stop it before it happens. This concept is not only the basic concept of good risk management, but also of the legal concept of foreseeability. It is essential to remember that when we travel all problems are seen as crises, and that people in a litigious society are fast in calling their lawyers. The problem may be a minor problem to the travel professional, but to his or her client it is not a problem but a crisis. Good customer service and a friendly smile are a lot less expensive than having to defend oneself in a court of law. Never forget that in tourism time is always of the essence. Thus, the faster you solve a problem the less chance it has of becoming a major crisis in the eyes of your customer and the less chance that you will have to defend yourself in court. When in doubt check with your legal team first rather than asking them to defend you once the lawsuit has been filed.

Remember, you are responsible not only to your customers, but also to the tourism community in which you work. Responsible tourism means taking the time to think about the impact of your tourism product on your employees and on the host community. Tourism officials must consider the economic and social impact on the host community, what the negative aspects of tourism are, and how does tourism act as a responsible agent within the total context of the community. The more responsible a tourism industry is, the less chance it has of having to deal with a class action lawsuit and with the negative publicity that may result.

Being responsible means that every tourism and travel business needs to provide full information, be that information about the environment or be it about safety and security. A major problem in the tourism industry is that critical information is often omitted and that people are not given full details. Tourists and visitors assume that travel experts, whether in transportation, hospitality, or in a travel agency, are looking out for them. All too often this belief is simply false. It is best to remember that many times our guests do not even know which questions they are to ask, and then become furious when they realize that they were not provided with full disclosure. Information needs to be given in precise, clear, and readable language. Putting something in the fine print may help in court, but it will cost your business a great deal of good will. Being responsible means caring for every aspect of tourism, from the visitor to the employee, from the site to the environment, from the host community to the business's reputation.

Being responsible also means that it is our job not to tolerate irresponsible behavior. Tourism cannot afford either from a moral or financial perspective to allow criminal behavior to become part of the industry. When human trafficking, child abuse, or use of illegal substances enter into the tourism system, the system is bound to collapse. Tourism officials must always be upright when dealing with their customers, local customs, and laws, and insist that to be responsible is to respect both our fellow citizens and the planet upon which we dwell.

REFERENCES

Anolik, A. (2010). Travel and tourism. *GPSolo Magazine*. Retrieved from https://www. americanbar.org/newsletter/publications/gp_solo_magazine_home/gp_solo_ magazine_index/anolik.html.

Anon., 2014. Economic Impact of Travel & Tourism 2014 Annual Update: Summary. World Travel and Tourism Council. Retrieved from http://www.wttc.org/site_ media/uploads/downloads/Economic_Impact_Summary_2014_2ppA4_FINAL.pdf.

Bischof, J. (2013). What to know before opening a bed and breakfast. *The Wall Street Journal*, January 13. Retrieved from http://blogs.wsj.com/metropolis/2013/01/31/what-to-know-before-opening-a-bed-and-breakfast/.

Fire safety in buildings (2011). *Fire Safe Europe*. Retrieved from http://www.firesafeeurope. eu/fire-safety.

Hotel fire safety (n.d.). *iklim*. Retrieved from http://www.iklimnet.com/hotelfires/ firesafety.html.

Hotel and motel fire safety act (2008). *American Hotel & Lodging Association*. Retrieved from http://www.ahla.com/issuebrief.aspx?id=20300.

Hotels and motels (2013). *National Fire Protection Association*. Retrieved from http://www. nfpa.org/safety-information/for-consumers/occupancies/hotels-and-motels.

Insurance solutions for the travel industry (2013). *AON*. Retrieved from http://www. berkely.com/sites/berkely/risk_management/Pages/service_fees.aspx.

Kim, J. (2011). *Exploring how employee empowerment impacts on hotel desk operations*. (Published dissertation). Retrieved from UNLV Theses/Dissertations/Professional Papers/Capstones. (Paper 1058).

McGee, B. (2013). When do airline passengers get their bill of rights? *USA Today, July 17*. *Retrieved from* http://www.usatoday.com/story/travel/columnist/mcgee/2013/07/17/ when-do-airline-passengers-get-their-bill-of-rights/2522117/.

Parrotta, L., & Peikin, D. (2013). Cruise industry adopts passenger bill of rights. *Cruise Lines International Association*. Retrieved from http://www.cruising.org/news/press_releases/ 2013/05/cruise-industry-adopts-passenger-bill-rights.

U.S. Department of Transportation expands airline passenger protections (2011). *United States Department of Transportation*. Retrieved from http://www.dot.gov/briefing-room/us-department-transportation-expands-airline-passenger-protections.

What should you do if you believe your passenger rights have been infringed? (n.d.). *European Commission*. Retrieved from http://ec.europa.eu/transport/passenger-rights/en/34-neb-air.html.

Your passenger rights when travelling by air (n.d.). *European Commission*. Retrieved from http://ec.europa.eu/transport/passenger-rights/en/03-air.html.

Case Studies: Four Tourism Cities

INTRODUCTION

Charles Dickens in 1859 published his famous novel, *A Tale of Two Cities*. The story was set in two cities and, although fiction, showed many of the differences between nineteenth-century London and Paris. This chapter is somewhat similar in that it may be called a tale of four cities. Although there is no fiction in the chapter, the chapter serves to underscore how tourism security is done in several representative cities around the world. Chapter 9 looks at tourism security in Charleston, South Carolina, a medium-size city that has invested heavily in tourism security and has become one of America's most successful cities. The chapter also looks at one of America's great tourism cities, Las Vegas, Nevada. From an international perspective the chapter looks at one of the best tourism-policing units in the Western Hemisphere, that of the Dominican Republic, and, finally, it examines perhaps the city that best represents mega-tourism events in the world, Rio de Janeiro. The chapter is divided into five subsections. Each subsection features one of the four locales mentioned above and then looks at a comparison between these cities. Subsection five seeks to understand what these cities have in common and what makes each of them unique, what their strong points are, and in what areas challenges still exist. Finally, the chapter ends with some words on the future of tourism security around the world, the challenges it faces, and how it can impact a city, state, or an entire nation.

TOURISM AND FREEDOM

Although the four case studies discussed in this chapter will show a great deal of differences, there are certain commonalities that touch upon all tourism cities. Tourism assumes that an individual enjoys freedom of travel and the freedom to be in a place where he or she is an unknown. As such, all tourism security professionals must work under the assumption that the individual can be kept safe and his or her worries for his or her personal welfare can be kept to a minimum. From the perspective of tourism security, we can read the Biblical book of Exodus as a story that not only tells of slaves traveling from slavery to freedom, but also as one of travel security.

Often tourism security professionals deal only in the present, but tourism security is more than dealing with a continuum of current problems, it is also the connection of the past to a future, a neverending interaction of human beings with their fellow humans in which time and places interconnect. When presented in such a manner, then the tourism security agent becomes more than a mere technician of safety, but an active part of the tourism marketing and economic development chain.

Tourism security professionals need to work under the assumption that visitors have the right to know the "other" without fear. Without this assumption, travel is merely a transferring of one "here" to another "here," a neverending cycle of motion that exists outside of the context of time. Travel then is more than mere motion, or displacement from one locale to another. For example, a prison inmate may be transferred from one incarceration center to another, but the prisoner is not a traveler. In this case, the inmate is merely an object being moved for the convenience of his or her jailer. In a like manner, one only needs to look at refugees on the run. No matter where these refugees may be, they are people who are traveling, but they are not travelers. Instead, they are people pushed by the forces of history, often against their will, from one locale to another, seeking nothing more than a return to their place of origin or a safe place in which to find refuge. Travelers then are different. To be a traveler-visitor, one has to fit into the following categories:

• Wishes to go from a "here" to a "there."
• Assumes that he or she is wanted in the new locale, that the locale is a temporary experience, and that he or she will be able to return home.
• Will be free to leave.
• Has the right to encounter sociologically and culturally the "other."
• Has the right to assume that he or she will be safe and comes under the protection of the "host community."
• Has the right to assume that the host society desires his or her presence.

Furthermore, modern tourism security specialists must not only worry about caring for the guest, but also caring for the host population. Both sexual tourism and at times sports tourism produce situations in which the local population lives in fear of what the traveler may do. For example, soccer fans often face forms of hooliganism that result in property damage and even sexual assault. This means that tourism security experts must worry not only about protecting their visitors, but also employees, locals, property, the community's culture and ecology, and its reputation.

The following locations have all dealt with many of these issues. Some have been more successful than others, but all have had to face the fact that tourism security is both a necessity and a challenge.

CHARLESTON, SOUTH CAROLINA
An Overview

Charleston is one of the oldest cities in the United States. The city dates back to the mid-seventeenth century. Despite the difficulties of surviving attacks from disease, European powers, and local Native Americans, the colony did survive. By 1680, Charles Town (as it was originally called) had a population of at least 1,000. Because the city was a place of religious tolerance, the city's population was composed of people from multiple Protestant denominations along with a sizeable Jewish and Catholic population.

Due to the fact that by the end of the seventeenth century it had good, secure port facilities, Charles Town became a major port along the U.S. Eastern Seaboard, and by 1740, the city became a major North American port. The economic prosperity did not mean that Charles Town was without its challenges. The city suffered from major fires throughout the eighteenth and nineteenth centuries, and epidemics such as small pox were a constant threat to the population's viability. Also, Charles Town has known its fair share of war. The British occupied the city during the Revolutionary War and Union soldiers reoccupied the city during its capture during and after the Civil War. In 1783, after being liberated from the British, the city was renamed "Charleston."

Charleston is perhaps best known in U.S. history as the place where the Civil War began. The city suffered from both physical and economic damage. The city had to maintain many of its older buildings, not due to a desire for historic preservation, but rather to severe poverty. In fact, preservation efforts did not begin until the 1940s. The twentieth century also presented Charleston with a series of challenges, including Hurricane Hugo. Despite the storm surge, the city lost or suffered damage to only 25 of its 3,500 historic buildings. These buildings are one of the pillars of modern Charleston's charm.

Over the last decade Charleston has become one of the top tourism cities in the United States. The city offers a wide variety of tourism experiences ranging from history and civil war, to beaches, golfing, African-American tourism, and a wide variety of culinary experiences. Its historic downtown and gardens has turned the city into a romantic location for weddings from around the world. Among the city's attractions are:

- Aquariums
- Downtown charm and photo opportunities
- Historic forts
- Historic homes and houses of worship
- Museums
- Plantations and gardens
- Restaurants and gastronomic tourism experiences

Charleston Survey

In order to understand how tourism security impacts each city studied, each of the locale's police departments were given the opportunity of answering a questionnaire. In order to avoid linguistic problems, the questionnaire was written in English, Portuguese, and Spanish. Chief Greg Mullen of the Charleston Police Department was kind enough to answer the questionnaire in detail. We note in Chief Mullen's answers his dedication to detail and why Charleston has become a leading tourism city within the United States (Figure 9.1).

- Tarlow: How major of a contributor to the economy of your city is tourism?

Figure 9.1 Charleston, South Carolina: downtown.

Mullen: Tourism is one of the largest economic engines in Charleston. Nearly five million visitors come to the city each year. The overall economic impact topped 3.5 billion in 2012 and is expanding. Occupancy rates are higher and room rates are again on the increase. For the third year in a row, Charleston was just named the number one destination in the USA by Condé Nast Traveler *magazine.*

- Tarlow: How many police officers work in tourism security?
  Mullen: Currently, there are 20 officers assigned full time to the tourist district. In addition, there are several other officers that work in tourism security–related assignments that include activities such as liaison with the Convention and Visitors Bureau (CVB), supporting the City's Tourism Commission, and addressing new laws and ordinances that enhance the tourist experience. All the officers work collectively with the business, residential, and college communities that are important components of Charleston's tourism experience. In October 2013, we hired an additional 12 officers that were approved by City Council in June 2013 to expand the tourism unit. Once the new officers have been trained, incumbent officers will be moved to the tourism unit to complete the expansion.
- Tarlow: How much training have they had/do they receive?
  Mullen: Several of the officers have attended sessions dealing with the tourism-oriented policing and protective services (TOPPS) concepts. In addition, they received instruction in customer service, communication, fair and impartial policing, dealing with the mentally ill and disabled, and judgment and decision making. Others have been involved with the Responsible Hospitality Institute (RHI) that focuses on environmental components of tourism and how they work collectively to improve the safety and vibrancy of the district. As part of the expanded program, all the officers will attend a formal program that includes elements of TOPPS and RHI in a combined program. We anticipate that the entire unit will be fully trained by June 2014.
- Tarlow: What special training do your officers receive regarding the tourism industry? Which officers (all/a special unit)?
  Mullen: The officers who receive specific training relating to the tourism industry are those who are assigned to the tourist district. That training is outlined in question number three. However, all officers attend training dealing with customer service and the importance of the tourist industry to the overall economic well-being of Charleston. We also provide roll-call training on a regular basis that involves dealing with tourism-related issues such as alcohol-induced sexual assaults, aggravated assaults, and personal injuries. This process focuses on the importance between prevention and enforcement and the critical thinking that is required to manage the polarities of enforcement and economic vitality. We constantly impress upon all officers the importance of communicating effectively with visitors and how

officers are truly ambassadors for the city. We also frequently discuss how our actions in one situation can create an image and reputation that permeates the minds and hearts of current and future guests to our city. Our training in this area primarily focuses on understanding the mindset of the visitors; creating a culture of service that is based on being fair, firm, and friendly; and the important role that we play in protecting the "golden goose" that supports the city's health and growth.

– Tarlow: What are your major tourism security challenges?

Mullen: The city sponsors over 200 special events per year. This ranges from small concerts to international art festivals. Each of these events creates their own challenges. As the world has changed, so have the requirements and expectations regarding tourist safety and security. Many of the events bring tens of thousands of visitors to the city and it is very manpower-intensive to plan and execute appropriate risk management protocols. The majority of the special events have been occurring for many years without any significant issues. Therefore, some do not understand the necessity of using new, restrictive regulations that change the way things have been done. As we began to implement new security requirements such as timelines for permitting, staffing requirements, screening procedures, and alcohol controls, we experienced pushback from organizers and some city officials. However, as we have worked through these issues, a very robust special events process has emerged and been implemented. This is still a work in progress and we are working through the growing pains; however, it is necessary to address the security challenges that are real in today's environment. We also battle the perception that nothing bad has happened in the tourist district so why do we need regulations that require businesses to be more responsible and take a proactive role in managing people and activities associated with their businesses. Tourist and business owners alike feel that the police is interfering in their business and limiting the ability for visitors to enjoy their visit. We have had success in adopting regulations that create a safer and more secure area and it is still a great deal to be done. While this may seem like unusual priorities for the police as it relates to tourism policing, it is critical. One of our biggest challenges currently is to manage an environment that is reaching a tipping point in terms of the number of bars, nightclubs, and restaurants that transition into bars. There is an expectation among patrons, business owners, parents of college students, city planners, and others that the police ensure the safety of everyone who frequents the area; however, there is reluctance to mitigate the potential for crime and violence by limiting density of alcohol establishments, changing zoning requirements, and placing strict accountability on operators for the activity associated with their establishments by some officials and business owners.

– Tarlow: Please describe the types of crime/violence that most commonly happen to tourists to your community.

Mullen: We are very fortunate that even as our tourist district has grown and seen substantial increases in visitation, we have not experienced increases in crime or violence. It is rare that we have a tourist who is the victim of crime or violence during their stay in Charleston. The most frequent crimes involving tourists are larcenies. The larcenies occur from individuals leaving valuables in their vehicles without securing the property or the vehicle. We frequently deal with visitors who feel very secure in the city and fail to take reasonable precautions that would be part of their normal behavior were they not on vacation. These crimes often occur in public parking garages or on street parking sites in neighborhoods adjacent to the tourist district. While we have worked collectively with the Convention and Visitor Bureau (CVB) and other hospitality associations to inform visitors to be aware of this situation and take steps to protect their belongings, we still receive reports about thefts occasionally. The few assaults that occur in the tourist district usually involve college-age adults who have visited local bars and nightclubs and engaged in binge drinking. At the end of the night when bars are closing there are thousands of people on the streets that were not originally developed for this type of business. When the intoxicated patrons exit the bars and nightclubs and overwhelm the sidewalk system that was developed for retail and small businesses, confrontations sometimes occur. On occasion, these confrontations turn into physical altercations and assaults happen. These incidents usually occur late in the evening and very quickly. Most involve groups of young people that feel a sense of anonymity as a result of the large crowds that consume the area during bar closing. While we do experience some robberies and sexual assaults within the district, they are infrequent. Most robberies do not involve tourists; however, some occur in neighborhoods surrounding the area, which can create concern because of the close proximity to the main tourist district. Our patrol commanders monitor this activity very closely and develop patrol strategies in the neighborhoods surrounding the tourist district to compliment and support the efforts conducted by the Tourism Unit. All officers working in these areas understand the importance of preventing crime that could negatively impact tourism and associated activities. We occasionally received reports about sexual assaults involving visitors to the city. They nearly always involve alcohol and occur between acquaintances or couples that have recently met. These cases are fully investigated and many cannot be prosecuted because of the difficulty in gaining details about the event from the parties involved. We have implemented several initiatives to educate students and visitors about the risk involved in heavy drinking and connecting with strangers while drinking. We have experienced a reduction of these incidents; however, they do still occur.

– Tarlow: What are the major complaints regarding tourism security?
Mullen: *The only complaint that we receive regarding tourist security comes from the parents of college students. They believe that the police do not do enough to manage rowdy behavior in the entertainment district. Unfortunately, their dialog regarding escalating crime is not supported by fact. Therefore, it is constantly a challenge to ensure accurate information is communicated and the real situation explained. The parents who do not live in Charleston get the information from their children or the local media, which is not always accurate or complete. The second complaint that we constantly deal with involves bicycles and skateboards. Visitors are concerned about the use of these devices on streets and sidewalks. This has created a unique situation. There is a big business and demand for bicycles in the city; however, the streets and sidewalks were not designed to accommodate these vehicles. Therefore, we are constantly balancing the tension between pedestrians and bicycle enthusiasts.*

– Tarlow: Does your department work with the tourism industry? If so, how?
Mullen: *Yes . . .the department has a very close and personal relationship with the tourism industry. There is a dedicated liaison officer who works directly with the various associations and CVB to identify and address issues and initiate new programs. Additionally, we have developed a Responsible Hospitality Group that is comprised of local tourism professionals from the major components that make up the tourism industry. Additionally, we have members from the college, residential community, and other city departments. We meet on a bimonthly basis to discuss issues, obtain feedback, brainstorm about new initiatives, and discuss training and legislative possibilities. This group has become a significant support mechanism for the police when we are asking for additional staffing, equipment, and regulations that impact the tourism industry. The meetings are hosted by the CVB and the Executive Director is an active participant. Some of the more important projects that have been shepherded by this group includes valet services, transportation enhancements, trash and cleaning enhancements for the district, implementation of CCTV safety and security systems, legislative changes, and bike and taxi ordinances. This group is very engaged and recognizes the importance of a substantial police/industry partnership.*

– Tarlow: Does the tourism industry aid your department? If so, how?
Mullen: *Yes. They are major supporters of the police in terms of legislative changes, program development and support, funding for training, and facilitators for partnership development. Additionally, they actively engage the Mayor and City Council to support funding requests that support the development and implementation of the TOPPS unit that has been in place for several years. They also*

sponsor training and most recently were advocates for the expansion of the unit and helped us win support for an additional 12 officers.

−   Tarlow: Does your police department view itself as having a special role in your tourism industry?

Mullen: Absolutely. We see ourselves as part of the economic development team. We understand the clear connection between our role of providing a safe and secure environment for tourism to thrive and the benefit we receive from the revenue generated by tourism dollars. If not for the robust tourism industry, the police department would not be able to purchase equipment and staff positions that are necessary to keep crime down and build relationships with businesses and visitors. We see ourselves as ambassadors for the city with a mission to prevent crime and offer a customer experience that builds memories and repeat visits.

−   Tarlow: What special problems do you have in protecting tourists?

Mullen: The major issue that drives behavioral issues that affect tourists, as well as local visitors to our destinations, involves alcohol consumption. We experience very little tourist-related crime or issues during the daytime and early-evening hours. The hours when challenges occur start around 11:00 P.M. This time coincides with the busiest time for bars and nightclubs and continues until 4:00 A.M. Because Charleston is an urban city, the tourist district interconnects with residential neighborhoods that possess a number of the accommodations. Therefore, there is a great deal of walking traffic throughout the area. Many of the areas are poorly lit due to concerns of residents and preservationists. They do not want the city to install high-intensity streetlights or additional lighting in their neighborhoods. While this would certainly offer better security for residents and visitors using the area, we must also consider the concerns of residents and preservationists who feel the increased lighting would negatively impact their quality of life and the feeling of the historic neighborhoods. Due to this situation, we extend the normal tourist district to manage the walking traffic that is found in dark, isolated, and mixed-use areas. Add to this equation the fact that many of these individuals are moderately to highly intoxicated; this creates an opportunity for victimization by offering a target-rich environment for those who wish to do harm. Compounding this challenge, as the city goes through a development explosion, many of the new and more popular restaurants are locating in areas adjacent to the main tourist districts and in some cases in the middle of areas that are going through significant transformation. Many of the owner/operators are pioneers who are taking risks and opening businesses in areas that are traditionally challenged from the perspective of crime and urban blight. These new and vibrant late-night establishments are bringing new opportunities to the city, as well as challenges to the police. We are attempting to encourage CPTED (Crime Prevention Through Environmental Design) principles as the development is occurring. Thus far, this has seen only limited successes because it is not mandated through the building code. A second challenge that adds to this situation is the lack of a late-night transportation system that can effectively handle the large number of tourists leaving the area during the late-night hours. The free shuttle in the area stops at 10:00 P.M. and the taxi system is not adequate to manage the ever-increasing demand. This has been identified as a major concern within the district and is being worked as a high-priority item.

- Tarlow: Are your tourism police a separate unit within the police department?

    Mullen: Currently, the Tourism Unit is not a separate entity. It is part of the team where the district is located. The rationale for this decision involves ownership by the commander who oversees the entire team. We believe that it is important that the commander who oversees the area within the city where the Tourist District is located has investment in this part of the team. Because of the unique atmosphere that is Charleston, it is imperative that a holistic approach be taken to police the district. As mentioned earlier, this district is expanding and there are no nature boundaries that clearly define the district. Therefore, it is necessary that the commander has the ability to identify issues and concerns and has the resources to quickly respond. As the areas continue to grow and eventually merge into a single geographic cluster, we currently have 1,500 new hotel rooms approved and thousands of square feet of retail and office space planned. I anticipate that we will create a separate team to cover the main tourist area.

- Tarlow: What are the major challenges that you have in protecting visitors?

    Mullen: The visitors themselves. They believe they are bulletproof. Charleston is an urban environment that has gone through a significant transformation in the last 20 years. As a result, the downtown area has become very vibrant and energized. This has also created an important balance for the police. We must create an environment where people can enjoy and have fun and also make sure that they do not become victims of crime. The city is a safe place to live and visit and it is important to be aware of your surroundings and not place yourself in risky situations. Unfortunately, because of the increase in bars and nightclubs in the downtown area this has become much more challenging. We have addressed this by implementing shuttles and taxi stands and expanded police coverage to ensure that our guests do have fun and we minimize the risk as much as possible. By training our officers to be as much ambassadors and crime preventers as they are crime-fighters, we have been able to enhance the visitors' experience while also increasing their safety.

- Tarlow: Does your department see its role as one of crime-solving/protection or does it define the problem in different terms? If so, what are they?

Mullen: We see ourselves as the most visible form of government within the city and our primary responsibility is to create a safe and secure environment for citizens and guests. To accomplish that, we operate under a philosophy that we treat the people in our city as we would want to be treated, or someone in our family treated, in a similar situation. That transcends many different layers of our response. First and foremost, we want people to see us as ambassadors who are here to help them enjoy their stay in Charleston. We reinforce constantly with all our officers the importance of being friendly, having neighborly chats with people on the street, and responding to requests for assistance in any form with a service-oriented mindset. We do this because we believe our best opportunity to support the city and our guests is by preventing bad things from happening to them. A golden thread that runs through all our training is this—we can never remove the trauma and negative feelings associated with being a victim. Therefore, we do everything that we can to prevent crime and create an atmosphere of positive energy. However, when events do occur, we respond quickly, with empathy and a sense of urgency. We want our visitors to understand that we take their issues seriously and will do our very best to help them recover from the negative experiences if they occur. Even if they are victimized in some way, we want them to leave our city with the assurance that we care about them.

– Tarlow: Does your department see its role as that of protectors of its city's image and reputation?
Mullen: Yes. This is a very important role for the police department as a whole. While we have a specialized unit that works in the tourism district, we impress upon all officers the importance of protecting the Charleston brand. We impress upon our officers how one bad event can destroy all the positive accolades that the city has enjoyed. Therefore, we constantly reinforce the requirement that customer service, professionalism, and all-around friendly hospitality is critical to the overall success of the department and the city.

– Tarlow: Does your department view the foreign tourist as having special needs?
Mullen: We recognize that foreign tourists have different needs and attempt to provide for them. We work with the CVB and other associations to identify the countries that frequent our area and do what we can to offer information, signage, and other instructional material that will assist them in their visit. This is an area of improvement that is being researched, especially since we are seeing more and more tourists from various countries. We are exploring the possibility of having frequently asked question cards be developed in different languages.

– Tarlow: Does your department believe that all tourists should be treated basically alike?

Mullen: At a foundational level yes. We also recognize that different visitors will have different needs. For example, we know that our interaction with the elderly will primary involve those that have started on a nice walk and realize they have overextended themselves. In these cases, officers are quick to offer rides or other transportation arrangements. Families are more interested in fun activities and want the police to be engaging and informational to assist them as they move about the city. Foreign tourists, as mentioned, may have needs that involve informational services, money exchange, not understanding the dangers or potential problems within an area, and the nightlife creates completely different demands. So, the answer is we want all tourists to be treated with respect, courtesy, and a welcoming attitude. We also recognize that depending on the purpose of their visit, they may need different services and responses.

- Tarlow: Has crime caused your community's image to suffer from negative media publicity due to crimes against tourists?

  Mullen: No.

- Tarlow: As a department, do you have adequate resources to protect tourists?

  Mullen: Yes. Our City Council has been very supportive. They recognize the importance of tourism safety and security to the financial health of the city. Recently, they added an additional 12 officers to our program that has allowed a more robust deployment that expands our ability to address the primary tourism areas as well as the surrounding environment.

- Tarlow: How well does your department cooperate with the media?

  Mullen: Very well. We have a very open and cooperative relationship with the media that allows us to share information about our operations and publicize important initiatives. This relationship also helps us to address misinformation or unfounded allegations that have the potential to harm our tourism image.

- Tarlow: Do you have any special tourism–policing programs that have worked well?

  Mullen: Our tourism programs are constantly evolving. We started with a small group of officers working a specific geographic area. Their method of operation was primarily bicycle patrols with a heavy emphasis on personal interaction with tourists and customer service. Over time, we have expanded the unit and become more involved in addressing issues surrounding nightlife venues that are expanding substantially in different geographic areas. As we expanded, we added foot patrols and T-3 devices to improve visibility and enhance the relationships between the police and business owners. Additionally, we hold regular meetings between the police and business owners to discuss items of concern and opportunities to improve the district. With the most recent expansion of the program, we will begin to develop a formal strategy that will provide foundational principles that support training and education and also provide commanders with flexibility to address the specific needs they identify within their own areas.

- Tarlow: What tourism-policing programs have you tried (if any) that were not successful?

  Mullen: We have not tried any programs that were not successful.

- Tarlow: Do you use an overall integrated plan in your tourism security? If so, please send me a copy; if not, why not?

  Mullen: The department has protocols and practices that have been instituted to address tourism safety and security. Until recently, most of our tourist activity was concentrated in a smaller geographic area. While there were overall plans and directives that provided guidance to officers, there was no formalized plan that encompassed tourism policing. However, with the evolution of our King Street corridor, which has become a very vibrant and energized shopping, eating, and nightlife area, we have started to develop a more integrated, structured, and formal process. The plan that is currently under development includes a sector system for officer deployment, expectations for growing business and visitor relationships, the role of officers in tourism policing, and specific skills and training required for officers working in the Tourism Unit. Once completed, this plan will serve as the roadmap for growth and development of the department's efforts relating to tourism policing, which will become an even higher priority as the district continues to grow and expand.

LAS VEGAS

Las Vegas Tourism

There can be little doubt that Las Vegas is not only one of America's premier tourism destinations, but it is also one of the world's great tourism meccas. According to the Las Vegas Convention and Visitor Authority's (LVCVA) official statistics, the city receives just under 40 million visitors a year. To serve these visitors, the local tourism industry generates over 380,000 jobs. Although the city brags that while others preserve their history, Las Vegas implodes its history with a giant party and even fireworks, in reality Las Vegas' history extends to the late eighteenth century when Spanish explorers first came through the Las Vegas valley. Spanish explorer Rafael Riviera may have been Las Vegas' first official visitor. By the mid-nineteenth century a band of Mormons arrived in the city, but they may have abandoned their "fort" in 1859. Although Nevada became a state in 1864, Las Vegas did not become a "city" until 1905 (and it only

Figure 9.2 The Las Vegas strip.

incorporated in 1911). The opening of the western railroads gave the city its
first *raison d'être*, or reason for existence (Figure 9.2).

The year 1931 may be seen as the city's tourism birth. In that year not
only was Hoover Dam construction begun, bringing thousands of men to
the Las Vegas valley, but the State of Nevada legalized gambling (gaming),
thus changing the face of Las Vegas forever. The 1940s saw the first of many
Las Vegas hotels open and by the end of the 1940s Las Vegas had a major
airport connecting it with much of the country. The first hotels to enter
the Las Vegas market turned into a tidal wave during the 1990s. With the
advent of air conditioning and the taming of the Colorado River, at least
for a while Las Vegas seemed to have conquered its environmental problems.
This can be seen by the fact that Las Vegas reported over 29 million visitors,
making it one of the world's most important tourism cities. Clark County (in
which Las Vegas is located) in 1995 produced $5.7 billion in gaming reve-
nue. Today, Las Vegas stands as a monument to human ingenuity. In a place
where no one should want to neither visit nor live we find a thriving community of almost 2 million residents. These people are joined by almost
40 million visitors yearly who spend almost $80 million per year, making
Las Vegas the number one tourism attraction in the United States.

Because Las Vegas pays careful attention to tourism security and realizes
that a security threat is more than a mere threat, it is also a threat to the city's
tourism economy and its business, the city holds a yearly international tourism safety and security conference. The conference attracts people from all

over the world and serves not only to provide information regarding tourism security issues, but also provides a great deal of networking opportunities. Although each year the Las Vegas conference has a different theme and has emphasized a different aspect of tourism security, each year's conference has shared some common themes. The conference seeks to unite academic research with security practitioners and public safety and security personnel with private security professionals. The goal is to allow people to exchange ideas, discuss mutual problems, and find ways to help each other. The conference also recognizes that the best crisis management is good risk management. That does not mean that all crises can be prevented, but rather that the less crises there are the better the tourism industry will fare. Las Vegas has taken the position that tourism security is not an issue of magic or mystery. Rather, it is an essential element within the tourism product. For this reason, Las Vegas has worked hard to create a safe and secure environment in which safety and security issues are examined thoroughly and in a scientific manner. The Las Vegas tourism authority understands that tourism crises do not just occur, they happen because of our own failures, and that tourism safety and security are too important not to be the subjects of the best academic and professional research. It is for this reason that Las Vegas has invested in its yearly tourism safety and security conference, and has tried to incorporate the conference's best ideas into its overall public tourism policy (Figure 9.3).

Figure 9.3 International Tourism Safety and Security Conference in Las Vegas.

The following is a compilation of some of the major themes that have been presented throughout the conferences.

1. Security must be maintained in an industry that sells magic and enchantment. The tourism industry can ill afford any act of violence that destroys a place's image. Tourism security leaders are continually preaching to tourism marketers that an interlocked world tourism security can be a major selling point.

2. Security requires a cooperative effort. Throughout the years conference speakers have addressed the need for interagency cooperation. Tourism security requires an integral plan that is both horizontal and vertical in nature. That is to say, tourism security must have interagency cooperation on both the management and applied levels, and that front-line personnel must have a clear understanding of management's goals.

3. Often speakers address the fact that the visitor neither knows little about nor cares about interagency rivalries or disputes. Instead, the tourist expects and has the right to expect a safe and secure vacation experience and does not expect to be in the middle of a turf war or an interagency dispute.

4. Tourism safety/security requires credibility. Throughout the years speaker after speaker has addressed the fact that from the consumers' perspective there is no difference between issues of safety and security. The consumer seeks a hassle-free vacation in which he or she does not need to be concerned about things such as poor food quality, room invasions, pickpockets, or health problems. Both contaminated water and being a victim of crime will ruin a leisure traveler's vacation. In both cases the visitor will most likely not only not return to the locale, but may well become a vehicle of negative publicity. To ensure against these problems, speakers emphasize the fact that tourism officials need to warn visitors of real situations and have the data to support their assertions.

5. Speakers often remind tourism officials that they dare not live in the past. Past battles and successes are merely passed battles and successes. The important thing is not what was, but what is and what will be. All too often tourism officials are so fixated by a success or crisis from previous years that they fail to note a new crisis that is brewing. Tourism safety experts need to be aware of the past but not prisoners to it. For example, if in a certain location identity theft crimes have replaced crimes of distraction, then officials need to be aware of the new situation and take measures to protect the traveling public. In a like manner a success does not mean that the problem will not occur again.

6. Tourism security requires first a vision then an assessment and finally, the development of an overall plan.

7. Throughout the years speakers have emphasized the importance of vision, data, and planning. Tourism security then begins with an overall realistic vision. The vision, however, is meaningless if it is not shared by all tourism stakeholders. This means that everyone from the local CVB to the local police department, from the local media to the local hotel association needs to become part of the overall tourism vision. Having a vision, however, is not enough; the vision must also be both practical and realizable.

8. Many of the conference speakers have spoken about the fact that a tourism industry that chooses to ignore security and safety is opening itself up to not only financial loss but also to major lawsuits and liability issues. A number of speakers have addressed the issue of liability, not only at places of lodging but also at attractions and transportation centers. From this perspective speakers noted that tourism safety and security do not subtract from the bottom line, but rather add a new marketing dimension to a tourism product.

Las Vegas is also an excellent example of an integrated security plan. Its police force is highly reinforced by a great number of private security professionals. These people include:

• Highly trained hotel and casino security professionals
• Much of the work done by the LVCVA

Because Las Vegas is not only a leisure destination but also a major convention center, the city must provide security to the leisure traveler as well as the convention attendee. Often Las Vegas' conventions are of the trade-show variety and this means that the city must not only protect the convention site and people attending the convention but also the goods and wares shown at the convention. In some cases these goods can be worth many millions of dollars.

Las Vegas Security

Because Las Vegas is such a large tourism convention destination, this chapter looks at some of the issues facing metro and then does an in-depth interview with Ray Suppe, who heads the security section of the LVCVA. The police material is derived from the author's having spent many years observing Metro and does not reflect an official position.

With almost 40 million tourists and a motto of "what happens in Vegas stays in Vegas," Las Vegas is a challenge to the security professional, both private and public. Tourism security professionals must find the way to allow the city to be safe while at the same time permitting the visitor the freedom to explore sides of his or her personality that may be different from those he or she chooses to show at home. Las Vegas then is the land where people often let their hair down, and at the same time still want to be safe and secure.

Metro has long recognized that travel and tourism is the heart of Las Vegas' economy. The LVCVA reports that the travel and tourism either directly or indirectly produced in 2012 some 382,000 jobs. The Las Vegas Police (called Metro) also recognizes that whenever a crime or other illegal incident occurs, the media surrounding the incident can hurt the city's image. Thus, Las Vegas is continually trying to balance the demands of the media to tell the truth as they see it, with the need for responsible reporting and the realization that the further one is from the incident's location, the longer it lasts in the public's mind and the worse it often seems.

Tourism and travel is a vital industry for Las Vegas; its police department recognizes this fact. One of the ways that it serves the local tourism industry is that Metro has, among other divisions, a dedicated area command police substation in the convention area and at the airport. Often police see crime as problems or events that need to be solved; tourism officials tend to see proactive policing measures as necessary. The discussion over a proactive or reactive police force then goes to the heart of the controversy. As this chapter is being written, this discussion is very much ongoing. Part of this can be seen in Las Vegas' police training. The police department does not offer special tourism security courses, but rather provides generalized police-created security training. It also does not use a special tourism uniform. The police department does offer special courses in counter-terrorism, and other topics that might impact tourism either directly or indirectly such as motorcycle or bicycle training. ·

Because philosophically Las Vegas Metro views tourism security as a normative part of its mission rather than a special mission, funding is often limited. These men and women deal with such "tourism crimes" as vehicle burglary and prostitution or issues of pickpocketing. The police department is continually developing new techniques to deal with these issues. For example, the Las Vegas police department uses *Lock, Take & Hide*, a prevention reminder program. Metro posts this program at the Las Vegas airport and several hotel resort properties. The police and security chiefs' association also has a fax notification system. They use this system to disseminate crime trend information and missing/wanted person information to all hotel resort and retail properties in real time.

To supplement the number of police officers in the tourism zone, Las Vegas also relies on a number of hotel properties whose own security staffs interact with the local police department. Many of these "private" security agents have been in law enforcement and/or the military and add thousands of extra eyes and ears to the tourism security mix. This private–public partnership approach provides Las Vegas with a great deal more security than the mere police numbers might reflect.

Las Vegas has a Tourism Security Chiefs Association. This committee allows both private and public security chiefs to exchange ideas, to network with each other, and to discuss any security or safety problems that may confront the city's tourism industry. For example, the city's security professionals are well aware of the fact that Las Vegas receives millions of visitors from around the world and not all of these people speak English or may have different attitudes toward law enforcement or security personnel. Even something as simple as taking a report may become a highly complicated matter when different languages are spoken.

The following is an interview with Ray Suppe, the head of security at the Las Vegas Visitors Convention Authority. He presents his analysis on how Metro (Las Vegas police) interacts with tourism and also how tourism security is seen from the civilian perspective. Because Las Vegas is such an important tourism city, Suppe's interview is especially important in our understanding of tourism security. It should be noted that Suppe is only speaking about the *Convention Center District Command of Las Vegas*. He is not an official representative of Las Vegas Metro and does not purport to speak for Metro. However, as a tourism security specialist and as the person who must oversee security at the city's main convention center, Suppe's interview affords us with a glimpse into the "intersection" of policing and tourism and security and business (Figure 9.4).

- Tarlow: How major of a contributor to the economy of your city is tourism?

  Suppe: The travel and tourism industry is the number one economic engine for Las Vegas. In 2011, 40 million visitors came to our city. The economic impact from tourism is $45 billion a year. Travel and tourism jobs make up almost one-half of our region's workforce and if you include both direct and indirect jobs, the industry supports 382,800 workers.

- Tarlow: How many police officers work in tourism security?

Figure 9.4 Las Vegas tourism police station; convention center district command.

Suppe: The Las Vegas Metropolitan Police Department (LVMPD) is the law enforcement agency responsible for policing the Las Vegas resort corridor with about 175 employees working out of the Convention Center Area Command station. Included in this number is the Tourist Crimes Unit (TCU).

– Tarlow: As far as you know, how much training do Metro tourism police officers receive?

Suppe: LVMPD is a law enforcement agency recognized with 6 Star Accreditation through Calea, the gold standard in public safety. This applies to all police department employees, not just the Tourist Crimes Unit. I am not aware of additional training to become part of the TCU.

– Tarlow: What special training do your officers receive regarding the tourism industry? Which officers (all/a special unit)?

Suppe: Tourism Oriented Policing and Protective Services (TOPPS) certification is offered by the Las Vegas Tourism Authority, but not required for Metro officers.

– Tarlow: From your perspective, what are Las Vegas' major tourism security challenges?

Suppe: Crimes of opportunity, sense of "freedom," alcohol, drugs, prostitution.

– Tarlow: Please describe the types of crime/violence that most commonly happen to tourists in your community.

Suppe: The most common criminal activity in the resort corridor includes street-level robberies and vehicle burglaries (stealing of items that are left in plain view inside the vehicle). Prostitution is another challenge and commonly includes robbing the victim instead of the act of sex. Street vendors are on the rise in Las Vegas. There are potential health concerns with street vendors selling drugs and attempting to resell bottled water using plastic bottles from the trash and water from a local building spout.

- Tarlow: What are the major complaints regarding tourism security?

Suppe: I am not aware of any specific complaints/concerns coming from visitors.

- Tarlow: Does your local police department work with the tourism industry? If so, how?

Suppe: LVMPD has a strong partnership with the agency tasked with marketing the destination, the Las Vegas Convention and Visitors Authority (LVCVA), as well as the Las Vegas Security Chiefs Association and the International Tourism Safety Association.

- Tarlow: Does the tourism industry aid your community's police department? If so, how?

Suppe: Currently, the LVMPD police station responsible for policing the resort corridor was funded by the tourism industry, specifically the LVCVA provided land and constructed the building. In addition, the tourism industry (LVCVA) provides financial resources to the Southern Nevada Counter Terrorism Center or Fusion Center. Each hotel along the tourism corridor also participates on varying levels.

- Tarlow: From your perspective, does your police department view itself as having a special role in your tourism industry?

Suppe: Las Vegas survives on tourism dollars. Each entity in the destination plays a role in keeping visitors returning by giving them a positive experience during their visit. The police department's role in establishing repeat visitation is to provide a safe and issue-free experience while in Las Vegas.

- Tarlow: What special problems do you believe that Metro has in protecting tourists?

Suppe: Our image is "Sin City" and one of our advertising campaigns is "What Happens Here, Stays Here." Visitors come to Las Vegas with a preconceived notion that they are coming to an adult Disneyland where there are essentially no rules. Alcohol is prevalent in the casinos and along Las Vegas Boulevard. Obviously alcohol lowers one's inhibitions and often makes them more vulnerable. I think we have difficulty with tourists realizing that they are just as susceptible for crime here as any other city.

- Tarlow: Is the tourism police a separate unit within the police department?

Suppe: The Convention Center Area Command was a successful product of the partnership between the Las Vegas Metropolitan Police Department (LVMPD) and the LVCVA. Although the police department does not have a "special unit" designated for tourism safety, geographically, the Convention Center Area

Command covers the majority of the tourist-populated areas and handles the tourism-related crimes. Conceptually thinking, Las Vegas could benefit by introducing a new type of enforcement officer dedicated to the safety and security of the tourist. In some prior international travels, I have seen police department units that were 100% dedicated to tourist safety. These were primarily in areas that have a history of violent crimes and yet these countries rely heavily on tourism dollars.

– Tarlow: What are the major challenges that you have in protecting visitors?

Suppe: Resources would be our biggest challenge. With the economy improving, we are seeing an increase in visitors, but unfortunately, the funding for our police department is actually decreasing. Decreased funding provides a challenge in supplying an appropriate amount of coverage, and limits our ability to specialize in tourist-based crimes. We currently do not have designated locations in the tourism corridor for tourists in need of assistance, i.e., a kiosk.

– Tarlow: Does your police department see its role as one of crime-solving/protection or does it define the problem in different terms? If so, what are they?

Suppe: The Tourist Crimes Unit primarily works in solving mode rather than preventative mode.

– Tarlow: Does your city's police department see its role as that of protectors of its city's image and reputation?

Suppe: Yes. Partnerships with the community are important in ensuring we are all on the same page with our goals of protecting the reputation and image of the destination.

– Tarlow: From what you have observed, does your police department view the foreign tourist as having special needs?

Suppe: Yes, not only are there language barriers, but there are cultural differences when it comes to interacting with foreign tourists. Even something as simple as providing directory assistance, all the way to taking an actual police report, can be very challenging. Currently, the international visitation is about 12% of the overall numbers. Tourism officials have a goal to increase that figure to 30% in the next ten years. With this increase in numbers, we need to prepare our police and security professionals with the tools to overcome the barriers through education and training.

– Tarlow: From what you have observed, does your police department believe that all tourists should be treated basically alike?

Suppe: We recognize that there are a wide variety of reasons why people choose Las Vegas to visit such as attending a conference, business travel, or for leisure. We also recognize there are varying cultures, languages, religious beliefs, etc. Although our visitors are here for a variety of reasons and come from varying backgrounds, the focus is to assure all visitors have a safe visit while in the destination.

– Tarlow: Has crime caused your community's image to suffer from negative media publicity due to crimes against tourists?

Suppe: Naturally whenever there is a newsworthy incident within the tourist corridor, it creates the possibility of someone opting out of Las Vegas as their next destination spot. The public affairs department within LVCVA makes great strides to minimize the impact it may have on future visitors. Honestly, I do not know of any specific crimes that have occurred in the destination that have created a negative impact on visitation.

– Tarlow: As a non-police officer, do you believe that your police department has adequate resources to protect tourists? If not, what additional resources do you need?

Suppe: There is always room for improvement. As referenced earlier, reduced funding sources create some challenges, but in general Las Vegas is a very safe destination.

– Tarlow: How well does your police department cooperate with the media?

Suppe: LVMPD has a Public Information Office who is the sole source for media communication. The public expects answers and information, and therefore, it is unreasonable to think the police department can remain tight-lipped on newsworthy crimes. The system appears to work well.

– Tarlow: From what you know, does Metro have any special tourism-policing programs that have worked well?

Suppe: The Police Department has a volunteer program called "Viva Patrol" (Visitor Information–Visitor Assistance). The program consists of using volunteer community citizens wearing visibly identifiable uniforms while walking the tourist areas. They provide directions and general assistance. This program works well for a number of reasons including being relatively low cost, providing heavy visibility in tourist areas, and gets our community members involved and interacting with our local police department. Another program that has worked well is an email notification system sent to all hotels and retail properties in the tourist areas. This system is used to relay information such as current crime trends, missing/wanted people information, sending surveillance camera photos, threat assessments for special events, etc. This is a quick and easy way for all hotels to be up to date on potential crimes, scams, or threats.

– Tarlow: From what you know, were there any tourism-policing programs Metro tried (if any) that were not successful?

Suppe: None to my knowledge.

THE DOMINICAN REPUBLIC

Tourism in the Dominican Republic is on a national rather than on a local scale. The Dominican Republic Tourism Police, known as *Politur* (now called CESTUR), is a national police department subdivided into a total unit of over 1,000 officers whose job is tourism safety and security. It is important to differentiate Politur from other Dominican Republic Police Forces. In fact, Politur is unique in that it is a hybrid of members of the army and police forces brought together to protect the nation's tourism industry (Figure 9.5, Figure 9.6).

Figure 9.5 Tourism police headquarters, Santo Domingo, Dominican Republic.

Figure 9.6 Dominican Republic beach.

Although the country emphasizes sand and sun tourism, it also has a rich historical and cultural life. Christopher Columbus is buried in the Dominican Republic and many of the basics of Western civilization were first constructed in the Dominican Republic. The Dominican Republic also has had a long history, despite periods of dictatorships, of caring for human and minority rights. As such, it was one of the few nations willing to accept refugees from Hitler's occupied Europe and visitors note its sense of hospitality throughout its national territory. The Dominican Republic is also heavily involved in the Caribbean cruise industry, and this means that its police must deal not only with land tourism security issues but also maritime tourism security issues. Besides its capital and largest city, Santo Domingo, the Dominican Republic boasts several other important tourism areas. Among these are (given in alphabetical order):

- Barahonra
- Boca Chica
- Puerto Plata
- Punta Cana
- La Romana
- Samana
- Sosua
- Las Terrenas

Unfortunately, as in other areas of the Caribbean region, crime and the perception of crime has been a major problem. Crime is one of the four "illnesses" from which many nations in the Caribbean suffer. These four illnesses are:

1. High cost of travel services
2. Irregular weather patterns due to hurricane season
3. Poor levels of customer service
4. High crime rates

Despite a major effort on the part of Dominican authorities, at the time of this writing the Dominican Republic is still under a travel advisory issued by the U.S. Department of State. It should be noted, however, that the Dominican Republic has made major strides in solving its tourism security issues. The U.S. Department of State (October 31, 2013) stated the following about the Dominican Republic and tourism security/safety. The following is merely a synopsis of the State Department's Website concerning the Dominican Republic.

CRIME: Crime continues to be a problem throughout the Dominican Republic. Street crime and petty theft involving U.S. tourists does occur, and you should take precautions to avoid becoming a target. While pickpocketing and mugging are the most common crimes against tourists, reports of violence against both foreigners and locals are growing. Valuables left unattended in parked automobiles, on beaches, and in other public places are vulnerable to theft, and car theft remains a problem.

The dangers present in the Dominican Republic are similar to those of many major U.S. cities. Criminals can be dangerous—many have weapons and are likely to use them if they meet resistance. Visitors walking the streets should always be aware of their surroundings. Be wary of strangers, especially those who seek you out at celebrations or nightspots. Travel with a partner or in a group if possible.

You should use credit cards judiciously while in the Dominican Republic. Credit card fraud is common, and recent reports indicate that its incidence has increased significantly in Santo Domingo as well as in the resort areas of the country.

If you elect to use your credit or debit cards, you should never let the cards leave your sight. You should also pay close attention to credit card bills following time spent in the Dominican Republic. There have been reports of fraudulent charges appearing months after card usage in the Dominican Republic. Victims of credit card fraud should contact the bank that issued the credit card immediately.

The State Department Website then goes on to say:

The Dominican Republic has taken these criticisms seriously, and to counter both crime and the negative consequences of crime, the Dominican Republic has created a special tourism police force called Politur. The U.S. embassy recognizes the importance of Politur on its website, stating:

TOURIST POLICE

The Dominican Republic has police that are specially trained to assist tourists who require assistance. This public institution is called Politur and represents a cooperative effort between the National Police, Secretary of the Armed Forces, and the Secretary of Tourism. Politur typically has personnel in tourist areas to provide first responder–type assistance to tourists. If you are the victim of a crime, Politur can help you get to a police station so that you may file a police report and seek further assistance.

As noted, perhaps no country in the Caribbean has done as much as the Dominican Republic in facing its problems and seeking workable solutions. For example, a tourist who walks along Santo Domingo's Malecón (seaside avenue) will note the presence of trained police officers. Many of these officers speak at least one foreign language and are trained in customer service.

Despite a chronic lack of funding, Politur should be considered the leading tourism security police force in the Caribbean, if not in all of Latin

America. This is especially important when one considers that a major national Dominican goal is to increase tourism to some 10 million annual visitors. In order to succeed, the Dominican Republic will need to demonstrate to the world that it has conquered its crime problem and has become a garden of safety in an area of the world known for its crime.

In the latter part of 2013 the name Politur was changed to CESTUR. CESTUR has produced a tourism-policing model that has either been copied or has influenced other Caribbean nations. CESTUR has a close working relationship with the President of the Dominican Republic and it is widely respected both within the tourism industry and in policing circles. CESTUR is a perfect example of both proactive security and classical reactive policing. It both educates and trains to prevent crime and it investigates and seeks to solve those crimes that have been committed. CESTUR also acts as an educational tool and is often a driving force in innovative ideas. For example, CESTUR has played a major role in lobbying for the new expressway between Punta Cana and Santo Domingo. The opening of this highway has played a considerable role in the reduction of road crime. CESTUR is known for its innovation. It has not only created a one of a kind tourism police academy, but it is also in the process of developing the first international school of tourism policing.

CESTUR representatives were asked the same questions as were asked of Charleston's and Las Vegas' police. Below are the answers CESTUR's representative Coronel Ambiorix Cepeda provided for this book. The answers were given in Spanish and have been translated by the author into English. It should be noted that where words were left out in the Spanish translation or where a literal translation made no sense, then the author took the liberty to translate it in such a way that the terms would make sense to an English-speaking/-reading audience.

- Tarlow: How major of a contributor to the economy of your city is tourism?
  Cepeda: Tourism is our nation's number one industry.
- Tarlow: How many police officers work in tourism security?
  Cepeda: Currently (2013) we have some 1,100 members of Politur working across the nation.
- Tarlow: How much training have they had/do they receive?
  Cepeda: They receive courses in the following areas:
  * *Some 500 hours in tourism security given over a 6-month period*
  * *Retraining and refresher courses (at 2-month intervals)*
  * *Additional continual education courses such as:*
    * *Diving*

- *Lifesaving*
- *Executive (VIP) protection*
- *Foreign language training in English, French, Mandarin Chinese, and Russian*
- Tarlow: What special training do your officers receive regarding the tourism industry? Which officers (all/a special unit)?

  Cepeda: During their training the officers receive 8 hours of daily training, 50% of which (4 hours each day) are dedicated to specific issues within the tourism industry. On a national level, all police officers are given at least some tourism police training.
- Tarlow: What are your major tourism security challenges?

  Cepeda: Our major challenges are:
  - *A stronger presence in the tourism areas*
  - *Integration of various national components within tourism security*
  - *Logistical and economic sufficiency*
  - *Increased training*
- Tarlow: Please describe the types of crime/violence that most commonly happen to tourists in your community.

  Cepeda: The principle types of crimes with which we have to deal are:
  - *Robbery*
  - *Assaults or fits of rage that turn violent*
  - *Scams committed both on and by tourists*
  - *Intentional loss of documents or insurance scam*
- Tarlow: What are the major complaints regarding tourism security?

  Cepeda: Our major complaints are:
  - *Lack of personnel*
  - *Lack of resources to provide safety to the public*
  - *Lack of motivation*
- Tarlow: Does your department work with the tourism industry? If so, how?

  Cepeda: The tourist industry provides us discretely with intelligence information and logistical support.
- Tarlow: Does the tourism industry (directly) aid your department? If so, how?

  Cepeda: No, we do not receive direct economic support from the tourism industry.
- Tarlow: Does you police department view itself as having a special role in your tourism industry?

  Cepeda: Yes, of course we do. We see security as the basis for tourism development.
- Tarlow: What special problems do you have in protecting tourists?

Cepeda: We need additional resources and logistical support. Often the law complicates our work.

-   Tarlow: Are your tourism police a separate unit within the police department?

Cepeda: CESTUR is a specialized and independent body (unit) that is directly under the Ministry of Defense.

-   Tarlow: What are the major challenges that you have in protecting visitors?

Cepeda: Our current goals are to:

-   *Lower the percentage of robberies, assaults, and battery incidents*
-   *Provide greater security in major tourism zone*
-   *Create the needed infrastructure so as to provide better tourism security*

-   Tarlow: Does your department see its role as one of crime-solving/protection or does it define the problem in different terms? If so, what are they?

Cepeda: We expect our officers to do the impossible. We understand that our nation's image often depends on what we do. We especially expect the officer to try and resolve all problems quickly and efficiently.

-   Tarlow: Does your department see its role as that of protectors of its city's image and reputation?

Cepeda: Yes, of course, the image and reputation (of the nation) is the responsibility of the tourism security officer in all tourism locations.

-   Tarlow: Does your department view the foreign tourist as having special needs?

Cepeda: Yes, because if a tourist arrives in the country seeking adventure, he or she leaves his common sense behind and often needs a "friend" who is the tourism security officer. This person can guide him and tell him what to do or where not to go. Many foreign tourists do not speak Spanish and therefore it is hard for them to communicate.

-   Tarlow: Does your department believe that all tourists should be treated basically alike?

Cepeda: Yes, of course. It does not matter what has happened, the treatment should be the same. Our conduct should be in accordance with the principles of human (rights) and the international laws and treaties to which we [the Dominican Republic] belong.

-   Tarlow: Has crime caused your community's image to suffer from negative media publicity due to crime against tourists?

Cepeda: No, but the press at times has created problems or magnified the situation, especially in some isolated cases.

- Tarlow: As a department, do you have adequate resources to protect tourists? If not, what additional resources do you need?

  Cepeda: We do not have sufficient resources considering the number of tourists who arrive and the cruises that are now coming to the Dominican Republic; however, we have excellent people working for us. We are lacking vehicles, communication apparatus, and other tools to provide the level of service that we would like to provide.

- Tarlow: How well does your department cooperate with the media?

  Cepeda: We usually have a good level of cooperation, but at times isolated cases have been sensationalized.

- Tarlow: Do you have any special tourism-policing programs that have worked well?

  Cepeda: Currently we have an "Integral Tourism Security Strategic Plan." It is from this plan that we develop our programming and principle strategies.

- Tarlow: What tourism-policing programs have you tried (if any) that were not successful?

  Cepeda: So far we have not had any programs that have failed; much to the contrary, the public has expressed a great deal of approval of our efforts.

- Tarlow: Do you use an overall integrated plan in your tourism security? If so, please send me a copy; if not, why not?

  Cepeda: Yes, we do, as has already been noted.

RIO DE JANEIRO

Rio de Janeiro (Figure 9.7) is one of the world's great tourism cities. The city will play host to some of soccer's 2014 World Cup (the final match will be played at Rio de Janeiro's Maracanã stadium, see Figure 9.8) and also will host the 2016 Olympic Games. As such, Rio de Janeiro is used to major events. In 2013 it hosted Pope Francis. *CBS News* reported about that event: "An estimated 3 million people poured onto Rio's Copacabana beach on Sunday for the final Mass of Pope Francis' historic trip to his home continent, cheering the first Latin American pope in one of the biggest turnouts for a papal Mass in recent history" ("Pope Francis wraps up Brazil trip," 2013, para. 1). The same article went on to report some of the problems that overwhelmed the city, stating:

> The numbers clearly overwhelmed the area's services: The stench of garbage and human waste hung in Rio's humid air, and the beach and adjoining chic Atlantic Avenue looked like an improvised refugee camp plunked down in the middle of one of the most beautiful cities in the world. Copacabana's famous mosaic

Figure 9.7 Rio de Janeiro from the air.

Figure 9.8 Maracanã Stadium.

sidewalks were strewn with trampled cardboard, plastic bags, empty water bottles and cookie wrappers as trash collectors in orange uniforms tried to restore order.
(para. 6)

Rio also hosts what may be the world's largest rock festival, known as *Rock in Rio*. *Festival Fever* even reported, "Rock in Rio has been the largest music festival in the world, with 1.5 million people in the first edition..." (Rock in Rio, 2013, para. 2). Also, Ben Tavener (2012), senior contributing reporter for the English-language *Rio Times*, reported that Brazil had reported having received a "record number of foreign tourists in 2011" (para. 1). The article noted that in 2011 the nation had received just over 5.43 million foreign visitors, coming both from neighboring nations and from Europe, Russia, and China.

It should be noted that despite the fact that Brazil has become perhaps the world's premier host nation for major events, the nation as a whole and Rio de Janeiro as a microcosm have multiple challenges. Among these challenges are:

1. Airports are lacking in basic terminal services.
2. Personal and media reports of police corruption.
3. Problems with the pacification of "*favelas*" (shanty towns), some of which are within walking distance to some of Rio's finest tourism areas.
4. Lack of internal transportation infrastructure that even in the best of times creates mammoth traffic jams.
5. Geographic challenges due to the fact that Rio's geography is a mixture of mountains, sea, and inlets.
6. Lack of hotel space resulting in excessive hotel costs.

Each of these is a serious problem and each interacts with tourism security issues, as discussed in Chapter 1. Not mentioned in this list is the potential for an act of terrorism and/or a natural disaster. Rio de Janeiro may be able to confront its challenges that lie ahead or may fail. Failure or success may depend on good planning and/or good luck and/or how the media decides to report these and future actions. The police interview given below, however, provides the careful reader with much room for thought.

Recent Negative Publicity

Despite major police efforts to lower Rio de Janeiro's crime rate, the year 2013 saw a number of highly publicized crimes or crime events that received a great deal of international publicity. These reported events produced a cumulative effect and gave the impression that the police efforts had been a failure. Although the reality is very much to the contrary, headlines and articles, such as "Brazilians wary over renewed mass beach robberies" (Barchfield, 2013), produced the impression that visitors needed to be wary of being on Rio de Janeiro's streets.

The following interview with Camilo D'Ornellas of the Police Academy of Rio de Janeiro's *Polícia Civil* (as shown in Figure 9.9) provides an overview of Rio de Janeiro's tourism policing efforts in November 2013. Once again, D'Ornellas received the same questions as did police representatives in

Figure 9.9 Members of the *Polícia Civil* studying tourism security in Rio de Janiero.

the other cities or locations studied in this chapter. The answers have been translated into English by the author. Once again, where words were omitted or concepts needed to be clarified, the Portuguese answers were adjusted so as to make sense to American readers.

– Tarlow: How major of a contributor to the economy of your city is tourism?

D'Ornellas: Tourism is a vital part of our economy. In the last few years Rio de Janeiro has become the country's cultural and sporting event capital, hosting such major events (mega events) as soccer's World Cup in 2014 and the 2016 Olympic Games along with such cultural events as Rock in Rio. Rock in Rio is the world's largest music festival. These events have created in the last 5 years multiple job opportunities in the hotel, restaurant, and nightlife industries. They have also caused the need for secondary expansion such as an expanded subway system, an improved road system, and urban renewal in such areas as the city's port. The port is now being totally revamped and revitalized and will in itself become a tourism attraction. Our major attractions such as the statue of Christ the Redeemer (Corcovado) and Sugarloaf Mountain have received in the past few years more tourists than other tourism centers in Brazil. Tourism has increased in all economic sectors of the population.

– Tarlow: How many police officers work in tourism security?

D'Ornellas: In the last few years the Civil Police Academy created a course specifically designed to train its agents to work in major and mega events. This course is designed specifically for the tourism and entertainment industries. It takes officers through every possible scenario, giving them a multidisciplinary approach to the peculiarities of working within these industries. Additionally, we have developed a working philosophy for police security in major events and in tourism. This means that we have created a new professionalism for our officers and for people in the private sector that demands high professional standards and an attitude that is innovative and efficient with an understanding that we must be able to compete on a worldwide stage and as a world-class tourism city.

– Tarlow: How much training have they had/do they receive?

  D'Ornellas: Their training is given over a 4-week period for 8 hours each day, for a total of 160 hours of both classroom and field training. Students receive both classroom theory and then practical real-life experience. We have trained some 1,600 students (both police and non-police officers).

– Tarlow: What special training do your officers receive regarding the tourism industry? Which officers (all/a special unit)?

  D'Ornellas: Our students come from the civil police officers, military police, constables, transit police officers, and private security. This mixing of students (from the various forces) allows us to integrate our security forces so as to understand their roles in securing our streets and major events. Those who participate in DEAT [Portuguese acronym for tourism police] and those in the Tourism Police Command (Batalhão de Polícia Turista) receive extra training, as they are special units dedicated to tourism policing.

– Tarlow: What are your major tourism security challenges?

  D'Ornellas: One of our major challenges is the lack of foreign language training. Foreign languages are especially important as Rio de Janeiro receives visitors from the entire world. Another challenge is our policy of rotating of police officers. This means that each time a police officer is given a new assignment he or she loses his or her specialized training in tourism and major event security. It also means that we have to begin to train a new officer who has replaced the other officer.

– Tarlow: Please describe the types of crime/violence that most commonly happen to tourists in your community.

  D'Ornellas: Outbreaks of violence and robberies are the most common. The current (2013) breakdown is as follows:

  • *Acts of violence, 65% of reported cases*
  • *Robberies, 25% of reported cases*
  • *Extortion, 0.5% of reported cases*
  • *Other crimes, 0.5% of reported cases*

– Tarlow: What are the major complaints regarding tourism security?

D'Ornellas: Recently the U.S. consulate in Rio sent out a warning alerting U.S. citizens (traveling in Rio de Janeiro) about the dangers of assaults within the tourism zones. Another complaint has concerned the growth of street people and the homeless on the city's streets.

- Tarlow: Does your department work with the tourism industry? If so, how?

D'Ornellas: Yes, there is a tourism-policing substation dedicated to tourism police.

- Tarlow: Does the tourism industry aid your department? If so, how?

D'Ornellas: Yes, there exist interactions between the tourism police units and the hotel industry. For example, each month we do an evaluation of police actions and if there are disagreements between the tourism industry and the police, then we discuss what new actions we need to take in order to avoid any crisis.

- Tarlow: Does you police department view itself as having a special role in your tourism industry?

D'Ornellas. We do not see a special role; there exists, however, a cooperative spirit between each section of Rio de Janeiro's policing and we all understand that we have a role to play in the tourism industry and in its protection.

- Tarlow: What special problems do you have in protecting tourists?

D'Ornellas: We need personnel who are both well trained and see this type of work as their vocation rather than as their job. We need greater amounts of training and we need to learn what others are doing abroad.

- Tarlow: Are your tourism police a separate unit within Rio de Janeiro's policing?

D'Ornellas: It is a separate entity from the rest of public security; there is a special tourism-policing task force.

- Tarlow: What are the major challenges that you have in protecting visitors?

D'Ornellas: There is no registry of who enters the country or who comes to Rio de Janeiro. There is no coordination between the hotel industry and the police.

- Tarlow: Does your department see its role as one of crime-solving/ protection or does it define the problem in different terms? If so, what are they?

D'Ornellas: Crimes against tourists are categorized in a similar fashion as the same crimes against Brazilian citizens. There is no differentiation or special protection given except in specific highly trafficked tourism points.

- Tarlow: Does your department see its role as that of protectors of its city's image and reputation?

D'Ornellas: Yes, a city's reputation depends a great deal on how the industry treats its visitors and if they want to return. We want them not only to return, but to recommend Rio de Janeiro to their friends and family.

- Tarlow: Does your department view the foreign tourist as having special needs?

D'Ornellas: Not special needs but rather special attention. We realize that visitors often leave their common sense behind, that they are fascinated by our city's natural beauty, and we understand that it is our role to guide the visitor and to be sure that our visitors feel isolated.

- Tarlow: Does your department believe that all tourists should be treated basically alike?

D'Ornellas: Yes, we want to do our best for all visitors.

- Tarlow: Has crime caused your community's image to suffer from negative media publicity due to crimes against tourists?

D'Ornellas: Yes.

- Tarlow: As a department, do you have adequate resources to protect tourists? If not, what additional resources do you need?

D'Ornellas: No, we ought to have (but do not have) adequate uniforms, more foreign language-speaking police officers, special vehicles that distinguish us from other police.

- Tarlow: How well does your department cooperate with the media?

D'Ornellas: We have a cordial relationship with the media and we try to be as open and honest with the media as possible.

- Tarlow: Do you have any special tourism-policing programs that have worked well?

D'Ornellas: Yes, our tourism course as mentioned above has been very successful. This is especially true for the seminars and courses given at our police academy.

- Tarlow: What tourism-policing programs have you tried (if any) that were not successful?

D'Ornellas: Our motorized policing did not yield the hoped-for results. In 1992 we tried a combined tourism police force that also was less successful than we would have hoped and our current efforts are based around both past successes and failures. We try to learn from our mistakes.

- Tarlow: Do you use an overall integrated plan in your tourism security? If so, please send me a copy; if not, why not?

D'Ornellas: We do not have an integral tourism security plan. We are in the development stage. We hope to develop methods by which all policing units can work together in a seamless fashion. We are not yet there.

SUMMARY

This chapter has examined two American cities and two Latin American tourism destinations. Las Vegas and Rio are major tourism cities and in both cases the police report that despite tourism being the city's major economic generator, security is often reduced to a second-tier investment. On the other hand, both the Dominican Republic and Charleston, although not perfect, seem to understand that without proper tourism security their industries cannot grow nor can their tourism locale prosper. All four locales are media-sensitive and understand that tourism surety is as much about policing and issues of safety as it is about economic viability and reputation. All four police departments also understand the importance of a professionalized tourism police and Charleston, the Dominican Republic, and Rio de Janeiro report special attention given to tourism police training that includes customer service and often foreign language skills. How well these locales act as examples of tourism surety may well help to decide the future of one of the world's youngest and largest industries.

REFERENCES

Barchfield, J. (2013). *Brazilians wary over renewed mass beach robberies.* Retrieved from AP, November 25, http://bigstory.ap.org/article/brazilians-wary-over-renewed-mass-beach-robberies.

Pope Francis wraps up Brazil trip with Mass for 3 million. (2013). *CBS News*, July 28. Retrieved from http://www.cbsnews.com/news/pope-francis-wraps-up-brazil-trip-with-mass-for-3-million/.

Rock in Rio. (2013). *Festival Outlook.* Retrieved from http://festival-outlook.consequenceofsound.net/fests/view/1069/rock-in-rio.

Tavener, B. (2012). Brazil reports record tourism: daily. *The Rio Times*, May 5. Retrieved from http://riotimesonline.com/brazil-news/rio-business/brazil-reports-record-tourism/.

AFTERWORD

As I finish writing this book at the beginning of 2014, I cannot help but wonder what the next few years will bring to the world of tourism security. Will we be more or less secure? How will the economy impact the state of tourism security both in the United States and in the world? What lessons have we learned from past successes and errors? Although it would be foolish to make predictions about a future that is yet to unfold, here are some guidelines and challenges to consider.

1. *Issues of Security.* Visitors and tourism on the whole are security sensitive. The coming years will present tourism security specialists with any number of challenges. Among these may be:

   a. Terrorism has not diminished, but rather it has mutated. Single-cell terrorist groups will increase their threat to the tourism industry and will be harder than ever to detect.

   b. Major events around the world will receive a great deal of publicity and publicity invites security issues. Tourism security specialists and professionals will have to be vigilant regarding potential acts of terrorism and acts of random violence. Tourism security specialists will have the continual problem of when they prevent an attack, few note the success, but when they fail, everyone knows it.

   c. Tourism-oriented policing and protection services (TOPPS) around the world will be needed more than ever. If security personnel can convince marketers of the importance of TOPPS units, then these forces may help to create a dent in international crimes against tourists. If, however, these forces remain underfunded, then additional problems may occur.

2. *Tourism is highly dependent on economic trends.* Often in the past, when tourism "sneezes," tourism security professionals have gotten "pneumonia." That is to say that often tourism security professionals have been some of the earliest people cut when there is a budget crisis. To avoid this pitfall, it is essential that tourism security professionals convince their industry colleagues that they are not only essential, but add to the bottom line. That means that part of their job is educating their colleagues as to what their job consists of and why they are an essential element in difficult economic times.

3. *Tourism marketing has placed its emphasis on the middle-class market.* In the latter half of the twentieth century and the first decade of the twenty-first century, these are the people who have traditionally thought about security issues and react negatively to a security threat. The middle class forms the largest travel group, is only moderately demanding, and sociologically tends to be forgiving of tourism mistakes and somewhat tolerant of less than perfect customer service. The middle class is perhaps the most vulnerable to economic highs and lows and tends to be the class that most easily panics during a downturn. Because the middle class often buys on credit, the cost of credit will have a major impact on its ability and willingness to purchase what appears to be nonessential services. On a positive note, in many of the developing economies there is a rising middle class, and these new middle classes appear to be following the same sociological patterns as the middle classes in the more traditionally established economies. Not only should tourism marketers and professionals do well to be alert to the following economic trends, but also so should tourism security professionals. Remember that part of security is being sure that our security professionals have sufficient manpower and equipment and none of this can be done without funding. Tourism security professionals would be wise to observe the following trends and compute how these trends will impact their economic well-being.

   a. *The cost of credit.* Because so much of the middle class's purchases for expendable items are dependent on credit, it is essential to track the trends in credit. If interest rates rise, then middle-class purchases become more expensive. When interest rates fall, the same item or service becomes less expensive.

   b. *The failures and successes of the middle class.* The middle class must live on some form of budget. That means that if there is a major rise in taxes or other required services, the middle class may tend to hold back on what it considers luxury items. For example, in the United States right now there is doubt as to what the cost of health care will be in 2014. Should the cost go down, then psychologically the public's willingness to travel may rise (assuming all else being the same). However, should health care costs spiral, the tourism industry may suffer, and tourism security professionals will have an additional problem with which to contend.

   c. *The stock markets around the world.* When the stock markets tend to rise, many people feel wealthier and are more willing to spend money. The opposite is true of a falling market. Note that the psychological macro impact is not connected to an individual's personal wealth. Members of the middle class tend to spend money as influenced by macro rather than micro trends.

4. *Tourism security officers and professionals need to be aware of transportation issues.* With the merger of airlines around the world, tourism leaders can expect higher costs and a continual downgrading of services. Will this lowering of services mean an angrier public and more security problems? Airlines have become the business that travelers love to hate, and road rage often turns into airline rage. Should the cost of fuel continue to climb, expect reductions in service, fewer flights, and lighter and less comfortable aircraft. The travel industry's dependency on air travel will continue to be a major problem. On the other hand, many nations have established functioning bus and train alternatives and these alternative forms of public transportation, along with private vehicles, may become a short-haul substitute for problems in air travel.

5. *Tourism security officials will need to adapt to travelers seeking new opportunities for alternative travel experiences.* Many of the legacy destinations will have to compete with new travel experiences. A new generation will seek combination tourism in which it can mix business with pleasure, short-term vacations that embrace long weekends, and boutique tourism experiences that are out of the ordinary. Many of the legacy destinations will suffer from the "been-there-done-that" syndrome and will have to offer more conveniences or tourism opportunities if they are to keep their status as premier destinations. How the tourism security industry will adapt itself to these needs is still an open question.

6. *Business travelers will expect more.* Business travelers around the world not only expect free Internet and Wi-Fi service, they are also aware that they are potential victims not only of assaults and larcenies, but also, in too many places around the world, of kidnappings. Female travelers will especially want to be careful when traveling alone and in locales that do not provide well-thought-out security at hotels, parking lots, and city streets. These people need access to free printing via the Internet, flexible check-in and check-out times, and dining options that are both affordable and varied. Travelers will continue to be concerned about pandemics and illnesses from contaminated food and water supplies.

Tourism professionals have always had to deal with challenges and in a number of cases security challenges have been met and overcome. A number of places around the world have come up with new creative measures in their tourism offerings. For example, Panama has created a program to provide visitors with 1 month of free health insurance. The Dominican Republic has created perhaps the world's best trained tourism police force, and the United States has begun to allow entrance, at least for returning U.S. citizens, via computers rather than forcing everyone to stand in line.

No one knows what the future will bring, but we can be sure that the world's largest and perhaps youngest industry is flexible enough to find creative solutions for challenges that will surely occur. Perhaps we can ask nothing more but to be vigilant and to face the world with a cheerful and caring countenance.

Peter E. Tarlow

Note: Page numbers followed by *f* indicate figures and *t* indicate tables.

A

Acceptable risk, 82, 86, 87, 91
Administrators, 57
Adversity, 83
"Afterlives", 87–88, 105
Agreements, 97
Airborne illnesses, 126
Airline industry, 171
Airline passenger bill of rights
  bumping, 212
  Department of Transportation's rules,
    213–214
  European Union (EU), 214–215
  full disclosure, additional fees, 212
  lost bags and bag fees, 212
  problems, 214
  tarmac delays, 213
Airlines, 98, 170, 172, 182
Airline security, 171
Air marshals, 171, 177, 178, 179
Air safety, 167
Air transportation
  airborne illnesses diseases, 183
  air travel risk, 182, 182*t*
  fast moving pandemic disease, 181–182
  fire issues, 178
  fly-drive vacation, 167
  health issues, 179–181
  newscasters and media journalists, 167
  SARS (*see* Severe acute respiratory
    syndrome (SARS))
  security and safety (*see* U.S. Hijackings)
  terrorism-based illnesses, 185–186
Air travel, 167, 168, 179
Alcohol and drugs
  age, crime, gangs and terrorism, 91–92
  safety and security, tourism, 92
Alcohol consumption, 133
Amusement, 111, 113
Amusement park, 111, 113
Analysis of risk, 81, 88
Anger management, 16, 20

Animals (pets), 128
Anna Karenina, 8
AON, 211
Aquatic sports, 137, 138, 140
Aquatic tourism, 138, 139, 141, 149
  beach/sea (*see* Beach/sea tourism)
  criminal and terrorism issues
    closed-circuit TV (CCTV) cameras,
      142
    sexual assaults, 141
    threats, children, 141
    visitor's incidentals, 141
  cruise (*see* Cruise tourism)
  lake, 140–141
  large-scale bodies, 137
  piracy and/or potential terrorist threats,
    138
  safety issues, 138
Armed robbery, 112
Athletic areas, 74
Attractions, 56

B

Background checks, 58
  aliases/nicknames, person, 117–118
  casino personnel, 116
  criminal investigation, 119
  document copies, 118
  financial history search, 118
  interview techniques, 119–121
  person's identities, 116–117
  person signing, release form, 117
  public records, 118
  social media, 119
  time and cost, 116
  types, inaccuracies, 118
Baggage/storage area, 69
Banquet, 72–73
Banquet staff, 72–73
Beaches, 137, 138, 139, 140, 141
Beach resorts, 59
Beach/sea/river tourism, 138–141

Beach/sea tourism
  aquatic options, 138
  defined, 138
  "do-it-yourself" safety, 139–140
  issues, 139
  lifeguard protection, 139
  signage confusion, 138–139
  sun protection, 140
  warning flags, 139
Beautification, 64, 73
Bed 'n breakfast, 53
Bed 'n Breakfast (B&B) challenges, 53
Boating safety, 140–141
Bombings, 69–70
Book of Genesis, 7
Bribery, 81–82
Bryan Eagle, 36
Budgetary restraints, 59
Budgets, 39–47
Building codes and restrictions, 128
Bush, G.W., 18–19
Business travelers, 25
Bus tourism, 190–193
  defined, 190–191
  disaster, Italy, 192–193
  Mexico attack, 192
  motor coaches, 191
  on- and off-bus security and safety
    challenges, 191, 191t

C
Car burglaries, 93
Cartels, 36, 93
Car travel, 167
Casino patron, 113, 116
Casinos, 52
  background checks (see Background
    checks)
  Bureau of Labor Statistics, 112
  CCTV cameras (see CCTV cameras)
  convention centers and trade shows
    (see Convention centers)
  Crime Report (Tapley, Lance), 110–111
  crimes of opportunity, 109–110
  description, 113
  and gaming, 109

homeland security issues, financial and
    social crimes, 112
  issues, professionals, 112
  local economy, 110
  local, state and/or federal regulation, 112
  scandals and criminal acts, 109
  security professional (see Security
    officers)
  spillover effect, general population, 110
  "The Effect of Casino Gambling on
    Crime in New Casino Jurisdictions",
    110
  Toronto Sun, 111
Casino security, 109, 111–112, 115–121
Casino security officers, 111–112
CCTV. See CCTV cameras
CCTV cameras
  casino gaming, 113
  criminal deterrent and evidence, 114
  dummy cameras, 115
  forms, 114
  installation, current and future needs, 115
  investment, 115
  issues, privacy rights, 114
  limitations, 115
  replacing and repairing, 115
  security vs. need for privacy, 113
  setup and maintenance costs, 114
  specific spaces/outside recording around
    outdoor space, 113
  tourism provider, customers' security, 114
Cepeda, A., 249–252
CESTUR, 246, 249
Chambermaids, 76
Charleston, South Carolina
  City's population, 225
  Civil War, 225
  community's image, 234
  crime/violence, 229
  CVB, 227
  economic development team, 231
  enforcement and economic vitality, 227
  locale's police departments, 226–235
  North American port, 225
  occupancy rates, 227
  pedestrians and bicycle enthusiasts, 230
  policing programs, 235

risk management protocols, 228
safe and secure environment, 233
TOPPS, 227
tourism industry, 230
transportation system, 231
Chicago, 23–24
Child trafficking, 55
Civil disturbances, 81–82
Civil unrest, 89
Cleaning staff, 57
CLIA. See Cruise Lines International
    Association (CLIA)
Closed-circuit television (CCTV), 113–115
Clustering, 63
Collateral crime, 27–28
Collateral damage, 105
Collective survival, 63
Columbus, C., 247
Commercial eateries, 94
Communication, 115–116, 130, 132
Communities, 17, 19
Community police, 36, 43
Comparative innocence, 93
Con artists, 7
Conferences, 15
Conflicts, 83
"Con" game, 86
Convention and Visitors Bureau (CVB), 227
Convention centers, 85, 121, 125–127, 128,
    129–130
  actual crimes, 125
  airborne illnesses and planned infections,
    126
  animals (pets), 128
  attacks, air and water system, 126
  attendees and/or participants, registration
    fees, 121
  attention shifts, 121
  building codes and restriction, 128
  capitalism forms, 121–122
  cybercrime issues, 125
  delegates and exhibitors, 122
  early exhibitors, 121–122
  event security plan (see Event security
    plan)
  fire and fire prevention issues, 126
  food poisoning issues, 126

gathering and community, 121
hazardous materials, 128
host community, 122–123
identity theft issues, 126
locale, 123–125
remote bombs issues, 126
safety and security plans, 127–128,
    129–130, 129f
security and safety departments, 123, 125
Conventions, 121–124
Copacabana beach, 252–253
Corruption, 83, 94
Counter-hijacking measures, 172–173
Country risk, 81
Credible information, 164
Crime, 11–12, 19–21
Crime and economic viability
  characteristics, 33
  classical Marxist theory, 28–29
  consumption growth, 31–32
  crime vs. terrorism acts, tourism, 28, 29t
  illegal narcotics, 27–28
  macro destruction, tourism industry, 28
  motivation effect, 32
  official and security specialist, 28
  opportunity effect, 32
  Robin Hood hypothesis, 32–33
  social inequality, 32–33
  theoretical Marxist perspective, 28–29
  and tourism, 30–31
  wealth accumulation, 30 31
Crime and terrorism
  economics and reputation, 12, 12f
  insurance industry, 14
  pre and post September 11, 2001, 12–13
  tourism security and safety, 11–12
Crime and violence
  cost, 39
  economic consequences, 39
  El Universal, 37–38
  JHTA, 37
  measurement modes, 39
  never-ending intercartel warfare, 36
  safety and security, 36–37
Crime issues, 27–28
Crime of distraction, 86
Crime prevention, 17

Crime rate, 39
Crime wave, 83
Criminal acts, 9–11
Criminal behavior, 8–9
Criminal deterrent, 114
Criminal history, 90
Criminal investigation, 119
Crisis, 79, 82–84, 84*t*, 89, 90, 97,
    103–107
Crisis afterlife, 105
Crisis expansion, 105
Crisis management, 40, 41*t*, 79, 82–84, 84*t*,
    103–106
  definition, 83
  negative event analysis, 104
  perceptions, 105–106
  plan structure
    coordination team, internal leader/
      external leader, 193
    inquiries, 194
    internal communications issues, 197
    legal/contract/finance, 196
    media team, 194–195
    on-site team, 195
    operations/logistics team, 195–196
  radical action, 82–83
  recovery, 106–107
  vs. risk management, 83, 84*t*
  terrorism and tourism, 79
  tourism location, 83–85
  types, 83
Crisis manager, 40
Crisis perceptions, 105–106
Crisis recovery, 105, 106–107
Crowd control, 126, 129*f*, 133
Cruise emergencies, 163–165
Cruise industry, 143–144, 145, 146, 149,
    151, 154–155, 157, 158, 161, 162
Cruise Lines International Association
    (CLIA), 215–216
Cruise Passenger Bill of Rights, 154–155
Cruise passengers, 145
Cruises, 142, 143–144, 156–157
Cruise safety, 154
Cruise security, 145–147
Cruise tourism, 142–143
  Book of Jonah (tale), 142, 143

description, 142
emergency procedures, 163–165
evacuations, 156
and health issues (*see* Health issues)
history, 143–144
passengers as tourists, sociology, 145
port security, 161–163
principles, ship passengers, 152–153
reference, Noah's, 142
sea experience, 143
security and safety, 145–147, 153–155
ship routes and, 156
surety (*see* Tourism surety (security))
terrorists attraction, passengers' profiles,
    156
Titanic (movie), 143
vulnerablility, ships' passengers, 156
Cruise vacationers, 155
Cultural habits, 57
Cultures, 57, 60
Customer service, 84*t*, 92, 93
CVB. *See* Convention and Visitors Bureau
    (CVB)
Cybercrime, 125

D
Dark tourism, 23
  city's tourism districts, 23–24
  negative economy, 24–25
  travel industry's ability, 25
  victimization, 24–25
Data analysis, 82
Destination, 6
Deviance, 29
Dickens, C., 223
Direct costs, 39
Disasters, 148
Diseases, 181–185
Disorderly conduct, 60
Dominican Republic, tourism
  beach, 246, 253*f*
  Caribbean cruise industry, 247
  crime, 247–248
  police (Politur), 246
  tourism police headquarters, 246, 246*f*
  tourism security/safety, 247–248
  Western civilization, 247

D'Ornellas, C., 254–259
Drink, 58
Drivers, 75
Drowning, 138, 139, 140
Drug dealer, 93
Drunken and lewd behavior, 160

E

Ecological management, 21, 151
Economic damage, 11
Economic declines, 27
Economic difficulties, 26–27
Economic downturn, 28
Economic loss, 171
Economic multiplier, 39
Economic protection, 21
Economics, 25, 26, 27–35
Economic security, 62, 63
Economic viability, 25, 27–34
Economic well-being, 31–32
EL AL Airlines, 176
Emergency, 57, 61
Employees, 58, 75, 77
Employee safety, 112
Employment theft, 112
Engineering, 167
The Entebbe Hijackings, 168–169
Entertainment, 109, 121
Entrance security, 51
Equipment, 53, 59, 66
Escorts, 59–60
Evacuated, 58
Evacuation, 126, 129, 133, 134
Evacuation procedures, 51
Event planning, 130, 131
Events, 40, 44–45
Event security plan, 129f, 130–134
    description, 130
    outdoor events, 130–134
    principles, 130
Exchange rate, 80
Exhibit areas, 127–128
Exhibitors, 127, 128
Exit doors, 58
Exits, 90, 97
Explosive and flammable materials, 177

F

FAA (*see* Federal Aviation Agency), 180
Fairs, 27
Fairs and festivals. *See* Outdoor events
Festival managers, 133
Festivals, 44–47
Financial crimes, 112
Financial history, 118
Financial risk, 80
Fire and tourism safety, 96–98
Fire department, 63
Fire fighters, 133
Fire prevention, 59
Fire regulations, codes and
    ordinances, 97
Fire safety, 53
Fire extinguishers, 97
First aid, 59
First aid department, 63
First aid kit, 181, 184
First aid squads, 133
Fitness centers, 61
Flight guard, 178
Food, 58, 72–73
Food and beverages
    medical checks and policies, 72
    safety and security
        professional, 72
    staffs, 72–73
Food consumption, 49
Food handlers, 72
Food illnesses, 95
Food industry, 94–95
Food poisoning, 55
Food preparation, 58, 72
Food preparer, 72
Food safety, 58
Food safety, tourism
    commercial eateries, 94
    food allergies, 95
    food supply chains, 94
    risk managers, 95–96
Food supplies, 94, 99
Food terrorism, 157
Foreign destination, 89
Foreign investors, 94
Foreign language, 33

Foreseeability
 tourism issues, court, 201
 tourism law, 204
 tourism risk management, 205
Fraud, 55
Front desk, 69
Front desk personnel, 70–71
 check-in and check-out times, 70
 guest's appearance, 70
 principles, 70–71
 tasks, 71
Frontline security professional, 59–60
Full-body scanner, 175, 176

G

Galapagos Islands, 199
Gambling, 109–111
Gaming regulations and laws, 111–112
Gang violence, 35–36, 86
Geographic locations, 37
Geography, 59
Government, 94
Government officials, 42
Guest injury, 81–82
Guest protection, 58
Guests, 50, 57, 59, 70, 77
Guest safety, 56
Guns and firearms, 176

H

Hallways, 71–72
Hardening, 173–175, 179
Hardening, air travel
 airport and security professionals, 173–175
 creative ideas, 179
 defined, 173
 security measurements, 173–175
Hard uniform, 2–3
Hazardous materials, 128
Health concerns, 81
Health issues
 crimes, ships, 158–160
 and cruises, 156–157, 157t
 cruise ship and airplane travelers, 158
 terrorism and piracy
  Africa and Red Sea, 160–161
  CNN report, 160

risk management plans, 160
South and Central America and
 Caribbean, 161
viruses, 157–158
Health problem, 34–35
Health regulations, 51
High rise, 50
Hijacking, 168–170, 171–173
Homeland security, 112
Hospitality program, 43
Hospitals, 101, 104
Hostage situations, 55
Hotel, 49, 49f, 52, 57, 66, 69, 75
Hotel and motel security
 categorization, 51–52
 definition, 52
 food and beverages, 72–73
 front desk personnel, 70–71
 Gold Coast, Australia, 49, 49f
 guest and lodging personnel safety, 50
 law/security enforcement, 77–78
 lobby area and front desk, 69
 lock types, 51
 lodging, tourism history,
  49–50
 outsourcing, 75–76
 physical facilities, 51
 pool and athletic safety, 74–75
 positive and negative aspects, 54t
 public areas, 73–74
 receiving and dispatch zone, 75
 reputation, lodging establishment, 51
 risk management, 50–51
 rooms and hallways, 71–72
 security challenges, 53, 54t
 sleep-oriented establishments, 52–53
 social systems, 69
 staff protection, 76–77
 tourism/lodging safety issues, 50–51
Hotel bedrooms, 113
Hotel challenges, 52
Hotel engineers, 57
Hotelier, 58
Hotel managers, 61–62
Hotel security, 50–51
Household consumption, 31–32
Huffington Post, 24

I

Identification, 52
Identity theft, 112, 126
Illegal drugs, 86, 90–91, 93–94
Illegal drug usage, 55
Illegal meetings, 55
Illegal sexual activity, 55
Incident, 87, 91–92, 100, 101–103
Indian Airlines Flight IC-814 hijacking, 170
Inhibitions, 149, 150*t*, 153
Insurance, 55
International tourism, 1–2, 2*t*
International travelers, 57
International war, 83
International waters, 145
Interview, 119–121

J

Jamaica, 37
Jamaica Hotel and Tourist Association
    (JHTA), 37
Journalism, 100
Journalists, 100, 101, 103
Journey, 49
Jumbo jets, 167

K

Kelly, R., 30
Key systems, 58
Kidnapping, 55

L

Lake tourism, 140–141
Larceny, 138, 139
Laredo, Texas, 35–36
Las Vegas Convention and Visitor
    Authority's (LVCVA), 235–236
Las Vegas Metro, 240–241
Las Vegas Metropolitan Police Department
    (LVMPD), 242
Las Vegas tourism
    city's tourism economy, 236–237
    convention center district, 241–246, 242*f*
    counter-terrorism, 240
    crime solving/protection, 244
    crisis management, 236–237
    economy, 241
    environmental problems, 236
    fax notification system, 240–241
    integrated security plan, 239
    interagency cooperation, 238
    international tourism safety, 236–237,
        237*f*
    intersection, policing and tourism,
        241–246
    LVCVA, 235–236
    LVMPD, 242
    management's goals, 238
    police material, 239
    private-public partnership, 241
    private security professionals, 236–237
    security conferences, 236–237, 237*f*
    TCU, 242
    TOPPS, 242
    tourism safety/security, 238
    vision, data and planning, 239
Latin America, 38
Law enforcement, 20–22
Legal vulnerability, 202–203
Leisure, 7–8
Leisure Travel, 7–8
Leisure travelers, 23
Lifeguards, 139, 142
Lighting, 84*t*, 89
Litigious society, 116, 128, 129–130
Loading docks, 75
Lobby area, 69
Local community, 25
Local customs, 33
Local environment, 56, 57
Local hotels, 63
Local markets, 94
Local police, 36
Local population, 27
Local, state and federal agencies, 112
Locker rooms, 113
Lodging, 49–50, 53, 54*t*, 56, 56*t*
Lodging security, 53–58, 59, 62–67
    age of electronic security, 53–54
    age of terrorism, 57
    analytical fictions, 63
    beautification projects, 63–64
    Bed 'n Breakfast (B&B) challenges, 53

Lodging security *(Continued)*
  broad-based community teams, 63
  campgrounds, 53
  caution, 69
  changeability rule, 69
  clustering power, 63
  crime and terrorism, 53
  economic security and viability, 63
  economic uncertainty, 62
  electrical blackout, 58
  food preparation services, 58
  guest safety and procedures, 56
  hospitality businesses, tourism, 56
  hotel's staff, 58
  job specialization, 67
  law enforcement agencies, 58
  Monetary inflow, 62
  physical knowledge, 67
  planning, 64–67
  priority calculator, 67, 68*t*
  product development, 63–64
  redundancy rule, 67
  safety material, 57, 58
  security plan, 62
  stealing, guest property, 55–56
  substance abuse, 57
  travel and tourism, 63
  types, public lodging, 56, 56*t*
Lodging tax, 63
Long-term officer, 59
Lowering of inhibitions, 150*t*, 153, 155
Low rise, 50
Luggage, 70
LVCVA. *See* Las Vegas Convention and
    Visitor Authority's (LVCVA)
LVMPD. *See* Las Vegas Metropolitan Police
    Department (LVMPD)

M
Mailroom, 75
Marketing, 82–83, 84*t*, 104, 105, 106–107
Marxism, 7–8
Marxists, 8
Mass casualties, 11, 98
Mass damage, 11
Media, 35
Media relations, 20

Medical emergencies, 59
Meetings, 117, 121–124, 129
Mexico, 36
Misinformation, 103
Modern capitalism, 7–8
Modern tourism, 3
Motel. *See* Hotel and motel security
Motel challenges, 52–53
Motel operator, 50
Motel security. *See* Hotel and motel
    security
Motor coaches, 187, 191
Mullen, G., 226–235
Murder, 86, 98, 99
Museums, 23, 36, 226

N
Natural disaster, 35
Negative publicity, 87
Negative publicity, tourism
  crime/violence, 256
  economy, 255
  foreign languages, 256
  image and reputation, 257
  international publicity, 254
  tourism security, Rio de Janiero,
    254, 255*f*
New York Times, 30
Non-monetary costs, 39
Notable hijackings, 168–170
Nudity, 138

O
Off-duty police officers, 53, 60
Opportunity effect, 32
Organized crime, 112
Outdoor events, 130–134
  alcohol consumption plan, 133
  casinos and convention/trade-show
    centers, 130
  critical factors, 132
  crowd control issues, 133, 134
  evaluation, 134
  festivals, 130–135
  festival type, 131
  local hospitality industry, 134
  organizational structure, 132

pre-event planning sessions, 131
risk levels, 132
security personnel, 133
security planners, 133
threat and risk assessment, 131
Outsourcing, 75–76

P

Pandemic potential, 55
Parking lot, 58
Parking spaces, 85
Parks, 85, 89
Perceptions, 18, 24–25
Petty cash, 70
Physical complaints, 60
Physical safety, 69
Pickpocket, 109–110, 112, 125
Piracy, 138, 146, 151, 153–154, 160–161
Planned infections, 126
Planning lodging security
  assessment, 67
  exterior and interior intrusion sensors,
    66–67
  forms, tourism security, 65
  hotel's security policies, 66
  personal histories, 65
  risk management, 64
  staff termination and departures, 66
Police officers, 5
Police, tourism cities
  city's image and reputation, 251
  community's image, 251
  crime/violence, 250
  Dominican Republic, 248
  economy, 249
  Integral Tourism Security Strategic Plan,
    252
  policing programs, 252
  road crimes, 249
  security, 250
  tourism industry, 250
Political risk, 81
Pool and athletic safety, 74–75
Port of call, 147, 150t, 151, 152, 162–163
Port protection, 151
Ports, 162, 163
Post-crisis recovery programs, 106–107

Press release, 101
Price fixing, 81–82
Privacy rights, 114
Property, 57, 75
Property maintenance, 73
Prostitution, 86
Protection of staff, 20, 149
Protection services, 94
Protestant Ethic, 7–8
Psychological profiling, 178
Psychological profiling, EL AL planes, 178
Public areas, 73–74
Public gathering places. *See* Casinos
Public health, 133
Publicity, 84t, 87, 99, 100
Public perception, 167

R

Remote bombs, 126
Report crimes, 39
Reporter, 100, 101, 102, 103
Reputation, 82, 87–88, 94
Reputation protection, 14, 21
Restaurants, 52–53, 72
Retired police, 60–61
Rio De Janeiro, tourism
  from air, 252–253, 253f
  challenges, 254
  rock festival, *Rock in Rio*, 253–254
Riot, 86
Risk, 40
Risk management
  alcohol and drugs, 90–92
  analysis, tourism, 81–82
  business, 80
  country/political, 81
  credit, 80
  and crisis, 103–106
  drugs, tourism and terrorism, 93–94
  elements, 79
  exchange rate, 80
  fire and tourism safety, 96–98
  food safety, tourism, 94–96
  guidelines, 88–90
  heat exhaustion, 81
  inflation/purchasing power, 80
  interest rate, 80

Risk management *(Continued)*
  market, 80
  model
    categorization, 87
    tourism risk manager, 87
    types, 87, 87*t*
  negative event prevention, 103
  performance, 85
  risk manager, 85
  sporting events, 79
  statistical data analysis, 82
  tourism entity's reputation, 82
Risk management specialists, 40
Risk manager, 40
Risk potential, 81–82
Robbery, 34–35
Robin Hood Scenario, 29
Room invasions, 53–54, 138
Rooms, 52–53, 59–60, 71–72
Room security, 72
Routine inspections, 157
Rule of changeability, 69
Rule of redundancy, 67

S
Safety, 14, 15
Safety issues, 139, 147, 153–155
Safety material, 57
Safety plans, 129–130
Safety precautions, 139–140
Sanitation inspections, 157
Sanitation standards, 157–158
SARS. *See* Severe acute respiratory
    syndrome (SARS)
Scandals, 83
Security, 11–12, 12*f*, 14, 19
Security agents, 74
Security assessment, 67
Security cameras, 58
Security department, 58
Security guards, 90
Security instructions, 89
Security officer, 59–62
Security officers
  alarm systems, 59
  casinos
    customer service, 116

    documentation, 116
    skill sets, 115
    tourism security and policies, 115–116
  categorization, 59
  cyber problem, 61
  equipment tests, 62
  fire prevention, 59
  first aid and medical emergencies, 59
  front-line security personnel, 59–60
  hotel security, 60
  legal emergencies, 60–61
  local legal system, 60
  lodging security, 59, 60–61
  payroll protection, 60–61
  physical complaints, 60
  post-employment training, 61
  prevention and proactive policy, 60
  risk management plans, 59, 61
  types, 59
Security officials, 42
Security personnel, 59, 61
Security planners, 133
Security plans, 58
Security policies, 56, 62
Security procedures, 56
Security professionals, 16
Security updates, 57
Senior staff, 59
Sepanski, Z., 207
Set-up and maintenance costs, 114
Severe acute respiratory syndrome
    (SARS)
  description, 183–185
  first-aid kit and preventative procedures,
    184
  security personnel, 184
  sick employees and families, 183
  tourism, highly vulnerable to panic
    situation, 183
Sexual assault, 53
Sexual harassment, 81–82
Ship concerns, 152–153
Ship protection, 151
Ship safety, 155–156
Ship travel, 144
Site protection, 21
Skimmers, 54–55

Social crimes, 112
Social inequality, 32–33
Social media, 119
Social multiplier, 39
Soft targets, 98
Soft Uniforms, 11–12
Soliciting, 127–128
Souvenirs, 35–36
Specialized contractors, 75
Sporting event, 79
Sports tourism, 79
Staff, 52, 57, 66
Staff background, 51
Staff termination, 66
Standards of care
    checklists, 202
    defined, 201
    events, 201
    industry-wide international regulations,
        201
    responsibility and legality issues, 200
    safety and security professional, 202
    tourism business, 201–202
    tourism surety and law, 199
    tour operator's responsibility, 201
Statistics, 82
Stealing, 55–56
Street vendors, 94
Strikes, 81–82
Substance abuse, 57
Suicides, 112
Sun bathing, 138, 140
Sun burning and poisoning, 139
Suppe, R., 241–246
Surety, 12, 14–17
Swim clubs, 138
Swimming pools, 74

T

Tale of two cities, 223
TCU. *See* Tourist Crimes Unit (TCU)
Technology change, 81–82
Tennis courts, 74–75
Terrorism, 9–12
Terrorism and tourism
    iconic settings, 98
    and media

before an incident, 101
    follow-up after incident, 102–103
    during the incident, 101–102
    risk management, 98–100
    terrorist attacks, 98–100
Terrorism-based illnesses
    biological warfare, 185
    contagious illnesses, 185–186
    health workers, 186
    interconnectivity, 185
    tourism security specialists and
        professionals, 186
Terrorism issues, 27–28
Terrorists, 9
Thieves, 6–7
Ticket booths, 89
Titanic, 143–144
TOPPS. *See* Tourism-oriented policing and
    protective services (TOPPS)
Tour buses, 190–193
Tourism, 1–3, 4–5
Tourism center, 11
Tourism cities
    Charleston, South Carolina
        (*see* Charleston, South Carolina)
    Dominican Republic, 246–248
    economic development chain, 224
    hooliganism, 224
    host community, 224
    Las Vegas (*see* Las Vegas Tourism)
    mega-tourism, 223
    negative publicity, 254–258
    never-ending cycle, 224
    police, 248–252
    Rio De Janeiro, 252–258
    security professionals, 223
Tourism crime, 9, 10*t*, 19–21
Tourism economy and security
    anticrime tool, 43
    architectural integrity, 44
    assumptions, crime and viability, 27–34
    beautification methods, 44
    changes and challenges, 25
    crime and violence, 35–38
    crime's impact measurement, 38–39
    crisis management, 40, 41*t*
    festivals and mega-events, 44–47

Tourism economy and security *(Continued)*
  forms and law enforcement, 39–40
  macro and micro economic trends, 46
  managers and government agencies,
    41–42
  marketing, 42
  monetary concerns, 45
  national/provincial, 42
  passive resistance, 40
  private officials and law enforcement, 42
  public transportation, 43
  resource allocation, 26, 26*t*
  risk management, 40, 41*t*
  terrorism, 44
  tourist information services, 43
  winners and losers, 26, 27*t*
Tourism history, 49–50
Tourism hospitality, 56
Tourism industry, 3, 4*f*, 18
Tourism law
  airline passenger "bill of rights", 204
  decisions, legal professionals, 204–207
  description, 203
  inconsistency, marijuana usage, 204
  physical, social and cultural borders, 203
Tourism-oriented policing and protective
    services (TOPPS)
  description, 227
  ecological management, 21
  economic protection, 21
  financial and social challenges, 22
  law enforcement, 20–22
  reputation protection, 21
  site protection, 21
  staff protection, 20
  visitor protection, 20
Tourism perspective, 27–28
Tourism policing, 15–16
Tourism professionals/officials, 8
Tourism security. *See* Tourism surety
    (security)
Tourism Security Chiefs Association, 241
Tourism security legal issues
  airline passenger bill of rights, 212–215
  California, 208–209
  decisions making, 200
  in Europe (EU), 218–219

  facts and figures, 216–218
  fire codes, 216–218
  Florida, 209
  Hawaii, 209
  Illinois, 209
  Iowa, 210
  issues, travel agencies, 211–212
  law (*see* Tourism law)
  legal vulnerability, 202–203
  Massachusetts, 210
  Nevada, 210
  responsibility, 200
  standards of care (*see* Standards of care)
  surety and law
    manager/professional, 199
    physical disasters, 199
    team, 199–200
  train and bus travel, 216
  travel agents, 207–208
  travelers' rights, 207
  U.S. cruise passengers bill of rights,
    215–216
  Washington, 210
Tourism surety (security)
  classical and modern travel challenges, 5–7
  CNN report, 147
  communicative disease, 8–9
  component parts/challenges, 148–149
  criminal and terrorism acts, 9–11, 10*t*
  cruise takers, 147
  definitions, 3, 5
  description, 147–148
  ecological management, 151
  economic protection, 151
  International Tourist Arrivals, 1–2, 2*t*
  issues host and cruise's risk manager, 148
  land *vs.* water tourism, 149, 150*t*
  leisure travel, 7–8
  peacetime industry, 1
  port protection, 151
  post-9/11 period, 17–19
  post-9/11 world, 14
  pre-9/11 years
    anger management, 16
    business decision, 16
    "Las Vegas Tourism Safety
      Seminar", 15

safety conferences, 16
travel and tourism industry, 14–15
reputation protection, 152
ship protection, 151
social phenomenon, 4–5
staff protection, 149
terminology and history, 2–3
TOPPs, 19–21
traveler protection, 149
unified vocabulary, 3–4
WTO, 1
Tourism well-being, 34–35
Tourist community, 25, 42
Tourist Crimes Unit (TCU), 242
Tourists, 1–2, 2*t*, 4, 13
Trade show/convention procedures,
    127–128
Trade shows, 127–128, 129–130.
    See also Convention centers
Training, 61, 72–73
Train travel tourism
bomb explosions, 190
crashes, 189–190
description, 187
economic and security issues, 188
Orient Express, 187
train trips, North America, 187–188
in United States, 187–188
worst train accidents, 188–189
Transportation, 11
air (*see* Air transportation)
bus tourism (*see* Bus tourism)
train travel (*see* Train travel tourism)
Transportation Security Administration
    (TSA) agents, 177
Transportation services, 121
Travel challenges, 5–7
Travel dilemmas, 81
Traveler protection, 149
Travelers, 6–7
Travel industry, 3
Traveling for business, 6–7
Traveling for meetings, 3
Traveling for pleasure, 3
Traveling public, 171
Travel schedules, 168
TWA Flight 847 hijacking, 169–170

U

U.S. cruise passengers bill of rights
Cruise Lines International Association
    (CLIA), 215–216
description, 215–216
U.S. Hijackings
commonality issues
    cost–benefit basis, 171
    immediate and long-term economic
        loss, 171
    media attention, 171
    national, international levels, 172
    nation's tourism industry, 172
counter-hijacking measurements, 172–173
description, 168, 169*t*
EL AL models, 177–178
The Entebbe, 168–169
hardening, terminal (*see* Hardening, air
    travel)
Indian Airlines Flight IC-814, 1999, 170
luggage examination
    categories, 175
    civil and professional manner, 175
    civil aviation authorities and law
        enforcement agencies, 175
    false-positives, 176
    full-body scanners, 176
    Transportation Security Administration
        (TSA), 175, 176–177
TWA Flight 847, 1985, 169–170

V

Vacation, 33
Vacationers, 57
Vandalism, 81–82, 86
Veblen, T., 30–31, 32–33
Venezuela, 37–38
Victimization, 99
Violence, 35–38, 40
Visitor protection, 20
Visitors, 3–4, 8

W

Waiters, 95, 96
Waitresses, 95, 96
Wall Street Journal, 219

Water sports, 137, 138, 140
Water system, 126
Weapons, 168, 169*t*, 170, 174, 176, 178
Weather, 81, 92
White collar crime, 81–82
World Cup, 9

World events, 92
World Health Organization, 39
World Tourism Organization (WTO), 1
Written policies, 74–75
WTO. *See* World Tourism Organization (WTO)

Printed in Great Britain
by Amazon

24689933R00175